Think Social!

A Social Thinking® Curriculum for School-Age Students

for Teaching Social Thinking and
Related Social Skills to Students with
High Functioning Autism, Asperger Syndrome,
PDD-NOS, ADHD, Nonverbal Learning Disability
and for all others in the murky
gray area of social thinking

by
Michelle Garcia Winner

Social Thinking Publishing, Inc.
3031 Tisch Way, Suite 800
San Jose, CA 95128
Telephone (408) 557-8595
Fax (408) 557-8594
information@socialthinking.com

1st Edition November 2005
2nd Printing 2008
Copyright©2008 Think Social Publishing, Inc.

ISBN-13: 978-0-97-013204-8

To order copies of this book or to learn about the workshops
Michelle Garcia Winner presents, visit **www.socialthinking.com**

Dedication

Dedicated to the clinicians, teachers, counselors, behaviorists, administrators, and parents around the world who are implementing a deeper, more thoughtful approach to teaching social thinking and related skills.

Contents

Special thanks and acknowledgements

Social thinking is a complex topic, one filled with thousands of nuances that make up how they relate, think about and connect with others. So many people across the country who have started social thinking programs – in their schools, private practices or at home – encouraged me to write this book.They wanted a guidebook to help them translate ideas into action and explain in more detail how social thinking lessons unfold at our clinic.They assured me they would not use this curriculum as the "be all and end all" to teach social thinking and related concepts, but would rather use it as a launching pad, a starting point to fuel creative ideas of their own. Trusting they would make good on their promises, I wrote this book for them and others who would follow in their wake. Use it as your guidebook but never let is become your bible. Students with social thinking challenges are as unique as snowflakes – no two are the same. They require us, above all, to be flexible in out mindset, continually adapting, changing and improving our own social thinking in order to develop theirs.

A special thank you to each and every person who has seen this curriculum and provided comments and opinions, whether or not you are named here. Your encouragement has sustained me through the often mind-numbing task involved in translating ideas into lesson plans. These people include, but are not limited to, three powerhouse women from Portland, Oregon: Patty O'Meara, Kathleen Davis and Tamara Haas, as well as a bevy of other ardent supporters there; Anita Strassman; the creative Chris Durbin and the team from San Francisco; the insightful Dr. Lauren Franke of Seal Beach. California. My thanks also go out to other pioneers and colleagues: Terri Jensen and Brittany Schmidt of South Dakota; Kathy Patton and Linda Hanson of Hopkins, Minnesota; Diane Taylor and Lisa Dillhunt of Green Bay, Wisconsin; Sandra Boehmiler and team from Montana; Sue Kish of Philomath, Oregon; the team from illinois; Jennifer Milette, Jan Petru and Vanessa Granato.

Tremendous thanks goes to the therapists at my clinic. Stephanie Madrigal (SLP) makes it possible for me to write this curriculum as she manages the clinic while continuing to work with students, provide training and consultations, as well as being my close friend. Randi Dodge (SLP), an enthusiastic member of the team, excels at transforming social thinking concepts into unique lessons tailored to her social thinking groups. Sue Day (SLP), Amy Miller (SLP) and Jaime Rivetts (Educator) are newer members of our team who have contributed significantly to the clinic's creativity in a relatively short period of time. Deborah Hoffman (SLP) is pioneering our preschool program after a very long career working with students of all ages; she brings a depth of insight, passion, and a magical ability to work with children and parents at the clinic on a daily basis. As always I must thank Cathy Hart, my personal assistant, cheerleader, friend, and clinic secretary for calming the clinic's chaos and giving me moments in which to focus.

My good friends in Orange County—Andrea Walker, Trisha Brady and Patty Schwartz—have continued to do more for my professional and personal social skill development than they could possibly know. Trisha gave direct feedback with regard to this curriculum's content and Andrea served as the initial editor of this work and helped to make these lessons more readable while also challenging me to think more deeply about the curriculum. Thanks also to all the other members of the "social butterflies" who continue to make work and travel fun.

The team involved in the SUCCESS Project of Orange County has impressed me so much by demonstrating we can make social thinking programs a reality in the schools. My best wishes to them for continued "success."

My sister, Tania Fowler, served as the second editor of this book, helping her speech language pathologist sister not appear so a-grammatical. She also added many worthy insights that helped make the text user-friendly.

Finally, my love and thanks to my precious daughters Heidi and Robyn. They continue to amaze me by pushing me into the next project and reassuring me the work is needed. They insist they don't feel all that bad about having meals as good as they used to before the clinic got started.

We live but once and touch people along the way. To all those who have touched my life in ways you will never know, my heartfelt thanks. Finally and especially, THANK YOU to readers everywhere, for being willing to climb this towering mountain of social understanding that affects our daily lives. You pave the way for our students to not only walk their path with greater ability and understanding, but to reach for the stars along the way.

Graphic Design, Typography, Production
Dion Desktop Publications
www.diondesktop.com

Introduction, Part 1

Understanding and Using This Curriculum

What is meant when I talk about someone "having good social skills"?

Having good social skills simply means people share their space with others effectively. Good social skills means following unwritten social rules of the environment, even outside of active social interaction within that environment. Examples of using good social skills outside interaction include stepping aside on an elevator to let another person on, or sitting quietly in a classroom while allowing the teacher to talk even if you have something you wish you could say.

Good social skills involve more that direct language-based interactions. Much of this curriculum explores sharing space with others, thinking about others in the shared environment, and learning to regulate one's own behavior to other people's thoughts or expectations.

The philosophy behind this curriculum

While teaching in the Campbell Union High School District in the 1990's, I began to appreciate that the social issues of high school students were much more complex than could be addressed by merely teaching simple social skills. I also noticed that these social thinking difficulties were spilling over into their academic work. Therefore in the late 1990s, I founded Michelle G. Winner's Center for Social Thinking, which specializes in addressing the needs of persons with social cognitive deficits. Since then, it has become even more clear to me the extent to which social thinking is infused into almost all parts of our home and school day.

Often persons with "weak" social skills do have reasonably developed, or even superior, academic, cognitive and language skills. Our goal is to help these individuals develop a deeper understanding of social relations and social communication while also learning to decode and encode related social skills. This is an area of development that they did not acquire intuitively, as did their neurotypical peers.

Absent from this curriculum is simply naming and teaching the social skills a student needs to be deemed socially competent. It is my strong belief these relatively high-functioning students can only truly become more socially competent if they understand **how** the social world works, and **why** specific social skills are important in differing contexts. To that end, this curriculum helps educators learn about and teach "social thinking and related social skills."

We all want our students to have personal problem solving, personal advocacy, and social relatedness skills. These are fundamental in lasting friendships and essential for working successfully with classroom peers. However, it is unrealistic to think we can do this easily or quickly. From my experience there is nothing more complex than teaching social thinking and related skills to persons born without solid and intuitive social cognition. We have to teach our students cognitively how to think socially!

Where can I learn more about the philosophy?

My first two books, *Inside Out: What Makes a Person With Social Cognitive Deficits Tick* (2000) and *Thinking About YOU Thinking About ME, 2nd Ed.* (2007), explain in detail the philosophy behind this curriculum. In these books I discuss core concepts related to understanding social thinking: the I LAUGH Model of Social Cognition, the "Four Steps of Communication," and perspective taking within the social context.

Educators not familiar with my core philosophy and related general treatment strategies for the school and home setting are strongly encouraged to read these two books, or at the very least, read the articles posted in the "Philosophy" section of my website:

www.socialthinking.com

A brief review of these concepts follows.

What is the scientific evidence for the information in this curriculum?

Teaching social thinking and related social skills is a developmental, behavioral approach that is utilizing cognitive behavioral strategies to teach core social thinking concepts. Cognitive Behavior Therapy (CBT) is a form of psychotherapy that was first developed in the 1960s and continues to evolve in its application. In a nutshell, CBT is based on the idea that our thoughts cause our feelings and behaviors, not the people, situations, and events in our environment, and that by changing the way we think, we can improve our life. CBT is anchored by three fundamental concepts (Dobson and Dozois, 2001):

1. Cognitive activity affects behavior.

2. Cognitive activity may be monitored and altered.

3. Desired behavior change may be influenced through CBT.

Researchers are beginning to demonstrate that CBT can be promising in the treatment of persons who function high on the autism spectrum and those with related social processing disabilities (Attwood, 2003; Anderson & Morris, 2006; Beebe & Risi, 2003; Perry & Condillac, 2003; Sofronoff, Attwood & Hinton, 2005). CBT is often referred to as a form of "talk therapy" that focuses on the present, rather than delving into the past to understand the origins of behavior. Marans, Rubin and Laurent (2005) discuss the role CBT

strategies, such as learning an "inner language" to help individuals cope with stressful events, can play for persons with Asperger Syndrome.

On a whole, cognitive interventions, as described by Simpson (2005, 2006), attempt to shift the focus of control from the therapists, educators and parents to the individual. Simpson explains that thought and other cognitive processes are generally assumed to mediate an individual's behavior and performance. Thus, changing these factors in a person is likely best accomplished by changing an individual's perceptions, self-understanding and beliefs.

Social Thinking is beginning to attract the attention of independent researchers. Crooke, Hendrix and Rachman (2007) demonstrated positive treatment/generalization effects with a small group, single subject design exploring social thinking treatment. Elementary-aged boys were taught social thinking concepts such as "expected/unexpected," "think with your eyes" and "listen with your whole body" in a small group therapeutic setting. Robust gains in both skills and generalization of skills were demonstrated when the boys were placed in a new setting, a pizza party. Crooke et al's research supports the theory that if we teach students to think socially they can take their thinking and use it effectively outside the therapy room.

The I LAUGH Model of Social Cognition

I LAUGH is an acronym representing the many different concepts we each need to consider and respond to in order to 1) relate to those around us, 2) interpret social information in academic lessons (such as reading comprehension), and 3) express ourselves in writing. The concepts represented in the I LAUGH Model describe how most moments during our home and school days require social interpretation and related social expression.

While this curriculum focuses explicitly on helping students develop better social thinking and related skills, the underlying lessons also teach improved social reasoning skills required for academic lessons. All educational lessons in this curriculum have roots in the I LAUGH model. (This model is explained in far more detail in my book *Inside Out: What Makes a Person With Social Cognitive Deficits Tick?*) A brief explanation, excerpted from that book, follows below:

I **I = Initiation of Language:** Initiation of language is the ability to use one's language skills to seek assistance and information, or to initiate social relations with others. A student's ability to talk about his own topics of interest can be in sharp contrast to how the student initiates language not related to these interests. Skills involved in the initiation of communication transform into self-advocacy skills as students age.

L **L= Listening With Eyes and Brain:** Most persons with social cognitive deficits have difficulty with auditory comprehension. Listening, however, requires more than just taking in auditory information—it also requires the person to integrate information he sees with what he hears to understand the deeper concept of the message, or make a smart guess about what is meant. Towards this end, we will explore how "listening with your eyes" helps all students be more receptive to reading people's thoughts, intentions, motives, emotions, etc.

A **A = Abstract and Inferential Language/Communication:** Communicative comprehension and expression also depends on the ability to recognize that most language/communication is not intended for literal interpretation. To interpret messages accurately, one must think flexibly and make smart guesses about the intended meaning of the message. Abstract and inferential meaning is often carried subtly through verbal and nonverbal communication. This skill emerges in the child's earliest moments of development and expands over the years as the messages we interpret — both socially and academically — become more abstract. Understanding these nuances of communication depends in part on one's ability to "make a guess" and take the perspective of another person.

U **U = Understanding Perspective:** This is the ability to understand the emotions, thoughts, beliefs, prior knowledge and experiences, motives and intentions of yourself as well as others. We generally acquire basic perspective-taking skills intuitively during early childhood. However, we continue to evolve in the sophistication of this skill across our entire lives!

Perspective taking is essential for participation in any type of group (social or academic) and for interpreting information that requires understanding other people's minds, such as reading comprehension, history, social studies, etc. Weakness in perspective taking is a significant part of the diagnosis of social cognitive deficits. However, this weakness can range from mild to severe. It is my belief that people on the autism spectrum represent this range of perspective-taking deficits.

G **G = Gestalt Processing/Getting The Big Picture:** Information is conveyed through concepts, not just facts. During a conversation, participants intuitively determine the underlying concept being discussed. When reading, the reader tracks the overall meaning (concept) of the material. Such information cannot be viewed as simply a series of facts, as is often the case in individuals with social thinking challenges. Conceptual processing is another key component to understanding social and academic information. Difficulty with organizational strategies is born from deficits in conceptual processing.

H **H= Humor and Human Relatedness:** Most of the clients I work with actually have a very good sense of humor, but it is often masked by the high levels of anxiety they experience. This anxiety results from the fact that they miss many of the subtle cues that would help them understand how to participate successfully with others. It is important for educators/parents to work compassionately and with humor to minimize this anxiety. At the same time, many of our clients use humor inappropriately; direct lessons about this topic are often needed.

The Four Steps of Communication

In addition to the I LAUGH Model of Social Cognition, we can also analyze the act of social communication and recognize that it has at least four definable parts. Face-to-face communication unfolds in a fairly routine and organized progression. It is important to explore the fact that communication is not solely based around language, but also involves thinking about other people, establishing a physical presence through our bodies and eyes, and elaborating through language what is meaningful to all involved. This progression is summarized in what I call "The Four Steps of Communication." These concepts are defined and discussed at length in my book *Thinking About YOU Thinking About ME,* and are reviewed briefly below. It is crucial that educators understand these four steps before embarking on teaching this social thinking curriculum.

Step 1: Think about the person(s) with whom you will communicate or share physical space. Consider their thoughts, emotions, motives, intentions, belief systems, prior knowledge, experiences and personality to better establish successful communication.

Step 2: Establish a physical presence: Approach the communicative partner and then use body language (such as shoulders, head and gestures) to further establish nonverbal communicative intent.

Step 3: Use your eyes to: consider more fully how people's body language and facial expression adds to their words; see what other people may be thinking about; evaluate the people around us to determine their intentions; explore the environment for additional cues to add meaning to what is being said. Also use your eyes to show people what you are thinking about as well as to demonstrate your continued interest in what they are saying.

Step 4: Use your language to show others that you are interested in them. Some examples include: asking about others, discussing topics of interest to them, making related comments, and adjusting what you say based on how you think other people will respond.

The Four Steps of Perspective Taking

As we learn to think about people in communicative contexts, one more model helps us think more clearly about this process: "The Four Steps of Perspective Taking" or "The Four Steps of Being Part of A Group" take abstract concepts and break them down into more concrete parts for each of us to consider. The Four Steps of Perspective Taking are reviewed below. This information is also available as a wall poster called "Being Part of a Group," a helpful visual tool. The poster reminds students how to regulate behavior while maintaining constant social thought about the people around us. The poster is available through our website:

www.socialthinking.com

Step 1
As soon as two people share a common space, they have a small thought about each other.

Step 2
As soon as they have a thought about each other, they consider the intention of the other person(s) in that space. Why is this person near me? What do they want from me?

Step 3
Each person considers what the other may be thinking about them, using their own thoughts as framework.

Step 4
The communication partners each monitor and possibly modify their own behavior to keep people thinking about them the way they want people to think about them.

This curriculum was created to help educators break down, teach and progress through a number of critical social concepts. It would be impossible to provide a curriculum that covers all, or even the majority, of experiences that ultimately need to be explored in a student's childhood.

Therefore, use this curriculum as a starting place, your rocket that launches you into your own personal study of the myriad aspects of the social world. Let your journey alongside your students begin!

Major themes of the curriculum

You will want to demonstrate and discuss some of the major themes introduced in these lessons during teachable moments across all lessons.

1. People who pay attention to others make others feel good. When you make other people feel good they want to be with you.

2. Students have to think about what others are thinking.

3. Students have to learn to observe other people's behaviors and form judgments about them.

4. Students have to realize that others are also thinking about them.

5. Students have to learn that social thinking is done in all environments (home, school, community) and the lessons need to walk with them out the door.

What is a Social Thinking Vocabulary?

In my earlier books I introduce a number of social concepts that can be taught more explicitly to students. As my staff of talented therapists and myself continued to learn how to better educate not only the students, but also the educators working with the students, we refined this material. We broke down concepts and assigned new vocabulary and terms to behaviors that most of us intuitively expect from each other but rarely discuss, such as "thinking about what people think," "keeping your body in the group," "keeping your mind in the group," "thinking with your eyes," "add-a-thought comments," etc.

In developing these vocabulary terms we realized how helpful it is to use them consistently across environments. This encourages students to observe the social connections between people and environments. Frequent use of the terms helps students take the concepts and apply them outside the therapy room.

As the list of vocabulary terms grew, we ultimately decided to call them the "Social Thinking Vocabulary."

The Social Thinking Vocabulary is appropriate for all educators to learn and use. The vocabulary, while developed for students with social learning challenges, has also proven to be helpful for other students. We encourage the regular education teacher, usually the person directly teaching these concepts, to use the vocabulary during teachable moments with her students. Social thinking is a vital part of education for every student.

Each lesson offers new social thinking vocabulary. Once a social thinking concept is introduced, it is then integrated into all the other lessons as appropriate. This vocabulary builds upon itself.

Who can teach this curriculum?

Any educator (defined as any adult who is interested in working with these students) can teach this curriculum. This can be parent, special education teacher, speech language pathologist, the psychologist or counselor, or a talented, experienced paraprofessional. In this curriculum, these people will be referred to as the "educator," "instructor," "teacher," or "therapist."

This curriculum is not taught in any university program, but is rather a gathering of forward thinking information not "owned" by a particular profession. I am a speech language pathologist, and my education in this field helped me develop my philosophy and related teaching strategies. However, I did not learn how to teach social thinking from my training as a speech language pathologist. The most important skills needed to work with these students is patience and the desire to understand their needs, strengths and weaknesses, and how they feel about themselves and others as they struggle to develop peer relations.

As I mentioned, parents can also teach this curriculum, but only to a child who is willing to have a parent teach in such a direct manner. The parent must be able to remain patient and calm as their child struggles to learn these concepts. Not all children are willing to let their parents take on multiple strong roles in their life. Not all parents are able to calmly handle this type of teaching.

Which students will benefit from this curriculum?

This curriculum is designed for students with social cognitive deficits who have near-normal to well above average verbal and nonverbal intelligence, and who also have a reasonable level of understanding that each person has a different set of thoughts. These students have the capacity to understand fairly quickly that people have different opinions and thoughts, even though they are not able to use or apply this knowledge in a socially competent manner.

The range of diagnostic labels this population represents includes but is not limited to: High Functioning Autism, Pervasive Developmental Disorder, Asperger Syndrome, Nonverbal Learning Disorder, Attention Deficit Hyperactivity Disorder, students with head injuries, Tourette Syndrome, etc.

The curriculum provides lessons for students across the school years. While the curriculum begins in a very basic manner, it is surprising how many older (above third grade) "smart" students lack basic social thinking and related social skills. It will be important for the educator to determine their students' social thinking strengths and weaknesses. It has been my experience that most of us err on the side of thinking our students have more skills than they actually do. Do not presume your student should start in the middle of this curriculum; none of my students ever have!

What are the primary tools educators need to be effective teachers?

- Creativity
- Flexibility
- Humor
- Patience

The curriculum begins with basic concepts and social thinking vocabulary that need to be introduced across the different ages of students in school. It provides detailed sample lessons to help the user learn how to "unfold" lessons and how to use one lesson to build on another. However, this curriculum is not intended to be the only way to teach these students, but rather as an example of one way in which to introduce the lessons. What is most important is providing the students, their educators and their parents access to the social thinking vocabulary.

Educators and parents who will do best with this curriculum are those who can grasp the lesson concept while being willing and able to adapt it to the specific student or group of students being taught. To do this well the instructor has to be adaptable and flexible.

The lessons, while appearing basic, are not quick and easy for our students to learn. Multiple lessons will be needed in order for students to learn the basic concepts. Creativity is essential to continue to teach the concepts in new ways once all the lessons in this curriculum have been used.

Another critical "educator" trait is patience and the ability to celebrate very small steps as genuine progress. Educators need to appreciate that any major shifts in social thinking will only evolve over a long period of time. It often takes two years for students to actively think socially about the world to the point where they actually modify their social behavior across a range of contexts.

Finally, a sense of humor cannot be undervalued. Even when you follow the curriculum and incorporate behavioral strategies, there are days when the lessons are just not going to gel. Being able to encourage laughter, even during the tricky moments, is helpful. That said, I still have days when I cannot access my humor during a "bad therapy session." In these instances I go back to the proverbial drawing board and spend some time figuring out what went wrong. Perhaps I was not flexible enough, or a student came into the session ready to explode, or I realize I have the wrong combination of kids working together. When things go wrong I have to be at my most creative to ensure that the next session will go well enough that we all continue to feel good about working together. Students learn social lessons best in a relaxed, fun, creative environment.

How is the curriculum organized?

The curriculum is divided into eight major sections. An educator can start on Lesson 1 and work through the sixty-plus lessons in order, or can mix lessons from different sections. Since the vocabulary concepts build from lesson to lesson, a sequential flow is recommended in most cases. The eight lesson sections, listed in order, are:

Section 1: Being Part of a Group and Recognizing Expectations

Section 2: Our Whole Body and Mind Help Us Be Part of the Group

Section 3: Self-awareness and Self-monitoring Our Behavior in a Group

Section 4: Starting the Detective Agency: Learning More About Observing Others

Section 5: The Super Detective Agency: Figuring Out What People Mean by What They Say

Section 6: Adjusting Our Participation and Language Based on What Other People Are Thinking, Imagining or Wondering

Section 7: Our Language Makes Others Have Different Thoughts and Feelings

Section 8: There is Still so Much More to Teach!

We suggest educators read through the entire curriculum to get a sense of the concepts before beginning to teach its parts. Section 8 is one the reader should consider carefully, as many of these concepts will need to be introduced ahead of time through the detailed lessons described in Sections 1-7.

Within each section, most of the lessons are connected to the previous lesson. However, it is certainly possible to teach concepts from more than one section simultaneously. For example, an educator can introduce lessons about helping students monitor behavior (Section 3), while they are also working on being social detectives (Sections 4 and 5). It is also possible to introduce concepts about using our imagination and wonder (Section 6) while we are trying to figure out what we mean by what we say (Section 5). Ultimately, you will find your compass on where you feel most comfortable working with your students, based on their individual needs.

This curriculum was written at the request of hundreds of people across the United States who asked that I create lessons that can help students develop their own paths to social understanding. I would not want anyone to think this curriculum is the only possible method for teaching social thinking and related skills.

Does this curriculum cover all possible areas of social interaction and communication?

NO!

The purpose of this curriculum is to introduce social thinking concepts in concrete ways so students can begin to explore and improve their own social thinking and related skills. In addition to the concepts discussed in this curriculum, many more exist that we have yet to find the words to describe or teach.

Section 8 introduces the educator to additional ideas that will eventually be embedded into lessons similar to those offered in this curriculum. Each group of students creates a unique social context and a unique set of problems related to social interaction. Learning the dynamics of your group will help you determine which lessons in Section 8 should be introduced and when. You may find it necessary or helpful to teach parallel lessons in organizational skills. Through careful observation you will be able to assess where and when additional lessons or training are needed.

Can this curriculum be used with all students on the autism spectrum?

NO.

It is my experience that all students on the autism spectrum can learn new information, but not all students can learn the same types of social thinking concepts. Even students who will be able to learn them cannot all learn them at the same speed, or at the same time in their life.

As mentioned earlier, this curriculum is best suited for people who are on the "high-functioning" end of the autism spectrum and recognize fairly quickly that people have different thoughts and opinions. That said, it is difficult for these same students to consider this information while they are communicating with others.

This curriculum requires students to think about thinking, which is called using one's "meta-cognition." We are helping younger students develop a very basic sense about thinking of others. As students get older, we encourage more complex thinking. As the curriculum progresses, the complexity of the ideas being explored increases.

The educator needs to learn to observe each student rather than depend on a diagnostic label to determine what type of teaching a student requires. But as a general rule, this curriculum is not designed to be used with students on the autism spectrum who are minimally verbal or nonverbal (for reasons other than pure apraxia). It is also inappropriate for those who are considered "moderate to low functioning autism." While I have successfully helped this type of student learn important social concepts, I did not use a meta-cognitive teaching approach. Instead, these students require directed fact-based methods that focus on teaching appropriate social skills without having to conceptually think about the social interpretation of others. It is possible for some younger students who require factually based teachings to mature and learn so they can eventually deal with more meta-cognitive teachings. Educators should be in the habit of doing "diagnostic therapy" every day with every child they work with, to determine what lessons are most appropriate.

Can this curriculum be used for students who are not on the autism spectrum or not labeled with NLD, ADHD, etc?

YES!

We find this curriculum helpful for many different types of students. We never use a student's label to determine what to teach a student, but rather base those decisions on individual needs. It always comes down to who the person you are teaching is, and what they need. This curriculum has been used successfully even with students who have no diagnostic labels, but could use a bit more information about the complex social world.

It is also important to remember that while people can be born with social cognitive deficits, such as those on the autism spectrum, people can acquire social deficits through a head injury or stroke, or can experience increased social challenges when born into significant poverty or exposed to drugs or prenatal alcohol.

How do we enhance generalization of these lessons outside the classroom where these lessons are taught?

Teaching students concepts to think about versus skills to perform increases the chances that students will naturally think about those concepts in other environments, while away from their teacher.

However, to expand the "generalization" of this curriculum's concepts beyond the room where they are taught, educators are encouraged to share these concepts with other adults and peers who co-exist in the same environments with the students. It is important for family members, mainstream and special education professionals and paraprofessionals to become familiar with these concepts so they can encourage the students to think about them and use the related skills across all environments. The concepts should also be introduced to any other person on campus who regularly interacts with the child (principal, secretaries, cafeteria workers, yard duty personnel, etc.).

We encourage social thinking by sharing a common vocabulary. At the end of each section is a handout called "Social Thinking Vocabulary and Concepts for Teachers and Parents" to be copied and shared with all people who will share space with the students of this curriculum. Please write in the student's name and date, as well as the primary educator's contact phone number, on the handout to encourage persons to not only use this information, but to also contact the educator with questions.

Furthermore, we are trying to enhance self-awareness and self-monitoring by having the students learn to observe and rate the behaviors they are seeing in their social thinking groups. The "Video Moments Check Sheet" is used with students to help them monitor their own or other people's behavior in the group and to generate thought about what they are observing.

It will be helpful for the user of this material to encourage students to make observations outside the therapy room as well.

Do we need to follow the curriculum lessons exactly as they are presented?

Yes and no.

The initial lessons explore nonverbal ways through which we communicate. We then build up to language. However, it is quite feasible to work on some concepts in Section 7 (language to relate to others) while also working on some lessons in Section 3, as long as these lessons are not worked on at the exact same time. This would overwhelm our students! A couple of lessons can be worked on within the same educational session.

As mentioned above, it is suitable to blend some lessons from different sections, but to do this I encourage the educator to read through all the sections first to gain a better overall picture of how the lessons build on each other.

How often should students work on this curriculum?

Ideally a student should work directly on this program each day for about 45 minutes. However, this is not generally realistic for most students who participate primarily in the mainstream environment or are receiving these lessons in after school private or public programs.

At our clinic, we generally work with students and parents for 60 minutes once per week; 50 minutes of this time is directly spent working with students in groups with similarly challenged students. The remaining 10 minutes is spent with the parents teaching them the concepts explored in the social thinking group on that day. The purpose of meeting with the parents is to provide them with the concepts and encourage them to carry on with the lessons during teachable moments at home.

The amount of time spent on social thinking should be based on the individual needs of the child and written into his individual education plan (IEP). It will vary from child to child. Providing students with 30 minutes of direct social thinking lessons a week with strong team consultation, while encouraging other adults at school and at home to continually work on the concepts across the day, can be more effective than individual 45- or 60-minute sessions. This is due to full integration of the curriculum into the student's life. Specific consultation time should be built into the IEP.

While students benefit tremendously from being part of a group with other high functioning students who share similar deficits, we also find there are strong benefits to working with students individually. This allows students to explore their own spin on concepts, personal emotions, and concerns in a more private atmosphere, resulting in the development of better coping skills when the student has to apply these same skills in the group context. Even in groups of three or four, social thinking can get complicated!

Some schools have begun to offer social thinking courses as an elective for their Special Education middle and high school students, and as part of the daily schedule for primary school kids. This is a good choice and provides a terrific opportunity for working with students consistently. We offer two notes of caution: 1) group size needs to remain small (1:3 or 1:4 adult to student ratio), and 2) do not attempt to teach all students on the autism spectrum in the same class. The different cognitive and social functioning levels of the autism spectrum demand very different teaching approaches.

How many students make for a good social thinking group and what ages?

Since so much of the curriculum focuses on trying to understand what other people are thinking or feeling, too many students working together make these lessons overwhelming. When beginning to work with students, generally keep the size of the group small: three to four students. We have some intellectually gifted students who have rigid social thinking and related skills; they can only start in a group size of two — they do not have the ability to think about more than one other person, nor the skills to remain calm and able to learn in a larger group. For younger students we often try and keep our group size to three, unless the child has serious speech and language issues or behavior rigidity requiring a smaller group size.

When two educators, such as one educator and one paraprofessional, or even two professionals are available to work with one group, there is a tendency to want to increase the group size to eight or 10 students. The problem with this situation is there can only be one group leader at any given time, Even though there are two adults in the room, there are still eight to 10 students who have to think about each other. When two adults are working with a larger group, the educators should divide the students into two smaller groups of four each, especially when group work is a relatively new concept for those involved. Age is not a factor in this regard; the same advice applies to groups of adults.

It is our experience once students have worked with us for a couple of years, the group size can be expanded as the students are better able to transfer the concepts and skills into a larger educational setting.

Students working in this curriculum can be grouped by grades, such as K-2, 3-5, middle school, and high school. In the primary years there is far more flexibility in grouping students. For example, you can group students in second to fourth grade, but obviously you don't want to group Kindergartners with students in third, fourth or fifth grades.

How do you decide on group composition?

Placing students in social thinking groups is the hardest part of the whole process! DO NOT place students into groups purely based on shared diagnostic label. While students may all have social weaknesses, it is very possible the similarities end there.

In my book *Thinking About YOU Thinking About ME, 2nd Ed.* (2007), I talk about a perspective taking spectrum. This is somewhat, but not exactly, aligned to the autism spectrum. However, in my book, I only defined two parts of the spectrum. In a perfect world, students with "classic" (lower functioning) autism would all be severely impaired perspective takers; students with labels such as "high-functioning autism" would have "emerging perspective taking skills" and students with Asperger Syndrome or PDD-NOS would have "impaired interactive perspective taking" skills. Keep in mind, however, the major tools used by doctors and public schools do not include a perspective-taking deficit as a direct way to diagnose or even better understand autism. An article I wrote entitled "Perspective Taking across the School and Adult Years for Persons with Social Cognitive Deficits: A proposal for a perspective taking spectrum and related critical curriculum and support to facilitate adult success," explains my evolving thoughts on the impact of perspective-taking deficits on social cognition, and ultimately prognosis, even with strong social educational programs. I encourage readers to review this article, which immediately follows this Introduction.

To summarize very briefly here:

Severely Impaired Perspective Takers (SIPT):

These students usually have tremendous developmental language challenges; most are nonverbal or minimally verbal. Not coincidentally, most also have a significant form of cognitive impairment (mental retardation). These students are aware of other people and enjoy others, but do not appear to consider the needs of others as part of their social relatedness skill set. Their communication is solely in response to getting their personal wants and needs met. Social thinking is not an appropriate curriculum for these students – they function best when information is delivered to them factually without the need to self-analyze or call on meta-cognitive social perspective taking skills. These students benefit from a more traditional "social skills" teaching approach.

Emerging Perspective Takers (EPT):

Students with EPT have usually developed language syntax to communicate a variety of wants and needs and they may comment on their own thoughts. These students generally have near normal to above normal intelligence, but are limited in the speed and efficiency with which they consider other people's wants and needs. They usually can understand the basic point of view of another person if they are allowed to think really long and really hard about it with direct explicit instruction. The problem is most communicative exchanges happen within seconds and do not allow enough time for these students to process and respond to the communicative partner. Students with EPT are always very literal and will struggle tremendously with reading literature for social meaning rather than fact. They may be able to quickly and efficiently answer the "who, what, where and when" questions about the reading material, but will struggle to summarize "why or how" questions, particularly when these plot lines involve understanding human emotion. These students always have very poor organizational skills and require clear, explicit social assistance to help them learn to engage in all levels of social interaction beyond their own wants and needs. What sets them apart from the SIPT is the fact the educators can discuss the concept of social thinking with the EPTs and they can learn to more clearly consider other people's perspective from a meta-cognitive level. EPTs usually look quirky; their peers know they don't understand the social world in the same way as the other kids at school.

These students can benefit from learning social thinking and related skills with very patient educators. It is a slow but rewarding process. Educators who work with these students must appreciate that helping these students learn the process of social thinking is a much stronger and more pivotal lesson over time than just teaching students specific social skills and reinforcing the performance of these skills. Remember, students cannot generalize social skills into a more natural environment if they don't understand why they are using these skills!

Impaired Interactive Perspective Takers (IIPT):

Students with IIPT often look just like their peers. They may lack social understanding or social nuance and appear "quirky." For this reason their peers identify them as socially "off" while adults often initially think they are fine. Students with IIPT may have near normal to advanced cognition. They quickly and efficiently recognize that people have different thoughts and opinions, and they may even describe what people expect from them with relative accuracy. Problems arise when students with IIPT try to engage at the rapid fire pace of normal social interaction, but become constrained by the speed of social communication. They tend to retreat to their own thoughts and opinions, failing to consider the needs or thoughts of their communicative partner. These students can be exasperating to parents and teachers since they seem to know so much, but make so many social errors. Parents often describe them as "smart but clueless," as they blurt out inappropriate comments in class, refuse to engage in class work they don't want to do, and tell on fellow students who break some of the same social rules they break themselves (not being fair, etc.).

In Summary:

Not all students fall neatly into three different categories. For example, I have a number of clients who I would describe as being high level EPT and low level IIPT. Perspective taking is a skill that develops across a continuum; it is important to use these descriptors as ways to better observe and perceive your students' needs, rather than as rigid categories to which everyone must be assigned. Nevertheless, if you have a student who clearly operates as an EPT and a student who clearly operates as an IIPT, these students will find little to no value being together in the same social thinking group. The educator will either have to move the pace of the group along to meet the needs of the IIPT while leaving the EPT student in the dust, or vice versa. Time spent trying to educate students simultaneously who have such different baselines of social understanding is time wasted.

This curriculum is mostly designed for the "Impaired Interactive Perspective Taker;" it has also been used with "Emerging Perspective Takers" effectively when taught at a slower pace.

How long should it take to get through an entire section?
How long will it take to get through the entire curriculum?

Each group is going to move at its own pace. Some groups will need lessons taught over and over before students grasp the major concept, while other groups will move through them more efficiently. It is not uncommon to spend an entire year or longer on Sections 1 and 2 with younger students or students with EPT.

As the book unfolds you will also notice that the sections become longer and more complex.

The basis of this curriculum could, and often does, span a childhood. The same type of lessons can also be used with young adults and adults. It is important to recognize, as mentioned in Section 8, that social rules change across our lives. Our social thinking lessons need to help students adapt their social knowledge to an increasingly sophisticated set of social rules as they age. We recycle lessons as students age while slightly modifying the content provided. For example, imagining and wondering with play (Section 6) for younger students evolves into imagining and wondering in conversation for older students and adults.

It is important to keep in mind that these lessons are rarely learned to full competence. This would be attempting to "cure," which I do not think educators/parents can do for students with social learning disabilities. The lessons here are offered to facilitate social thinking and related skills. The goal is for the child to advance in his personal understanding and use of these skills. The goal is not to cure or make the child "normal," but to improve his functional skills. The reality is that teaching social thinking and related skills to a student who does not intuitively develop them is one of the hardest things we could possibly teach a person.

To summarize, there are no time limits on teaching these concepts. Many times we may teach a set of lessons and then go back through and review them again.

Introduction Part 2

Goal Ideas for Each Social Thinking Section: Demonstrating a Relationship to Education Content Standards

Goal Suggestions Related to Each Chapter

At the end of each chapter, you will find goals related to the social thinking concepts presented. These suggestions will guide you in developing goals that are not only measurable, but also incorporate ample time for students to process the complicated social information. This processing phase (learning to apply and synthesize the knowledge) is critical. It needs to be encouraged and monitored prior to having students demonstrate their knowledge simply through 'rote' skill production. The suggested goals are meant to encourage you to expand your teaching and interventions beyond the educational sessions and settings, and to encourage you to measure generalization of the concepts across the home and school day.

As previously mentioned, these ideas should not be considered "mandates" in using this curriculum. Instead, view them as one way of defining goals and objectives and measuring progress in your students.

You, as educators, are encouraged to develop a variety of goals that expand these ideas without feeling you are restricted to simply using those included in this curriculum. Goal writing should be personal to each student's unique needs and circumstances.

Goals Without Benchmarks

New requirements affecting students' Individualized Education Plan (IEP) became effective nationally in July, 2005. They are mandated by the Individuals with Disabilities Education Improvement Act of 2004 (IDEA 2004). One proposed regulation addresses the issue of paperwork reduction by eliminating writing benchmarks related to goals (except for students with moderate to severe handicaps). Current information on reauthorization of IDEA can be obtained by searching the Internet.

In light of the paperwork reduction regulation, benchmarks have not been provided in this curriculum. If your IEP team chooses to incorporate benchmarks into a student's IEP, consider writing benchmarks that can be broken down into the following areas:

Benchmark 1: Processing the social thinking concepts

Benchmark 2: Performing the related social skill

Benchmark 3: Carrying over social thinking and related skills to other environments.

Making the Goals Measurable (Yikes!)

Each suggested goal includes a place to write the targeted percentage of concept or skill development towards the stated goal. Goals should be measurable, and quantifying social thinking is difficult. This is not what most of us data collectors want to hear, but it is the truth.

When students are sitting around a table practicing a specific concept repeatedly, it is pretty easy to take data about how the child performs the concept. However, when students are learning to think socially and are actively moving around an environment trying to be alert to what other people are thinking, saying and how they themselves are responding, data collection becomes much more difficult.

Goals are included in this curriculum for generalizing concepts into mainstream environments; in the mainstream setting it is far more difficult to take data. It is also more difficult for the student to demonstrate the targeted social thinking or related concepts when not being closely monitored by an adult.

Therefore, there are times data will be easier to take than others. As a general rule, always set the achievement percentages in more structured, specialized educational environments higher than those in less structured, mainstream environments. For example, we might say we want a child to produce a certain skill 60% of the time in the therapy room, but in the mainstream room we may only expect the child to produce the same skill about 35% of the time. While 35% may seem low, it is progress if the student was initially only producing it 15% of the time in the regular education classroom.

Remember, goal writing is not about curing a problem; it is about teaching the student to develop more skills over time.

Our goal as educators is to provide students with an educational foundation upon which we can document growth. When teaching students to become better social thinkers, the only way we may be able to show growth is through a narrative description documenting change in attitude or actions over time. Therefore, at times it may be helpful for the baseline to be descriptive or narrative. Then this baseline can be compared to narrative descriptions of student performance in a similar context later in the year. In my opinion, you have the freedom to measure progress in a variety of ways. A percentage is not the only way, nor is it often the best way, when trying to measure the growth in someone's capacity to think socially.

Goal Suggestions as They Relate to Essential Education Content Standards

An important message repeated over and over again within this curriculum is that social thinking and related skills impact far more than just a student's social play or conversation. The need to teach these specific social thinking skills is therefore, essential.

Following the suggested goals for each chapter, you will find a list of educational content standards relevant to that section's material. These Content Standards, adopted by the California State Board of Education for grades K-12, define the knowledge, concepts and skills students should acquire at each grade level.

If we consider these Content Standards to be the "essential building blocks" of education, then social thinking and related skills are the "mortar" that binds these blocks together.

Of particular interest for our population are the English-Language Arts Content Standards. The following excerpts are from that section. The complete document encompasses a variety of curriculum areas and can be found at:

www.cde.ca.gov/be/st/ss/engmain.asp

"An Essential Discipline: The ability to communicate well - to read, write, listen, and speak, runs to the core of human experience. Language skills are essential tools not only because they serve as the necessary basis for further learning and career development but also because they enable the human spirit to be enriched, foster responsible citizenship, and preserve the collective memory of a nation.

Students who read well learn the tempo and structure of language early in their development. They master vocabulary, variance in expression, and organization and skill in marshaling evidence to support an idea.

Fluent Readers and Skilled Writers: Through reading and writing students may share perspectives on enduring questions, understand and learn how to impart essential information, and even obtain a glimpse of human motivation. Reading and writing offer incomparable experiences of shared conflict, wisdom, understanding, and beauty.

Confident Speakers and Thoughtful Listeners: ... Speaking and listening skills have never been more important. Most Americans now talk for a living at least part of the time. The abilities to express ideas cogently and to construct valid and truthful arguments are as important to speaking well as to writing well. Honing the ability to express defensible reflections about literature will ensure comprehension and understanding."

California's Content Standards of Education are derived from those generated at the federal level; users of this curriculum guide within the U.S. should find their state's educational standards to be similar. More information can be obtained about your state's interpretation of the Content Standards from your state's Department of Education.

Not All Students are Intuitively Able to Learn the Content Standards

I am a parent of two "neurotypical" (e.g. normally developing) teenage girls. I have watched them work through their school curriculum towards graduation from high school. As I reviewed the Content Standards and Framework for all students, I considered my daughters' cognitive development and whether their teachers actually taught them the Content Standards for Language Arts. I reflected on whether each daughter's own neurological development provided them with the intuitive understanding and foundation to develop the knowledge to support the Standards or whether the Standards were directly taught to them by the teachers. My conclusion was my children actually had the knowledge to support the Standards prior to their teacher addressing it in class; the teachers functioned to sharpen and expand their knowledge and skills related to the Standards.

For example, by preschool, language learners are beginning to play with words that have literal versus figurative meaning. They love reading books demonstrating word play. While preschoolers may still be very literal in their language-based interpretation, they are actively expanding their capacity to move towards figurative understanding of language. This continues as they move into kindergarten, first, second grade, etc. However, it is not until fourth grade that teachers focus on the concept of figurative language. When the teacher introduces figurative language as an educational concept, most children have had years of experience playing with language meaning prior to having to meet this standard.

However, children with impaired social thinking may not intuitively acquire the Standards or have experiences prior to the time their teacher introduces concepts. Most of these children have some type of learning disability. Students on the autism spectrum demonstrate this reality repeatedly. For example, "smart" students with Asperger Syndrome may have good factual knowledge, but cannot efficiently figure out other people's motives. As a result of their social cognition learning disability, sixth graders with Asperger Syndrome may have never met or mastered an expected fourth grade Standard: to figure out a character's motivations.

Students do not all have the same capacity to learn the Standards in the same way or on the same time line. It is important for teachers, parents and administrators to discuss this formally (IEP meetings) and informally. The implications are pervasive and emphasize the need to teach students with social cognitive deficits very differently from neurotypical students. This introductory curriculum for teaching social thinking and related skills is a starting point.

As students acquire more knowledge related to social thinking (and the ability to apply and synthesize that knowledge), they are gaining the mortar to help them utilize the building blocks inherent in the Content Standards. For this reason, and this reason alone, students using this curriculum must have access to an educational environment that removes them from their neurotypical peers for part of the day. This provides them with access to a different type of education—one that aligned to their unique social learning abilities, to help them develop skills for use at school, home, and in the adult world.

To Summarize About Goals and Standards

The information within this curriculum is offered as a means for parents, educators and administrators to think about and learn how social thinking is essential to so many of the education Content Standards. This curriculum is a first step in exploring the complex landscape of social thinking and teaching it to students who do not learn it intuitively. Educators must discuss, in administrative, parent conferences and IEP meetings, how children's weak "social skills" are not just a problem on the playground or campus, but are actually part of a deeper problem in the classroom as well. Let's remove the idea that social relatedness problems are secondary to an education. These complicated deficits impact our students' education. Addressing them is essential for helping our students move towards independent living skills as adults.

Introduction Part 3
Sharing Social Thinking Concepts with Other Educators

How do we encourage staff to realize the importance of what we are teaching?

Educators using these materials are providing very important lessons to students, not only about coping better at school and at home, but also how to function as a member of our larger society (community, work, leisure, etc.).

Social thinking educators should consider themselves a "ripple in the pond," meaning it is also our duty to share what we are teaching and learning about these students with other people on campus. Consider giving a brief update about your group and a social thinking concept at each of your monthly staff meetings.

Teachers will find that these social thinking concepts apply to all students, not just those who are recognized as impaired.

School and program administrators grapple with justifying the inclusion of social thinking instruction during an academically based curriculum day. We must remind our administrators and teachers that every single moment of academic teaching is done within a social context. Students only learn when they can socially regulate as a group. Teaching social thinking and related skills is far more than teaching a child how to play with others on the playground. As more and more students with social cognitive learning disabilities are included in the mainstream classroom, we must explore ways to help teachers develop social cooperation in the classroom among all students.

Perspective Taking Across the School and Adult Years For Persons With Social Cognitive Deficits

A proposal for a perspective taking spectrum and related critical curriculum and support to facilitate adult success, by Michelle Garcia Winner.

Joe, a 6-year-old boy, with a passion for chemistry, was working with a therapist in my office for difficulties related to Asperger Syndrome. Joe had an amazingly sophisticated vocabulary and language skills that reflected his strong intelligence, measured to be in the superior range. While a number of Joe's academic skills were incredibly high when compared to his developmental age, he also presented with complex deficits in his ability to relate to others, especially his peers. In an effort to help one of my clinicians understand Joe's limited perspective-taking abilities and how they impacted his social interactions I asked her to observe me interact with Joe. I then asked Joe to tell me everything he knew about chemistry. This delighted Joe and he enthusiastically began to tell me all about the topic. As he did so I initially responded with active listening, then slowly I got up out of my chair, walked out a door and stood on the other side of the door only to have Joe continue to look at my chair and talk about chemistry.

Joe's difficulty in regulating his interaction with me was directly related to his inability to speak while considering his listener's point of view. From my years of clinical work with persons who have diagnostic labels that reflect weaknesses in social cognition (e.g. Autism Spectrum Disorders, Nonverbal Learning Disabilities, ADHD), it is apparent to me that perspective taking plays a key role in our ability to relate to others not only for the purpose of socialization but also to interpret meaning that is critical for academic work and personal problem solving skills critical for living independently as an adult.

The term "perspective taking" (PT) is an informal way to discuss what is often described in the literature as "Theory of Mind" (ToM). PT was introduced into my clinical work to override the difficulties educators and parents experienced when trying to understand the concept of ToM. It is my belief that most people can begin to make a guess about the implied meaning of perspective-taking given that the general population acknowledges that each person has his own "perspective".

PT is a social executive function task as it requires processing and responding to multiple levels of information simultaneously and within an incredibly limited time frame (1-2 seconds). Perspective-taking requires one to consider not only a person's own thoughts but also those of the person(s) he or she is communicating with. The following bullets very briefly describe many of the critical elements involved in the act of perspective taking required whenever one is in the presence of another person, even if there is no direct interaction:

- Actively considering and adjusting to the thoughts and emotions of one's self as well as the person(s) one is communicating with.

- Actively considering and then comparing and contrasting beliefs (e.g. religious, political, and cultural) of one's self as well as the person(s) one is communicating with.

- Actively considering and then adjusting one's message given the prior knowledge or experiences of one's communicative partner(s).

- Actively considering and then adjusting given the motives and intentions of one's self and/or their communicative partner.

Natural abilities to sustain attention and engage in the multiple tasks involved in perspective taking is at the heart of each person's ability to interact at a level that is perceived as fulfilling for all persons in the communicative environment. Some of the results of PT include the abilities to: interpret the needs and wants of others; provide responses that are considered empathetic; safely navigate around persons who may have ill intentions; interact with nuance so that others do not perceive you to be too demanding or too straightforward; interpret assignments at school by understanding the perspective of the characters studied or those of the teacher who is grading the assignment; share in the passions or delights of others even without sharing the same level of interest in the topic purely because one can enjoy the underlying relationship that is evolving; and engage in acts of socially related critical thinking and personal problem solving.

Persons with the same labels do not necessarily share the same skills:

Most people are born with solid perspective-taking skills that begin in utero and then develop intuitively though basic human interactions shortly after birth through early childhood and ultimately across our adult lives. The growth of perspective-taking skills continues across all persons' lives, thus unlike many skills we learn in school, this one is evolutionary with each developmental perspective-taking lesson leading to a deepening of awareness that allows for more mature and wiser interpretations and responses. For persons born with social-cognitive deficits, or those who acquire them through accident or injury, the evolution of this critical process is not guaranteed.

In my clinical experience I have observed that the perspective-taking abilities one develops by early elementary school has a direct impact on one's ability to develop and functionally use verbal and nonverbal language and nuance to engage in increasingly sophisticated interactions as our students age. Those with sustained weaknesses in this area, even if they have solid cognitive and emerging language learning abilities, often demonstrate difficulty with higher level forms of language, including abstract interpretation of meaning, as well as forming an overall conceptual understanding of what is being discussed or read. Those with severe deficits in PT may be unable to develop verbal and nonverbal communication skills that move them beyond the initial but important ability to focus on their own desires, needs and thoughts during communicative interaction.[1]

Although the act of perspective taking is deeply embedded in our eventual success as communicators and personal problem solvers, the ability to measure it through standardized tests remains elusive. Given its very abstract nature, one's ability or lack of ability to take perspective of others is not currently associated with the official diagnostic descriptions of persons with Autism Spectrum Disorders as defined in the DSM-IV or for persons with Nonverbal Learning Disabilities. While a lack of development in perspective taking directly impacts one's ability to develop social skills and language, professionals often only refer to "social skill problems" and "difficulties with verbal or nonverbal communicative development" in the anecdotal descriptions of a larger label such as "autism" or "Asperger Syndrome." Thus, the Autism Spectrum diagnostic labels are given to persons who represent extremely wide learning abilities when it comes to their potential development for social and communicative skills which directly impact their ability to function or not to function as independent adults.

The great divide between a traditional education and a functional education:

My motivation to understand the depth of perspective taking deficits comes from a concern about how we educate children across their school years with the supposed intent to help them develop into adults who can feel satisfied with their ability to participate in and contribute to society. It is my belief that we can do a better job recognizing the strengths and weaknesses of our students with the goal of designing a curriculum that facilitates growth towards functioning as an adult. PT deficits, whether manifested in a person with low or high cognition and language, strongly increase the likelihood that the student will have difficulty transitioning into adulthood without direct educational intervention. However, I have come to the conclusion that we can do a better job at predicting the intensity of life skills curriculum (work, daily living and leisure) that should be defined and explored at school and home based on the different levels of PT skills a student demonstrates.

In recognizing that every single person has the ability to learn, I also recognize that all persons do not have the ability to learn the same information. Given that I have always worked with adults as well as children, I have had many opportunities to observe what happens

---

[1]Severe deficits in perspective-taking ability may ultimately limit one's ability to function with complete independence as an adult. However it does not mean the child is not able to learn a great range of practical skills across a lifetime that will help him to function with increasing independence as he ages.

when children are taught a standard educational curriculum without regard to their level of perspective-taking/ social interpretive skills. These standards of education are highly regarded currently in the United States; however they were established with the belief that all children have solid social communicative skills. From my work with persons from ages five to 65, I have had many opportunities to learn backwards what we should have taught students to help them work towards achieving increasing or full independence in adulthood, which is an implied goal of public education.

Sarah, a 22-year-old young woman was recently diagnosed with Asperger Syndrome at her university medical center. She graduated from high school as a merit scholar with confident hopes for success in college given her academic accomplishments in high school. Her first year at a four-year university resulted in dismal failure, as she could not keep on top of the organizational and communicative demands expected of the university student. Sure that this experience was due to problems with the university personnel, she was transferred to a different university where once again she was met with the same difficulties. During her third year out of school she moved back home and worked for a small non-profit agency where she could focus on her computer knowledge. There she was able to succeed given the small nurturing environment of the company while she was also able to contribute given her strong technical knowledge. During this time she also continued to take a couple of classes at the local junior college. This combination of working in an environment that supported her cognitive skills while taking a reduced number of classes provided for a successful year. Armed with success she moved back to the four-year university that she last attended. While initially doing well, as soon as she felt overwhelmed by an assignment she described that she "completely shut down". Once again her lack of communication, problem solving and organizational skills led to her academic failure across her classes. This time the university asked her not to return. Left on her own while barred from attending her university, she had become secluded in her apartment refusing to leave even for a community Asperger support group meeting. At the same time she tried to assure her family that she would work it out all by herself. Her parents ultimately insisted that she move back home. Upon returning home she had to cope with the humiliation of academic failure and the realization that she had not learned to develop skills for independence at college even though she received awards for her academic accomplishments in high school.

It is critical that educators, administrators and parents realize persons with social cognitive deficits, even those with exceptionally strong cognitive and language skills, have to learn much more than the standard curriculum in their elementary through high school years, to prepare them for adult independent living.

The spectrum of perspective-taking skills and related adult outcomes:

Given that special education is based on helping students learn to thrive in "least restrictive environments" where they can live with "increasing independence," it is not uncommon for adults to interpret these concepts to mean that all children will be able to function independently as adults as long as the they are blessed with good teachers who are familiar with the latest educational techniques. While I strongly believe all students can learn and improve their functioning relative to who they are today, I realize that not all students have the ability to learn at the same pace or the same lessons. In fact, if we try and teach all children the same lessons we easily can overwhelm some of our students and send them into behavioral and mental health spirals. When a parent of a 12-year-old child with significant mental retardation, very limited communication skills and extremely limited perspective-taking abilities told me: "If my child is not able to live and hold a job in the community independently by the time he is 18 years old, I will personally hold the director of special education accountable," I realized that we have not done a sufficient job helping parents learn how their children's learning differences will likely impact their children's outcome even with the best of teaching.

As researchers struggle to define perspective-taking deficits, it is becoming increasingly clear that perspective-taking skills are not entities that you are or are not born with; instead there is a spectrum of perspective-taking deficits. I propose three levels of perspective-taking functioning and the related outcomes for persons with these deficits. The purpose of the proposal of this spectrum is to establish more realistic goals and potential outcomes that will allow us to celebrate the smaller steps of progress a student achieves, regardless of functioning level. I believe that in our attempt to treat all students the same, we set unrealistic goals for many. Unrealistic goals establish unrealistic expectations making it more difficult to celebrate the critical, smaller foundational steps of learning that should be celebrated with the students, their parents and teachers.

The three levels on the spectrum of perspective taking:

Children with social cognitive deficits can experience enormous changes in their language, behavioral and relational abilities during their early developmental years (ages 0-5). A child with very weak communication and behavior skills at age three may have a very different command of the world by age five. However, once children enter the first or second grade we begin to see some consistency in their learning abilities across their life. The following three different levels of perspective taking are to be considered for children who are at least in first or second grade. Since no one model applies to all people, this information should be perceived as a guide rather than as a set of facts.

1. Severely Impaired Perspective Takers (SIPD)

Students with SIPD generally have mental retardation that accompanies a diagnosis of autism. These students have extremely limited abilities to understand the perspective of others even if given clear explanation, visual information and time to consider the information. However, they enjoy being in the presence of others, much of the time, as long it is clear what others want from them in the environment. The following bullets notate some specific traits that might be observed in elementary school and beyond:

a. Generally they learn about the expectations others have for them through routinized experiences. Changes in expectations/routines even if explained can be very distressing and cause significant behavioral reactions.

b. Weak development of language. Nearly all of these students are nonverbal or minimally verbal. These students are prone to behavioral distress given their lack of functional receptive and expressive communication skills.

c. They can make gains in communication with augmentative communication systems and/or verbal language, however most spontaneous communication is related to the students' specific wants and needs in the form of making requests. Comments with language, if the student does comment, are usually to reference a thought he is having without the ability to explain clearly to his listener what he is thinking.

d. Loves and enjoys persons in his family as well as familiar educators, friends, and so forth. Has great difficulty relating to persons based on what other persons might enjoy doing. However, they are often happy to receive and give hugs when they feel good. The presence of their loved ones can help to relax them.

e. Unless highly routinized, participation in reciprocal communication or interactions with adults requires a highly structured environment to help the student follow through with an activity.

f. Given their very limited ability to consider the perspective of others, they have great difficulty learning and maintaining their attention as part of a large group. Most of these students do best in a 1:1 learning environment or in a very small group.

g. Very limited expressive and receptive interpretive language skills. These students are very literal in how they perceive the world and how they express themselves.

h. Great difficulty engaging in a discussion about the different belief systems of two or more people, given that this type of concept is not apparent to them.

i. Can learn skills that are factually based. In addition to learning to use a communication system (verbal, augmentative or both), many of them have abilities to do basic math, basic writing, and acquire reading, decoding and basic comprehension skills.

j. Will do best when their education focuses on their own understanding of the world and introduces them to community events and expectations. They usually enjoy being out in the community and are best at learning when provided with opportunities to participate in events that are highly structured and fulfilling to them. This may include grocery shopping, food preparation, functional math skills, and job skills in an environment they enjoy. Learning in these environments is the most efficient given the intrinsic motivation that community and functional experiences provide.

k. Difficulty learning conceptual information that they cannot relate to. This includes learning from textbook or other types of information that do not intrinsically make sense in their daily experiences.

l. Clearly have cognitive strengths in specific areas of academics, sports, arts or leisure. These should be celebrated and encouraged.

Students with the above profiles will most likely need strong supported living across their adult years in all environments: community/work, leisure and home. Due to their tremendous difficulty learning as part of a larger group, they generally require close supervision in the teaching environment. Paraprofessionals are important members of their educational treatment team. Progress will continue to be celebrated across their lives as long as adults are there to continue to encourage and support new learning. They are wonderful people who can exhibit enjoyment, love and good sense of humor when they feel comfortable and secure.

2. Emerging Perspective Takers (EPT):

Emerging perspective takers may have mild mental retardation to advanced cognitive skills with a solid emergence in the use of verbal or augmentative expressive and receptive language skills to communicate their daily needs. By upper elementary school they understand that other people have some level of different thoughts, emotions and experiences, however they need to think long and hard about this before they can figure out what those might be. Perspective taking for the EPT student might be considered "social algebra." It is not that they are without the ability to consider other people's thoughts and emotions, they just often need guidance to consider, incorporate and react to the information they are acquiring. From my clinical work it appears that one of the critical issues with this population is the amount of time and guidance it takes to think through what others might be thinking. Normally a communicative message is processed and responded to within three seconds, so students who require 20 minutes to consider and respond to others are perceived as having a serious disability that impacts their social and academic functioning. This perception exists even when cognitive and academic testing may reveal a number of areas where they function in the normal to above normal range. The following bullets notate some specific traits that might be observed in elementary school and beyond:

a. The students use verbal language or sophisticated computer driven augmentative communication systems to convey their ideas to others. However, given their deficits in perspective taking they will exhibit difficulty in the following areas:

   i. Narrative language skills: being able to consider other people's prior knowledge to describe clearly and efficiently information for others to comprehend about their life.

ii. Pronoun referencing: will most likely have difficulty understanding pronoun references and use them appropriately in their own early communication in early elementary school and possibly beyond that time.

iii. Grammar may be immature and lack elaboration.

iv. Tendency towards strong literal expressive and receptive language.

v. Language is often self-focused with difficulty focusing on the thoughts or needs of others.

vi. Difficulty answering "how" and "why" questions, strikingly better at answering the factual "who, what, when, where" questions.

b. Tendency towards an over-focus on detail rather than conceptualization of ideas. For example:

i. Communication may be highly tangential as they have difficulty tracking the underlying concept of what is being discussed.

ii. Reading comprehension is best at the factual level, great difficulty understanding the main idea of a passage or book.

c. Tremendous difficulty with social pragmatic skills even though they may attempt to spontaneously engage in social interaction with others. Interactions tend to be perseverative.

d. Given the social nature of group learning, they have difficulty participating and learning as part of the larger group in classrooms even though they may be educated in a large group setting given their stronger cognitive abilities. Generally they need directed instruction from a paraprofessional or educational specialist within the large group setting to help them maintain attention and break down concepts so that they can understand what they need to do.

e. Overwhelmed by organizational tasks.

f. Difficulty with personal problem solving and asking for help.

g. Difficulty with written expression.

h. Need direct instruction about life skills such as hygiene, shopping, money management, employment, cooking, cleaning, budgeting since they do not easily infer information or learn through observation.

i. Demonstrate love, companionship and personal preferences with regard to the people they choose to share their friendship. They desire social interaction but have difficulty initiating and sustaining it particularly with their own peer group. Do best with highly structured social situations.

j. Clearly have cognitive strengths in specific areas of academics, sports, arts or leisure. These should be celebrated and encouraged.

Given this description, these students show potential for directed instruction about the concept of perspective taking using very explicit and visual teaching techniques such as comic strip conversations, social stories, clear explanations and role play. While they continue to struggle in this area, small gains are wonderful experiences as they can relate better to others with each small step of learning. They also have good abilities to continue to learn across their lives; however they will need to have alternative curriculum lessons during their school years to help them learn directly about life skills for work, college, leisure and home life. While in school, if taught in large group classrooms they generally need a paraprofessional or special educator nearby to help them better conceptualize the information being taught.

Adults with emerging perspective taking skills may be able to live and work with relative independence in the community, after a routine has been established across these environments. At the same time, they will need a support team nearby throughout their life to assist with problem solving complex situations that arise in daily life such as changes in job demands, job searches, budgeting, moving living environments or difficulties encountered in personal relations at work or in the community. These folks, as long as they are motivated and have helpful adults near by, will continue to learn more sophisticated concepts. They need assistance with breaking down complicated concepts into small, more concrete parts. These adults seek friendship, have a great sense of humor and can celebrate the progress they are making.

3. Impaired Interactive Perspective Takers (IIPT)

The impaired interactive perspective taker (IIPT) is the student who looks like everyone else at school, at least initially. The IIPT students have solid to advanced cognitive skills with solid language development. They have a lot of information about the world and will comment openly about their areas of interest. Socially they are very interested in pursuing peer relationships and they understand the "superficial social rules," meaning they are aware that there is an underlying rule-based system that helps to negotiate social situations. They can tell you the more concrete social rules "stand in line," "say please," "don't interrupt." However, they have a great deal of difficulty perceiving how those rules apply to them. They have poor self-awareness. They are far less aware of the more subtle or sophisticated rules or non-verbal signals that help to mitigate social relationships as students' age. While these students may appear "normal" on the outside, there are differences in how they process and respond to the more socially abstract information. It is not uncommon for younger students with IIPT to turn in their peers for breaking rules on the playground, while not being aware that the act of turning in a peer breaks a far greater social rule. Their struggles with social interpretation and abstraction become more evident as they age given the increasing complexity of social interaction and academic interpretation.

They are called "impaired interactive perspective takers" because their greatest deficits become apparent at the moment of interaction with their peers. Adults are far more flexible in accommodating to a single-minded conversation, but peers are unrelenting in their requirements that interactions be reciprocal. Peer based interaction requires not only the formulation of thoughts one might wish to communicate, but also persistent monitoring of how others might be interpreting or responding to the message so that the message can be adjusted as needed to meet the needs of the communicative partner. This is a social executive function task.

Sue was a beautiful middle school girl who had worked with me in an individual and group session to help her develop social thinking and related skills. During our individual sessions we worked actively on perspective-taking concepts, the length of a message, how to adjust a message in response to another, etc. One day in our group session with other middle school girls, all of the girls were told that the goal for the day was to "ask questions of other girls about their life".

We reviewed the importance of focusing their communication on the needs of others and using their own language as an avenue to explore others, which directly positively impacts how other people feel about them. After a thorough review of the concepts I asked who wanted to start. Sue raised her hand and said, "I had to audition in the school play. I had to learn 50 lines" and then she recited many of the 50 lines in her audition. Upon retelling of her audition she added, "I even get to sing in the school play" and then she started to sing. She only stopped when another girl in the group gave her a very blunt non-verbal cue to stop talking. This was on videotape and we used it during our next individual session to increase her awareness of the perspective of others during a spontaneous social exchange.

In addition to difficulty with reciprocal peer interaction, the following bullets point out other issues common for this group. However, given their strong academic and language skills demonstrated on test taking, the challenges to these students are not easily revealed. More commonly their challenges come to light in late childhood or early adolescence when they start to demonstrate feelings of depression, inadequacy or lack of being able to relate to others through sustained friendships.

a. Great difficulty with organizational tasks; their organizational struggles are deep and require a lengthy intervention to help them conceptualize, task analyze, manage time. They also need assistance with perspective taking, functional communication and problem solving.

b. Difficulty with written expression. This relates to weaknesses in fine motor control (penmanship) as well as conceptualizing and pre-organizing the material.

c. Deeper reading comprehension that requires a strong analysis of the social-emotional nature of the characters being explored in literature or history.

d. Some students have tremendous difficulty understanding math concepts.

e. Abstract thinking and making inferences. They tend towards more literal interpretation, making it difficult to be flexible in deriving meaning (verbally and nonverbally) quickly during communication.

f. Social relatedness as described above. Given that they do have "superficial" knowledge of social interactions they generally do well on standardized tests exploring social pragmatic knowledge, however functionally they struggle tremendously. It is difficult for them to get adults to understand the level of their deficits as they have a good vocabulary and physically look like their peers. Unfortunately, their peer group very quickly notices subtle "quirks" and can be very unforgiving.

g. Tendency towards perseveration on specific themes or topics both in their spoken and written expression.

h. Limited social experiences in the community. May need assistance learning to navigate shopping, job interviews, adjusting to the "hidden curriculum" of the job as well as pursuing social relationships in less structured environments.

i. Very confused when it comes to dating, despite a strong desire to develop these relationships.

j. May lie to avoid dealing with situations that overwhelm them.

k. Difficulty participating in group activities, including in larger classroom groups and smaller academic workgroups with peers.

l. Most likely of all the three levels of perspective takers to get teased/taunted by their peers.

These students are generally taught in the mainstream educational environment, however they benefit from direct instruction in social thinking and related skills for managing the complex requirements of the older child and young adult. They may be the least likely group to require the assistance of a paraprofessional, but they do benefit from special educators who offer insight into strategies that help them break down tasks, (academic and social) to prevent them from feeling overwhelmed.

In addition to the social challenges (which often lighten up a bit in high school), as these bright students go to college some of their greatest challenges will come from their failure to seek assistance or clarification, and from their organizational/problem solving weaknesses. While we might describe these folks as having a "mild" disability, given their many academic or cognitive strengths, actually due to their difficulties learning the complex skills of functioning as adults, their deficits are not at all mild. Many parents call my clinic to seek assistance for a 20 or 30-year-old child with IIPT who has not developed skills for independence with regard to life and work skills.

This group has the greatest likelihood for full adult independence; however, they may be slower than their neurotypical peers at achieving it. As they get older they also become more keenly aware that they are not able to process social information quickly and efficiently. This can be a source of great frustration that does not wane just because they are getting older.

Even if these folks make the choice to live with fewer opportunities for social interaction, they desire to be able to function in groups and to have close friends. They are generally terrific, friendly people with a good sense of humor when they feel comfortable.

Summary:

The intention of this article has been to explore different levels of perspective-taking deficits in persons with weaknesses in social cognitive processing. This information is intended to better understand reasonable educational expectations while also promoting the need to create a more functional curriculum to meet the social, organizational, and life skills needs according to their different levels of need. The three levels of perspective taking functioning included:

1. Severely Impaired Perspective Takers (SIPT)

2. Emerging Perspective Takers (EPT)

3. Impaired Interactive Perspective Takers (IIPT)

Ultimately all students should be provided, at the very least, with an education that facilitates the development of skills for success in life, whether this is to achieve a higher level of education, participate with increasing independence in the work environment and seek leisure activities in the community. Given that students have different learning abilities we have to be reminded that they also need different curricular standards to facilitate this goal of education: to live and work successfully in our communities.

We, as parents and educators, need to improve our own abilities to describe and discuss our children's'/students' level of functioning to create realistic expectations and more finely tuned educational treatment plans. This article was written with the intention of providing a framework to foster more specific instruction for our wide range of students with social cognitive deficits.

This article was published in The Educational Therapist; The Journal of the Association of Educational Therapists *(Winner, 2004, Vol 24, number 1); Burbank, California, under the title* "A Proposal for a Perspective Taking Spectrum"

It was also published in Social Spectrum: Social Understanding *(Volume 4 -03/04) The Gap; Australia, under the title* "Perspective Taking Across the School and Adult Years for Persons With Social Cognitive Deficits."

Being Part of a Group and Recognizing Expectations

The purpose of this section is to explore how people create a group and how they work together within that structure. Working together means there are "hidden" expected and unexpected behaviors within the group that people are subconsciously aware of and regulate their behavior around. We say they are "hidden" expectations since we adults often don't explicitly state them.

Being in a group is more complicated than most of us realize. For neurotypical students, these abilities evolve from birth. However, our students with social cognitive learning challenges do not experience a natural development of the skills needed to co-exist easily in a group. This entire curriculum helps to teach concepts to support this type of learning.

Learning these skills, however, does not address all the issues related to sharing other people's space. We also have to work with kids on "personal problem solving". One of our opening lessons helps students learn that we don't react to all problems with the same level of emotional and behavioral response because problems come in different sizes: big and little.

Through these lessons we will also explore that when we play in a group, structure is needed to create and sustain the play itself.

How do these lessons relate to classroom participation?

The lessons in this section are basic to working as part of a group. For example, most children intuitively learn there are "expected" and "unexpected" behaviors in a setting such as a classroom. They realize that one's behavior may impact the emotions of others.

However, students with social cognitive deficits need to be directly taught the social skills that appear to be "obvious" to the rest of us. These lessons, while seemingly simple, are NOT simple to our students. Students with social cognitive deficits may take months or years to explore, process, and eventually develop skills towards coping effectively in groups.

In this section we focus on these first steps — being aware of participating within a group and the need to increase awareness of those around them.

Tools & Materials

• Video camera

• Poster of different emotions (optional)

• A passage or book that demonstrates how one person's behavior impacts another person's feelings causing them to have their own behavioral reactions.

• Objects for the "Drumming Game" (See Lesson 3)

• Time-Timer (A visual timer – optional.) Go to www.timetimer.com to learn more.

Critical Vocabulary & Concepts

• Doing what is expected in the group

• Doing what is unexpected in a group

• "You can change my feelings."

• Observing others through imitation

• Identifying whether there is a "big problem - little problem"

• Feeling "safe" within a group

• Three parts of play: set up, play and clean up

• Various "feeling" words

Lesson 1: Expected and Unexpected Behavior in a Group

Critical Vocabulary

Doing what is *expected* in the group
Doing what is *unexpected* in the group

You can adapt the vocabulary to more explicitly state what behaviors are **expected** versus **unexpected** within the group. This informs students that people actually notice other people's behavior and recognize whether they are abiding by the unwritten social rules or hidden rules.

How to use this lesson in the classroom:

1. Give the students free time when they first come into your room. Videotape them playing or just existing in this new social thinking group (3-4 minutes).

2. Encourage the students to join together in a group:

A. Sit with the students in a circle on a mat on the floor (preferred) but a table is ok. Providing concrete visual cues (such as a small mat to sit on) is useful so each child knows where his body belongs. Use mats even with third and fourth graders!

B. You may experience problems when getting students to work and play together. The students may fight about what color or type of mat each of them receives or who sits next to whom. This may lead to a side lesson on "big problem, little problem." You can either interrupt your current lesson plan to do this now or you can plan do it during another lesson.

C. You will also want to work with your group on discovering there are three distinct parts to play. See Lesson 5 on page 47.

3. Observe who is looking like he or she is ready to be part of the group.

4. You, the teacher, will now perform a series of socially bizarre or unexpected behaviors while you introduce yourself to the group.

    A. Lie down on the floor, or have your body turned out of the group or splayed across the worktable.

    B. Begin to talk to the students about learning how to be part of a group. Talk to them as if nothing unexpected is happening.

    C. Observe the students' reactions. If they look puzzled or start to ask you what you are doing, just let them continue to ask. Ignore their weird looks.

5. After a few minutes, ask the students if they think there is anything wrong or odd with the way you are behaving. You are going to encourage them to participate in Step 6, so they can more explicitly state exactly what it is that you were doing right versus wrong.

    A. Allow the students to tell you how they feel about you doing these unexpected behaviors.

    B. Encourage them to talk about what you are doing "wrong".

    C. Verbally praise them for figuring out that this behavior is unexpected and it makes them feel "weird" or "nervous".

6. On the blackboard, draw two columns. At the top of one column, write the words "Expected Behavior" and at the top of the other column, write the words "Unexpected Behavior." If the children are too young to read, then draw a happy face on one column and an unhappy face on the other column.

A. Using the students' feedback, make a list of what behaviors they might expect of you and the others who are in a group.

B. Now make a list of behaviors that are unexpected (see example below). For younger students, draw sample pictures to illustrate the concepts.

Expected behaviors in the group

• Sitting on the mat

• Facing the teacher

• Making comments only about what the group is talking about (staying on topic)

• Using good eye contact

Unexpected behaviors in the group

• Lying on the floor

• Body turned around

• Saying things that have nothing to do with what the group is talking about

• Not looking at people in the group

7. Foster discussion about what students are expected to do with their:

A. Eyes

B. Head

C. Shoulder

D. Legs

E. Hands

8. Acknowledge the students for sharing what they know about being in a group. Work with them on how "smart" they are for being aware of what makes people feel safe within groups of other people.

 Use vocabulary that is appropriate to their age and current jargon such as "cool," "awesome," "right-on," etc.

Lesson 2:
Our Behavior Impacts the Feelings of Those Around Us

 Critical Vocabulary

"You can change (impact/affect) my feelings."

You can now talk about the fact that when you see students doing *expected* behavior it makes you feel more positive (proud, happy, etc). You can also explicitly make the connection that when you see a student doing what is *unexpected* this makes you feel more negative (frustrated, uncomfortable, angry, etc). To have this lesson be effective you MUST emphasize observing and talking about students who are doing what is expected or justified in the situation. Students are more likely to work towards making others feel good when they are aware of their own impact, even if they won't admit it.

How to use this lesson in the classroom:

1. Use a poster or pictures that show various emotions to help students think of 'feeling' words.

2. Discuss the fact that all people have feelings. Explain that even right now, while in the group, the students have reactions and feelings about the room, the people, and the lesson.

3. List emotion words describing how the students feel when you or they are doing what is expected (e.g. safe, good, happy).

4. List emotion words about how students feel when you or they are doing what is unexpected (e.g. yucky, bad, sad, mixed-up).

5. Discuss that people's feelings can be changed by the behavior of others around them. Read aloud a passage or story where people's behavior changes based on how they feel. One example is *Miss Nelson is Missing* (1977). In this book a teacher is frustrated by the behavior of the students in her classroom so she comes back disguised as a witch. This subsequently impacts how the children behave, and once they start to follow the rules, Miss Nelson, the teacher returns.

 What books can you think of that provide examples of how one's behavior impacts another's feelings? Discuss the connections between behavior and feelings.

6. Use the concept "you can change (impact/affect) my feelings." For younger children address the simple concept that "you can change my feelings." For older students, use more sophisticated terminology by saying "you can impact or affect my feelings." Identify students whose recent behaviors give you a positive reaction/feeling. Identify students whose recent behaviors give you negative reactions/feelings. For example, you can point out a student who looks like he is not listening. Explain that this makes you feel worried that he is not working with the group, and that it can even make you feel frustrated since it does not appear that he is listening.

If the student replies by saying he was listening, and then he proceeds to tell you everything you just said, point out to him or her that it was great that he was listening, but that when you observed that he was distracted, you FELT like he was not listening. Explain that his behavior caused a change in your own emotions. It is always important to get the idea across that your feelings are very real to you, even if the other person felt that you were not correct in feeling them to begin with!

Lesson 3: Play Games of Imitation to Show How a Group Works Together

 Critical Vocabulary

Learning to observe others through imitation

Play imitation games with body movement. Ask the students to sit in a circle or stand. Have them watch and imitate you (the teacher). If they are doing well, have each student take turns being the leader. This is basically "follow the leader" but, at first, start by just standing in a circle. Begin moving around only when the group is ready to move while still thinking about being part of the group. While this sounds easy, it often is not. Plan to play this game many times over the coming sessions. This will help the students pay attention to the other members of the group. You may need to exaggerate the movements at first.

How to use this lesson in the classroom:

1. Once you have the children imitating you with reasonable success, allow each of the students to become "the leader."

2. You, the teacher, should help the children be aware that they need to go slowly so the other children, who are imitating the leader, can keep up. The leader will have to make a point of modeling slow movements the others can think about. Encourage the leader to make big (exaggerated) and slow movements so that others can figure out what the leader is going to do next.

3. Reward students who cooperate. While the leaders may try and compete with the other students by modeling difficult or complicated movements, thereby making it difficult for the others to keep up, reinforce the leaders' slow, exaggerated movements.

4. Provide specific praise/feedback for students who respond to the leader by imitating the leader accurately. Also pay attention to the leader (e.g. "I like the way Joe is thinking about Sam. Joe is watching Sam really carefully and he is also going just as slow as Sam when he imitates his movements. Nice job, Joe!")

5. Allow each child to become a leader. Provide positive and constructive feedback to the leaders and imitators. Help each child want to work together as part of a group. Limit the time of the imitation to just 1-2 minutes so everyone gets a turn.

Drumming Game Activities

Have the students use their hands on the top of the table to make drumming sounds. While you can use drumming sticks and drum heads, these objects often become distractions.

Use a simple beat/pattern and have the students follow that beat. Compliment the students who are keeping their body in the group, watching the others and keeping close to the same beat. (Make the beats simple, only advance at the level of the group.)

The goal is for the students to develop an awareness of working together by observing, listening and imitating each other, but first they start by just imitating you.

Once the students can follow your beat/patterns (this may take many sessions), allow each of the students to take turns being a leader. Encourage the students to talk about the fact that being a leader means they think about the others in the group and don't go too fast so that everyone can keep pace with them as leader.

 This skill may be too advanced for your group. If they are not ready to be able to lead or take direction from one of the other students, remember this and come back to it later when you are in Section 2.

Lesson 4: Problem Solving

Critical Vocabulary

• **What is the size of the problem?**

• **Is it a big problem or a little problem (also known as a glitch)?**

• **Learning to sort out/analyze the situation**

• **Matching the level of expected responses and reactions to the level of the problem**

When students participate within group activities, they often get upset when someone else gets something they wanted such as the color game piece, mat or being chosen first. We want to start working with them on the fact that some problems are really big while others are little or simply glitches. Problems require different reactions, emotions and solutions based on their size.

How to use this lesson in the classroom:

You can use the "big problem/little problem" strategy to help students sort out what is important to them given their personal ability to cope. You can ask students to sort out or analyze the following: "is this a 'big problem,' 'little problem,' or a glitch?" and then help them learn there are many strategies and coping mechanisms available to them regarding such problems. Well formed strategies help to deal with life's bumps and hurdles.

1. Determine the size of a problem:

  A. Write a scale from 1-10 on the white board or chart paper.

  B. Have the students list what type of problem is a **10** (earthquakes, car accidents, being seriously hurt, etc.); a **5** (getting in a big fight with their sibling); or a **1** (not getting the color mat you want to sit on).

  C. Facilitate the students' discussion to generate descriptions of problems and then determine where they fit on the scale.

2. Define what makes a problem large or small. Some of our bigger problems are problems that many people share and which have no easy, quick or pleasant solution.

3. Discuss what types of emotions are associated with different levels of problems.

4. Discuss how different problem levels impact a situation over time. Come up with clear examples such as how the results of a tornado can last for years (big problem) or arguing can make people upset for hours and make them feel physically bad (moderate size problem, depending on the situation). With a little problem or glitch, such as not getting the color of the game piece they want, the feeling ends as soon as the game is over and perhaps as soon as they start playing the game.

5. Discuss how the students can start to sort out and analyze that little problems or glitches actually merit smaller emotional responses and reactions. Point out that this relatively quick recovery from feeling frustrated to being fine is what other people expect as well.

6. Discuss with students their own emotions.

    A. What happens when they have emotional responses that are at the level of a big problem when actually it was just a little problem or glitch? For example, what if the student screams and kicks and cries when he did not get the color game piece he or she desired?

    B. Did children recover quickly or did they end up not being able to play at all? We slowly want to work with students on understanding that their emotional response prevented them from getting to play at all. In the next lesson the students will explore how play has at least three parts, and some parts are more important than others!

 This will be an ongoing lesson that will not be completely learned by doing this activity once or twice. However this activity will establish basic vocabulary about the size of a problem and how it relates to the levels of emotions people experience and expect within various situations.

Lesson 5: Understanding How Play Unfolds

 Critical Vocabulary

Three parts of play:

1. Set up

2. Play

3. Clean up

Where and how do you want to spend your time?

There are three parts to playing a game. In this lesson, you want your students to understand that playing a game involves the SET UP, PLAY and CLEAN UP. You want to stress that the real pleasure in the game is the part where the kids get to PLAY, so it is in their best interest to be as efficient as possible in moving through set-up and clean-up. You want to teach them that the longer they take to set up or clean up, the less time they get for play.

When setting up the game, students choose a game piece (or sitting mat or chair color) to help identify their choice during the game or activity.

Challenge: Students with social cognitive deficits in elementary school often start to cry or protest when they don't get the color or item desired.

How to use this lesson in the classroom:

Establish a clear time frame for play, so the students can explore how to budget their time when moving through the three parts of play: Work with the students on setting time limits for the activity. "We are going to play this game for 10 minutes."

1. You can remind students during game based activities there are three parts to play. Ask them where they want to spend most of the time: setting up, playing, or cleaning up?

---

2. Since all students will answer "playing", you can help them realize that the color piece they choose or who goes first are likely all "little problems," "no big deal," or "no problem at all." Once the students make a good choice or demonstrate this skill, acknowledge them with specific performance praise ("You were able to make a fast, good choice." or "I liked the way you decided to choose another color and started the game quickly. Jeff liked the way you let him go first, way to go!").

3. For students who can do basic math, ask the students to decide how much time should be spent in set up, play and clean up. The students are usually very good establishing that the set-up and clean-up times should be less than two minutes each to allow a full six minutes for play. For students who cannot do basic math, use blocks to represent each minute of the time. Ask them how many of the blocks should represent the amount of time for set up and how many of the blocks should represent the play time, etc.

4. Discuss what happens when the group argues about the set up. This should be a little problem or glitch (i.e. the color of the item for the game). Does this still only take two minutes or is the set up now taking five minutes with people getting really mad, frustrated or sad? (Use various emotion vocabularies as needed). Using the Time-Timer (visual timer) or the blocks, show that if they take five minutes to set up then they only have three minutes to play before they need two more minutes to clean up.

5. If needed, put the time increments on a board or paper as a math problem or have other concrete ways, beyond the use of the blocks or visual timer, to show the time increments.

6. Discuss how they feel when they cry or have other emotions. Is this the feeling they were seeking, expecting or wanting, when they looked forward to playing?

7. Discuss a resolution: How important is the color of the game piece? Is it worth getting really sad and leaving the group for, with no time left to really play, or is it not very important at all? Most students can cognitively discuss that a little problem is not important.

8. Encourage the group to focus on what is important in play, such as having fun doing an activity together.

9. Remind them, each time they are exposed to a "play" type of situation, to think about where they want to spend their time. Is it in setting up the activity, playing the activity, or cleaning it up?

Video Moments Self-Monitoring Checklist - Section 1

Being Part of a Group and Recognizing Expectations

Student's Name _____ Date _____

We are learning to watch people's social behavior and figure out how these behaviors are making other people feel.

Every once in a while you are going to be a **"behavior checker,"** meaning you will be checking on someone's behavior in the group.

Sometimes the person you are going to check on is **you**, other times it is someone else in the group.

The person you are going to check on today is _____

Behavior to monitor or watch	Put a check here if the student is doing a good job.	Put a check here if the student is NOT doing a good job.
Doing what is expected in the group.		For example, put a check here if the student looks like he or she is really distracted.
Identifying whether there is a big problem or a little problem.		
Following the three parts of play: set up, play, and clean up		

Based on what you checked, do you think this person would be a good person to work with on a project?

Circle: YES or NO

If not, what is one behavior the student could try and think about more to help people want to work with him?

Review for Teachers & Parents
🔊 ## Section 1

Being Part of a Group and Recognizing Expectations

Teaching social communication skills and behaviors is quite complicated. We can introduce these lessons in the therapy room, resource room, special needs classroom, and even the regular classroom, but to have the student really learn to grasp how these skills impact him all day, every day, we need educational professionals and paraprofessionals, along with family members, to become acquainted with how to break down the information, teach and reinforce these skills on a regular basis as the need comes up in the environment.

We have developed a set of lessons for the student to become more efficient at social thinking and understanding the related social skills. We need all persons who work or live with the student to also become familiar with the social thinking concepts and to use them during "teachable moments."

Please review the vocabulary terms and concepts on the other side of this sheet and use them with the student as they apply.

If you have any questions on how to use these terms please contact your child's teacher:

_____

at (phone number) _____.

Thanks for helping _____ learn to use these skills throughout his/her day, at home and school!

Review for Teachers & Parents - Section 1

VOCABULARY & CONCEPTS

Being Part of a Group and Recognizing Expectations

We are currently exploring the following terms. Remember to use them with the student now and over time to help them generalize the concepts beyond the room where the lesson was first taught.

Critical Vocabulary	Definitions
Expected behaviors, unexpected behaviors	Every environment has a set of unwritten rules that people expect to be followed such as talking when it is your turn, respecting personal space, etc. When people follow these rules, some of which are not always explained to the student, then he is considered to be "doing what is **expected**". Students who don't follow the rules are doing what is **unexpected** and people may have "weird" thoughts about them.
You can change my feelings	People have feelings/reactions about other people's behavior. Sometimes people have good feelings when people behave by doing what is **expected** and other times they have annoyed or angry feelings when others do what is **unexpected**. Students learn that their behavior affects other people's feelings.
Observing other people through imitation	When you're in a group and you are not sure what to do, you often observe the people around you. If you see what they are doing and it looks like the teacher is pleased, then you can imitate their behavior and the teacher will likely be pleased with you!
Big problem - Little problem	Not all problems merit the same concern or reaction. Discuss with the student if it was a truly big problem (near a crisis) or a smaller problem (a glitch).
Three parts to play	Playing involves three steps: set up, play and clean up. Many of our students take way too long setting up since they insist things have to be done a certain way. We want them to learn that this takes away from the play time which is what the students really want.

Goal Suggestions - Section 1
Being Part of a Group and Recognizing Expectations

 Based on curriculum activities in Section 1 and California Content Standards

Goal #   <u>**Goal Suggestions**</u>

1-1   Student will be able to use the terms "expected and unexpected" related to behaviors observed in his or her presence, and then describe his own behaviors as expected or unexpected, ____% of intervention session, and then using these concepts beyond the intervention room ____% of the time.

     1-1a   When in a small intervention group situation and provided a range of behaviors to critique, _____ will label observed behaviors of others as "expected or unexpected" ____% of intervention session.

             Take this skill beyond the intervention setting: There the student is expected to label observed "expected or unexpected" behavior in others, when asked by teachers or parents ____% of the time.

     1-1b   When in a small intervention group situation and provided a range of situations, _____ will describe his own behaviors as "expected or unexpected," ____% of intervention session.

             Take this skill beyond the intervention setting: There the student is expected to label his own behavior as "expected or unexpected," when asked by teachers or parents ____% of the time.

1-2   Student will be able to explain how expected and unexpected behaviors can impact how someone else feels, when observing others and then when describing how people are reacting to this student, ____% of intervention session, and then using these concepts beyond the intervention room ____% of the time.

     1-2a   When in a social situation and observing others, _____ will be able to explain how "expected and unexpected" behavior can impact how someone else feels, _____% of the intervention session.

             Take this skill beyond the intervention setting: There the student is expected to explain how "expected and unexpected" behaviors can change how someone else feels, when asked by teachers or parents ____% of the time.

     1-2b   When in a small group session and asked, _____ will describe how other group members are reacting to him during _____% of intervention session.

             Take this skill beyond the intervention setting: There the student is expected to describe how others are reacting to him, when asked by teachers or parents _____% of the time.

Goal #	Goal Suggestions

1-3

The student will predict how people will feel based on the possible presence of certain behaviors and then the child will modify his own behavior to help create specific positive/desired feelings in other people, ____% of intervention session, and then using these concepts beyond the intervention room ____% of the time.

1-3a   When in a structured intervention group session, _____ will predict how people will feel based on the presence of certain behaviors, ____% of the intervention setting.

Take this skill beyond the intervention setting: There the student is expected to predict how others will feel based on the presence of certain behaviors, ____ % of the time.

1-3b   When in an intervention group situation, _____ will modify his own behavior to help create specific positive/desired feelings in other people, ____% of intervention session.

Take this skill beyond the intervention setting: There the student is expected to modify his/her behavior to create positive and desired feelings in others, ____ % of the time.

1-4

The student will observe other students and imitate discrete group play skills (group drumming, etc), with verbal or physical cues to maintain attention and synchronize movements and timing with the other members of the group, ____% of intervention session, and then using these concepts beyond the intervention room ____% of the time.

1-4a   After observing other students' actions and being given verbal or physical cues to maintain attention, or to synchronize movements and timing with the other members, _____ will imitate specific group play skills (ie. group drumming, etc), ____% of intervention session.

Take this skill beyond the intervention setting: There the student is expected to appropriately imitate the specific actions of others when participating in a social game, ____% of the time.

Goal #	Goal Suggestions
1-5	When getting frustrated, the student will determine the size of the problem (big problem, little problem), describe their own and others emotional reactions to problems based on the size and then minimize their own emotional response to problems they acknowledge to be relatively small, ____% of intervention session, and then using these concepts beyond the intervention room ____% of the time.

1-5a   Given a situation that involves a "glitch" or problem that is frustrating to the student, _____ will accurately determine the size of the problem (big problem, little problem), ____% within the intervention setting.

Take this skill beyond the intervention setting: There the student is expected to determine the "appropriate" size of a frustrating situation ((big problem/little problem) when asked to evaluate the situation by his teachers or parents, ____ % of the time.

1-5b   When in a frustrating situation, _____ will describe <u>his/her own</u> <u>emotional reactions</u> to their own problems based on the perceived size of the problem, ____% of the time within the intervention setting.

1-5c   When in a frustrating situation, _____ will describe <u>other people's</u> <u>emotional reactions</u> to their own problems based on the perceived size of the problem, ____% of the time within the intervention setting.

Take this skill beyond the intervention setting: There the student is expected to describe the emotional reactions of himself or others based upon the size of the problem encountered, when asked by teachers or parents, ____ % of the time.

1-5d   When faced with a "small" problem or glitch, _____ will display a minimized emotional response to problems they acknowledge to be relatively small, ____% within an intervention session.

Take this skill beyond the intervention setting: There the student is expected to display a minimized emotional response to a "small" problem, ____ % of the time.

Goal #	Goal Suggestions

1-6   The student will be able to describe the three parts of play and then will regulate his or her own behavioral reactions during the "set up of play" to allow more time for all students to enjoy play, ____% of intervention session, and then use these concepts beyond the intervention room ____% of the time.

1-6a   After a structured play session, _____ will label or describe the three parts of play, ____% of the time within the intervention setting.

1-6b   During a play session or group activity, _____ will regulate his own behavioral reactions during the "set up of play" to allow more time for all students to enjoy play, ____% of intervention session.

Take this skill beyond the intervention setting: There the student is expected to regulate his behavior during the three different steps of play during group activities, _____% of the time, to allow for the most play time.

California Content Standards -Section 1
Being Part of a Group and Recognizing Expectations

Grade	Area of the curriculum	California Content Standards
1	Listening and Speaking: Pragmatics	Listen attentively
2	Listening and Speaking: Pragmatics	Determine purpose for listening/ Problem solve/ enjoyment

Bibliography and References - Section 1
Being Part of a Group and Recognizing Expectations

Allard, H. & Marshall, J. (1977). *Miss Nelson is Missing!* Houghton-Mifflin Company: New York, NY.

Our Whole Body and Mind
Help Us be Part of the Group

The purpose of this section is to explore how our whole bodies are used while being part of a group. We will explore the concept of thinking with our brains as well as thinking with our eyes. We will focus on thinking about what other people are thinking.

How does the information in these lessons impact the classroom setting?

In Section 1 we explored what it means to be in a group. Now in this section we will explore how each of us gains information from the world and people around us while functioning in the group. Again, the information may seem very basic but these are important lessons for our students, especially if we expect them to succeed in the classroom setting, even if they have a paraprofessional to help them! The educator will also find these are good lessons to use with ALL children. They encourage insight into how we relate and evaluate those around us.

Tools & Materials

- Lunch bags or some blindfolds to cover their eyes
- Provide things with a distinct and pleasant smell like mint extract
- A ball (a large ball is more fun)
- A set of square and rectangle building blocks (avoid using shapes that are hard to stack, e.g. triangles)
- Book: *Can You Listen With Your Eyes?* (Everly, 2005) or a similar book on how we listen with our whole body
- Puppets and/or dolls for younger children

Critical Vocabulary & Concepts

- Whole body listening
- Think and thinking with our brains
- Thinking with our eyes
- Thinking about what other people are thinking.

Use these vocabulary concepts learned in previous lessons while teaching new concepts!

- Doing what is **"expected"** in the group
- Doing what is **"unexpected"** in a group
- "You can impact/affect my feelings"
- Observing others through imitation
- Big problem - little problem
- Three parts of play: set up, play and clean up

Lesson 6: Listening With our Whole Body

Critical Vocabulary

Whole Body Listening

You can adapt the vocabulary to more explicitly state what behaviors are expected versus unexpected within the group. This informs students that people actually notice other people's behavior and recognize whether they are abiding by the unwritten social rules or hidden rules.

How to use this lesson in the classroom:

1. **Explain that "whole body listening" requires that when we pay attention to others it means our hands, feet, heart, brain, fingers, eyes all pay attention to what other people or members of the group are doing.**

   A. For young students (Kindergarten to second grade), read the book on whole body listening, *Can You Listen with Your Eyes?* (Everly, 2005). This book is a large poster board type book that demonstrates how a bear listens with all parts of his body (brain, hands, feet, heart, etc.). If you know of a similar type of book, feel free to use it instead!

   B. Write the word "listening" on the board and draw a body with ears, eyes, hands and feet. Discuss what listening is. Talk with the students about how they listen with their whole body (hence, "whole body listening").

   C. Play games of observing other people in the group and figuring out who looks like they are listening and who does not appear to be listening based on what people are doing with their whole body. The important lesson is that listening is much more than just hearing people say the words.

---

2. After the children have developed the ability to identify the different components, you, the teacher, should act like you are not listening.

    A. Turn your body or head or legs out of the group. The students will likely start to tell you what you are doing is wrong before you have a chance to ask them if they think everything you are doing is ok.

    B. If a student says to you, "your eyes are not in the group," then only turn your head back into the group but keep the rest of your body out of the group. They will then cue you to move your shoulders back into the group.

    C. At this point only move your shoulders back in the group, but keep your legs turned in the other direction. The more they can break down and describe what is wrong, the more they are thinking about this information.

3. Have the students display specific behaviors of whole body listening.

    A. Copy the "Using Our Body & Mind" form on the next page and then cut it up and put the pieces of paper into a cup. For pre-readers, you can whisper what they are to do in their ears.

    B. Have the children take turns taking a piece of paper from the cup and have them act out either being a good listener, or act out what makes them a not-so-good listener. Have the other students define what parts of the "actor's" bodies are not listening.

Using Our Body and Mind
Student Worksheet

Listening well with your whole body.
Your eyes are not helping you to listen (no eye-contact).
Your feet and legs are not helping you to listen.
Your hands are not helping you to listen.
Your body is not in the group but you are looking at the teacher.
Your body is facing the wall while you sit in the group.
You are talking about airplanes while you are in the group.
You are doing a good job listening with your whole body.

Lesson 7: Using Our Brains to Think About Others

Critical Vocabulary

Think and Thinking With Our Brains

How to use this lesson in the classroom:

1. Discuss what it means to "think" and use this vocabulary word to really get the students connected to the abstraction of "thinking."

♫

2. Discuss where the brain is located in the body.

♫

3. Discuss what it means to "think with our brains" This is a very hard concept to define. The most basic definition of think is "to have an idea."

♫

4. Have the students discuss the difference between dreaming at night and thinking during the school day.

♫

---

5. The concept of thinking about others in school has to do with paying attention to people and the surrounding context/environment; figuring out new ideas related to what people say, what you read about other people or what you experience.

A. Read a short passage from one of the student's current literature books; facilitate a discussion about what the main character was thinking about. What was the character feeling? Why was he feeling that way? Each time a student gives an appropriate answer, tell him, "nice job thinking through that!"

B. Show pictures of people with different emotions. Ask the students to describe how the people in the pictures feel. Also ask them to make a guess as to what could have happened that made the person feel that way. Each time a student gives an appropriate answer, provide him with appropriate praise.

C. Ask the student if he would feel the same way in the same situation. At times it is important to point out that we actually may have different types of feelings in similar situations.

 Teachers, what other games can you develop to help students learn to think about what other people think?

6. Discuss how other parts of our bodies help us think.

A. Have the students cover their eyes. Place an item in their hands. Can they think about what they are touching/holding? Can they make a guess about what it is they are touching?

B. Put a scented item close to them. Can they think about what they smell? Can they make a guess about what they smell?

C. Can they think about who is talking from what they are hearing?

7. Play a game about figuring out who is talking just by using our ears.

   A. All the students should keep their heads on the desk and keep their eyes closed.

   B. On an index card write the words "I am over here."

   C. Give the index card to one student, by quietly patting him on the shoulder.

   D. Explain when you tap the person on the back, they are to read the index card quietly and then read it out loud in a regular tone of voice. Practice this step if needed.

   E. All of the other students are to keep their heads down on the desk with their eyes closed.

   F. Once the selected child reads the card aloud, the other students are then to guess who just read the card.

   G. Discuss how they could figure out who was talking.

   H. Take turns until all students get a chance to be the reader, and all the other students are the guessers.

   I. You can talk about what clues they used to figure out who read the card. Did they hear you approach a student, did they listen to you and the student talk, or did they recognize the student's voice?

8. What do the students like to think about when they are not in school? Discuss...

    A. Do they think about other people?

    B. Who do they like to think about?

    C. What do they like about that person?

    D. Can they think about people who are not in the room?

    E. Can they think about people they do not know?

♫

9. Part of thinking is remembering. What do they remember about their moms, dads, friends, etc.

→ *Teachers, what other ways can you explore the concept of how our students are constantly expected to think about their environment and the people in their environment? Be creative and have fun!*

Lesson 8: Thinking With Our Eyes

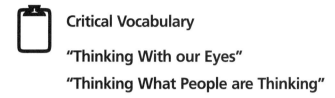

Critical Vocabulary

"Thinking With our Eyes"
"Thinking What People are Thinking"

Discuss what it means to "think with our eyes". We use the term "think with our eyes" as a more concrete way to explore eye-contact. We often give students social directions such as "look at me" or give me "eye-contact," but this directive does not tell students what they are supposed to do once they look in that direction. If you are interested in exploring this concept further, please refer to Chapter 3 in the book *Thinking About YOU Thinking About ME.* (Winner, 2002).

When students start to use their eyes to consider where others are looking and how that relates to what others are possibly thinking, we are making progress with our students' ability to be social thinkers. The key to thinking with our eyes is to help students learn they can make a guess about what someone else might be thinking. When they do this they have more information to understand others and to regulate their own behavior based on what others might be thinking.

A prerequisite skill for this lesson is to make sure your students understand how to follow a person's directed eye-gaze, so they can consider what someone might be thinking about based on where they are looking. Some of our students with high-functioning autism may not know to track people's eye gaze. Normally this skill is learned in the first year of life. If this skill is not in place, you need to teach it directly. More is written on teaching this skill in Chapter 3 of the above mentioned book.

NOTE: While the lessons below may seem basic, they are often useful for middle school kids and even those in high school. You can play many of the games mentioned below as you are teaching these older students an awareness of these critical social thinking skills.

How to use this lesson in the classroom:

1. Introduce the concept "you think with your eyes."

    A. Have the students close their eyes.

    B. While their eyes are closed, give them vague instructions, like "look over there to see what I have on the wall," or "why did you wear that today?" or "who is that?"

    C. Ask them what it is you are talking about with each question you ask. Ask them to describe why they don't know. Encourage them to realize they don't know what you are talking about because they cannot see what you are referring to. Have them keep their eyes closed while you discuss this.

    D. Have the students open their eyes. Introduce the concept **"you think with your eyes"**. (We also describe this as "listening with your eyes".)

    E. Have the students discuss how they use their eyes to think about what's in the room.

2. Further explore "thinking with your eyes."

    A. Introduce the social thinking concept that you can "think about what other people are thinking" if you **"think with your eyes."**

    B. Have the students play games of trying to figure out what you are thinking about based on where you are looking. Stare at objects around the room and see if the students can figure out what you are looking at and therefore, thinking about. Start by looking at things or people very close to you. BE OBVIOUS!!! Remember, in this step, you only want the students to identify what you are looking at (we are not yet identifying what you might be thinking about).

C. Explain to the students that what you are looking at often reflects what you are thinking about. Play the same type of game as above but now have the students guess what you are thinking about based on where you are looking. Start by looking at each of the students and see if they notice when you are thinking about each of them. Next, start to look at objects around the room, including the clock. See if they can figure out that when you look at a clock, you are thinking about the time, or when you look at a picture you are thinking about what's in the picture.

3. **Infer someone's plans/intent based on where they are looking by playing "Who Wants the Ball?"**

   A. Have the students sit or stand on their designated mats.

   B. Bring a ball into the group; the children often like the great big soft-sided balls.

   C. Start this lesson by having the teacher hold the ball. The students are told if they want to get the ball rolled to them, they have to show the person who has the ball they are thinking about the person with the ball. Remind the students that we can see that someone is thinking about us if they are looking at us.

   D. Watch the students' eyes. Choose to roll the ball only to one of the students who is looking at the ball you are holding, or your eyes.

   E. The student who now has the ball is in charge of deciding who to roll the ball to next.

   F. Coach this student to look at other students' eyes and only roll the ball to someone who is showing they are thinking about the student who is holding the ball.

   G. Play this game through numerous turns, trying to allow each child to have a turn getting the ball and then deciding who to give the ball to next.

H.If a child is really struggling, work closely with that student to help him stay focused on the person with the ball. For students who do not look at the person holding the ball, cue them by saying, "you have to show Megan you want the ball by looking at Megan's eyes or at the ball." As soon as a student does this, reward him for showing Megan that he was thinking about her.

I. As the instructor, continue to facilitate success by saying things like, "I can see Brandon is looking at the ball. That means he is thinking about wanting the ball." When a student rolls the ball to a child who is looking at him, say "good job figuring out who is thinking about you," or "Good job seeing that Tom wants the ball."

4. **Determine whose turn it is to speak, based on who people are looking at, playing "Who am I Talking To?"**

A.Tell the students that you or other selected students are going to ask them questions and they are only allowed to respond if the question is asked directly of them.

B. When asking questions, do NOT use the student's name!

C. Ask a question to a student only when looking at him or her. Only the person you are looking at should answer.

D.Rotate turns so everyone has a chance. Remember, BE OBVIOUS at first!

E. Encourage your group of students to take turns asking questions to someone in the group by looking directly at that person. However, you likely have to provide the questions they are going to ask, since generating questions can be a very difficult skill. (This skill is addressed in Section 7).

5. Guess what people are thinking by watching movie clips.

A. Select clips from the movies Toy Story 1 or 2, or any other computer generated animation film where the characters have large eyes and exaggerated facial expressions. Play the clips on a VCR or DVD.

B. Show a clip of the movie to the students and pause the clip on a part where one of the characters is clearly looking at something specific.

C. Ask the students to figure out what the character is thinking about. You can further explore this by asking what they think the character will do next and how different characters will feel or react. For example, in Toy Story 2, in one scene, the main character "Woody" is staring at the heating grate in a room. In the context of the movie, he is looking at this because he is thinking about escaping from the apartment through this grate. After you pause on Woody staring at the grate, ask the students, "What is Woody thinking about?" What might happen next? How do you think the other toys will feel if Woody leaves?

D. You can do this type of "prediction" with any number of movie clips.

E. As the students become more skilled, show them movies of real life characters that do not have large, exaggerated eyes and have them practice making the same type of predictions. Any movie, cartoon or commercial that is age appropriate for your group can be used.

F. You can also do this same type of activity with pictures of people who are looking at different things in the environment around them.

→ *Teachers, what are some other ideas you have for teaching this concept?*

6. Take Turns by Looking: "Build a Block Tower"

The block "tower" that is being constructed should not just be one block on top of the other to make one tall column of blocks. Instead, the tower can have multiple blocks at the base so it allows for a range of "building" choices.

A. Explain to students they are going to play a "no talking game." Pass around a cup and have them pretend to throw their voices in the cup, to indicate stripping them of their voices.

B. Explain they can only show each other whose turn it is by having the person who is in charge use his or her eyes to think about someone else.

C. Ask one of the students to pass out five blocks to each person at the table including you, the educator.

D. At first, allow each child to build his or her own tower with the blocks.

E. Explain if they use the blocks to build one big block tower it will be a much bigger, more interesting tower than the towers they created with their five blocks.

F. Explain that the rule is that once a child puts his block on the tower, no one is allowed to move that block for the rest of the game.

G. You (educator) start by taking your block and putting it on the center of the table.

H. Just like with the game "Who wants the ball?" you start by telling the students they should look at you to show they want to put one of their blocks on the tower.

I. Whoever you look at next gets to take a turn. The child then puts his block on the tower.

J. That child then looks to see who is looking at him. Whomever he looks back at next gets to take his or her turn by putting a block on the tower.

K. Continue having students take turns. Compliment students who are doing a good job showing they want a turn by looking with their eyes at the student who just put his block on the tower. Also compliment the students who took a turn and then successfully looked at another child in the group.

L. Coach the students who are not paying attention. Remind them that in order for them to get a turn putting a block on the tower they will have to "think with your eyes."

M. When everyone has used up his or her blocks, talk about how "neat" (great, awesome, cool, etc.) the tower is now that everyone worked together to build it.

N. Count to three and let everyone knock it down together.

 Teachers, what other ways can you encourage your students to explore how they "think with your eyes" and "think about what other people are thinking?"

 Keep some notes on the students' ability to grasp the concepts.

Keep track of what games work well in helping your students learn the concepts. Also keep track of where a student is "getting lost". You will need to think about what part of the task was hard for the student, and then break that task down further the next time you work with him or her.

For example, did the child have a hard time with the block building because he was not paying attention to other people's eyes when he was with others? If so, you may need to really work with the child on this game but only with one other person in the group. This makes the game less complicated than when you are waiting for your turn with three other students.

Video Moments Self-Monitoring Checklist - Section 2

Our Whole Body and Mind Help Us Be Part of the Group

Student's Name _____ Date _____

We are learning to watch people's social behavior and figure out how these behaviors are making other people feel.

Every once in a while you are going to be a **"behavior checker,"** meaning you will be checking on someone's behavior in the group.

Sometimes the person you are going to check on is **you**, other times it is someone else in the group.

The person you are going to check on today is _____

Behavior to monitor or watch	Put a check here if the student is making others feel like he is doing a good job.	Put a check here if the student is not doing a good job.
Whole body listening.		
Thinking with your eyes to figure out what someone else is thinking.		

Based on what you checked, do you think this person would be a good person to work with on a project?

Circle: YES or NO

If not, what is one behavior the student could try and think about more to help people want to work with him?

Review for Teachers & Parents
🔊 Section 2

Our Whole Body and Mind Help Us Be Part of the Group

Teaching social communication skills and behaviors is quite complicated. We can introduce these lessons in the therapy room, resource room, special needs classroom, and even the regular classroom, but to have the student really learn to grasp how these skills impact him all day, every day, we need educational professionals and paraprofessionals, along with family members, to become acquainted with how to break down the information, teach and reinforce these skills on a regular basis as the need comes up in the environment.

We have developed a set of lessons for the student to become more efficient at social thinking and understanding the related social skills. We need all persons who work or live with the student to also become familiar with the social thinking concepts and to use them during "teachable moments."

Please review the vocabulary terms and concepts on the other side of this sheet and use them with the student as they apply.

If you have any questions on how to use these terms please contact your child's teacher:

_____

at (phone number) _____.

Thanks for helping _____ learn to use these skills throughout his/her day, at home and school!

Remember the concepts we have introduced in previous lessons:

- Doing what is **"expected"** in the group.
- Doing what is **"unexpected"** in a group.
- "You can impact/affect my feelings."

- Observing others through imitation.
- Big problem – little problem.
- Three parts of play: set up, play and clean up.

VOCABULARY & CONCEPTS

Our Whole Body and Mind
Help Us Be Part of the Group

We are currently exploring the following terms. Remember to use them with the student now and over time to help them generalize the concepts beyond the room where the lesson was first taught.

Critical Vocabulary	Definitions
Whole body listening	The whole body (eyes, ears, mouth, hands, feet, bottom and brain) needs to be focused on others in order to listen and show you are listening.
Thinking with our eyes	Use your eyes to figure out what non-verbal messages others are sending as well as what they might be thinking about. (This provides more information than just telling the student to "use good eye-contact" or "look at me".) When we are aware that others have thoughts and we "think with our eyes" to watch people's faces and eyes, we can begin to see some of the thoughts other people are having.
Thinking about what people are thinking *(in terms of what they expect from others)*	Taking into consideration the thoughts of others is an important way to decipher what they expect from you. Encourage students in classrooms and at home to be more actively aware of the thoughts of others.

Goal Suggestions - Section 2
Our Whole Body and Mind Help Us Be Part of the Group

 Based on curriculum activities in Section 2 and the California Content Standards

Goal #	Goal Suggestions

2.1 The student will be able to identify how effectively others are using whole body listening and then be able to monitor and modify his or her own behavior with verbal cues to use whole body listening, ____% of intervention session, and then using these concepts beyond the intervention room ____% of the time.

2-1a While participating in a small group setting, _____ will describe how effectively others are using "whole body listening" ____% of the time within the intervention setting.

Take this skill beyond the intervention setting: There the student is expected to observe and describe how others use whole body listening when asked by a teacher or parents ____% of the time.

2-1b Given verbal cues to use whole body listening, _____ will monitor and modify his own behavior _____% of intervention session.

Take this skill beyond the intervention setting: There the student is expected to monitor and modify his whole body listening, when cued by teachers or parents ____% of the time.

2-2 The student will be able to predict what other people are looking at and thinking about based on where the student observes them to be looking, ____% of intervention session, and then using these concepts beyond the intervention room ____% of the time.

2-2a While observing the eye gaze and eye directions of others, _____ will determine and state what that person is looking at and maybe thinking about ____% of intervention session.

Take this skill beyond the intervention setting: There the student is expected to observe and predict what others are looking at and thinking ____% of the time.

Goal #	Goal Suggestions

2.3 The student will modify his or her own behavior based on what he sees others looking at/possibly thinking about (e.g. will think with his/her eyes to determine whose turn it is in a game, etc.), ____% of intervention session, and then using these concepts beyond the intervention room ____% of the time.

2-3a When in a structured situation (e.g. a game which involves turn taking), _____ will modify his behavior based on what he sees others looking at/possibly thinking about ____% of the opportunities within the intervention session.

Take this skill beyond the intervention setting: There the student is expected to modify his behavior by watching for the eye gaze of others in a turn-taking activity with peers, teachers or parents ____% of the time.

California Content Standards
Section 2: Our Whole Body and Mind Help Us Be Part of the Group

Grade	Area of the curriculum	California Content Standards
1	Listening and Speaking: Pragmatics	Listen attentively
2	Listening and Speaking: Pragmatics	Determine purpose for listening/Problem solve/ enjoyment

Bibliography and References
Section 2: Our Whole Body and Mind Help Us Be Part of the Group

Everly, N. (2005) *Can You Think With Your Eyes?* Linguisystems Inc.: East Moline, IL.
www.linguisystems.com

Section 3

Self-awareness and Self-monitoring Our Behavior in a Group

Another critical skill for being part of a group is being able to be aware of our own social behavior and how it impacts others. In this section we will work on the idea that people's thoughts about us are often created from our behavioral presentation. Furthermore, we want to teach that we have the power to control some of the thoughts people have about us by learning to monitor and control our own social behavior. In this lesson we will explore the need to adjust our behaviors when we are in a group compared to how we behave when we are by ourselves.

How does this lesson impact the classroom?

Just like the lessons in Sections 1 and 2, this is another critical set of skills we expect all children to be actively developing by the time they enter kindergarten. Behavioral awareness and control is at the heart of people who can work well together for play, learning and simply sharing space. Again, in this section we are taking information that is intuitive to most children and explicitly teaching concepts ALL teachers can review with ALL students. A successful classroom teacher will encourage all students to become better observers of their own behavior, its impact on others and understand why they should work to monitor and then control it.

Tools & Materials

• Play dough   • Colored Popsicle sticks (available at arts and crafts stores)

• Index cards   • Transparent cups

• Large Rubber Chickens (or any soft playful toy you choose to use).
  Rubber chickens can be purchased in most party or magic stores or on the internet.

Critical Vocabulary & Concepts

• Your body is in the group! Your body is out of the group!

• Your brain is in the group! Your brain is out of the group!

• Just ME/Thinking of You

• Good thoughts/Weird thoughts

• "I've got a secret"

• "Video moment" to watch what others are doing

Lesson 9: Is Your Body in the Group or Out of the Group?

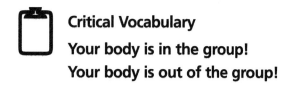

Critical Vocabulary
Your body is in the group!
Your body is out of the group!

This activity develops awareness of how others know you are part of a group through your physical presence. These concepts are reviewed in greater detail in *Thinking about YOU Thinking about ME, 2nd Ed.* (2007). This "play dough lesson" about your "body being in the group" is described in Chapter 5 of the book.

How to use this lesson in the classroom:

1. Make a small ball out of play dough (about the size of a large marble) to represent each student in the group.

2. Make a different shape, like a short column, to represent the adults in the room.

3. In the center of the table place the play dough balls and columns in the same configuration as the people who are sitting around the table. For example, if you have four kids in the group, seat two of them on one side of a rectangular table and two on the other side; you sit on the end. In the center of the table, place two balls of play dough next to each other and facing the other two balls of play dough. Place the column that represents you at the end of this group of play dough, centered.

---

4. Tell the students that the play dough demonstrates how our bodies look in our group.

☆

5. Have a student leave the group and go stand by the door. Then say to the group, "Oops, now our group is broken because _____'s (say the student's name) body is out of the group."

☆

6. Roll his play dough ball off the table.

☆

7. Have the student come back to the table and sit down. Then put his play dough ball back in the group and say to the group, "Now _____'s body is back in the group."

☆

8. Discuss the idea that the physical location of our bodies is one of the primary ways we decide who is in our group. Therefore, the location of each person's body, relative to the group, helps everyone else, in and out of the group, figure out who is in the group. For example, kids at recess can look over and see who is in a group and who is not.

☆

9. You can expand on this lesson by having a student move his chair back from the table and having the group determine how far back his chair has to be for him to be considered "out of the group". (Another option: "No longer an "active" part of the situation/activity".) When a child moves his or her chair backwards, also move the play dough the related distance out of the group.

Keep this lesson in mind for other "teachable moments." When you are working within groups across the day, and you see a student wander out of a group say, "I see _____'s body is out of the group." Use this lesson positively.

When you notice students are keeping their bodies in the group say, "I like how _____'s keeping his or her body in the group."

Share this simple vocabulary concept (e.g. "your body is in the group" or "your body is out of the group") with the other educators/parents so all can frequently comment on who is doing a good job keeping their body in the group and who is not actively being a part of the group.

Lesson 10: Is Your Brain in the Group or Out of the Group?

Critical Vocabulary
Your brain is in the group!
Your brain is out of the group!

Follow the same steps introduced in Activity 9 in this Section, with the play dough balls and columns on the table representing what the group looks like.

During this lesson, one of the students within the group is going to "space out." You notice this because while their body is still physically in the group it does not appear their brain is connected to the group or activity.

How to use this lesson in the classroom:

1. When you see this happen, take a small piece of play dough, (about the size of a grain of rice), off the ball that represents the student and put it back into the group of play dough balls on the table. You now have a much smaller piece of play dough representing the child's body.

2. Take the rest of the ball of play dough (a fairly sizeable piece) and say, "I see _____'s body is still in the group, but his brain has rolled away" and roll the rest of the remaining larger ball of play dough off the table. If there is need, you can explain that the brain represents the larger part of the clay ball since the brain is responsible for everything our body ends up doing.

3. Most of the students will usually become more alert and they will immediately say that they want their brain to be part of the group.

4. Tell the students "we can see when your brain is not in the group!" Discuss the fact that people in the group can see when someone's brain is in the group or when it has rolled away. Remind the students that each of our jobs in a group is to try and keep our brains focused on the group so people want to keep working with each of us.

5. Use the vocabulary concepts "your brain is in the group" or "your brain has rolled out of the group" frequently to comment on who is doing a good job keeping their brain in the group or whose brain appears to be out of the group.

6. Invariably a student will tell you that he or she was "listening." When that happens, explain to the student that you felt like the student was not paying attention because he did not look like he was thinking about anyone else in the group. It is always important to help students understand that our own personal feelings, in response to another person's behavior, are very real to us, even if the other person says they should not feel that way! If a student understands that his behavior (staring at the ceiling when others are talking) makes people feel like he is not part of the group, then he can make the connection to modify his own behavior to ensure that other people feel good about his participation.

7. Remember to try and find times to compliment, as well as redirect, the students. Avoid always praising the same student or being consistently critical about the behavior of another student. The reality is most everyone in the group has times they do this well and times they don't do this well.

8. Once you have taught these vocabulary concepts at the table, you will find you can use them when the students are doing activities away from the table as well. You only need to demonstrate the play dough lessons a couple of times for a group to understand the meaning of the concepts.

9. Teach this set of vocabulary to other educators and parents, so we can all work on it consistently across environments.

Lesson 11: Just ME versus Thinking of You

Critical Vocabulary

Are you a "Just ME" or a "Thinking of You" kid?

The Just ME/Thinking of You lesson is written in full detail, with an example of the story we use to teach these concepts in *Thinking About YOU Thinking About ME, 2nd Ed.* (2007). The focus of this lesson is that people behave differently in a group than they do when alone, by themselves.

This concept is adapted from the book *Fair Play* (1939 by Munro Leaf, now out of print). The main aspects of the story are summarized below. Try drawing simple pictures to go along with the text when you present it to the students. Pictures in the original book are simple line drawings.

How to use this lesson in the classroom:

1. Read the story summary on page 94 to the students; guide them through the "teach-able moment" tasks as discussed below for each of the three parts of the story.

2. Once the story is read and the teachable moment lessons reviewed, create index cards for each student. On one index card write, "Just ME." On the remaining index cards write, "Thinking of You."

---

3. Give an index card to each student in the group. Usually my groups have about four students in them, so there are four index cards.

4. Explain to students they are going to each get a turn being "Just ME."

5. Instruct the student who has the "Just ME" card to do or play with whatever he wants in the room (except be violent, unsafe or careless with materials). He is not allowed to observe or play with the other students who are the Thinking of You students.

6. Each of the "Thinking of You" students get to play together in a cooperative (not competitive) game you have organized. Some examples of cooperative games are taking turns climbing through a tunnel, jumping on a small exercise trampoline, and bouncing a ball to each other.

7. Prior to the students playing out the description on the index card they were given, discuss the role of the "Thinking of You" students. Since they are part of a group, their job is to think about the possible needs or wants of the other people in the group. Discuss what the "Thinking of You" students might need to think about while they are playing; write this information on the board. For example: they all might discuss that kids like it when they take turns, since then everyone gets a chance. They also like it if we wait for our turn patiently so kids are not rushed through their turns unfairly; while waiting we don't push or cut in line, etc. Once the play begins the students may think of more "Thinking of You" ideas; add these to the board.

8. Slowly transition the students in and out of the role of the "Just ME" and "Thinking of You" student. At times, the child who is "Just Me" will ask to be a "Thinking of You" student. When the students are transitioning from being the "Just ME" to the "Thinking of You" student, remind them their job is to now think about all the others in the group. This usually means that a child transitioning into the "Thinking of You" group needs to go to the end of the line, look to see if others need help, and be patient, etc.

9. Remind the "Just ME" student he doesn't have to be patient or thoughtful because he doesn't get to play with anyone. When he is by himself he really doesn't have to think too much about others, but he doesn't have anyone else to play with either!

10. Talk to the students about the differences between being a "Just ME" and a "Thinking of You" student. Which one do people want to be friends with or work with? Work in groups with? Which type of student does the teacher need to help her classroom succeed? Why?

11. Use this vocabulary in teachable moments across the rest of the lessons. When you see students cooperating, praise them for being a "Thinking of You" student. When you see someone only doing what he wants to do, talk to him about acting like a "Just ME." Try to find times when a "Just ME" student notices how he is behaving and tries to be a "Thinking of You" student. Verbally praise the students for any attempts at being a "Thinking of You" person.

12. Teach students there are times it is fine to be a "Just ME." These are times when a student is allowed to completely do his own thing, such as playing alone at home. Problems arise when a person exhibits "Just ME" behaviors when others expect the student to be a "Thinking of You" person. This results in people having weird thoughts about the student. There is really NO time at school when students are expected to be "Just MEs" since part of the school experience is to constantly share space with others!

13. Teach this set of vocabulary to other educators and parents, so we can all work on it consistently across environments.

Summary of Initial Story in the book *Fair Play* (1936) by Munro Leaf
(Lesson plan notes in italics)

First part of the story:

"Imagine you are the only person in the United States. It is just you and no one else except the wild animals. There are no grocery stores, school, hospitals, homes, etc., because there are no grocery clerks, teachers, doctors or parents. It is just you and the wild animals."

Teachable Moment:

Have students take off their shoes and stand on their chairs to get a sense of being deprived of something. Encourage the students to talk about what it would be like to live all by themselves without any adults. What types of things would they have to do to survive? Would they enjoy it?

Second part of the story:

"But the good news is that you do not live by yourself, you are surrounded by people who help you out and with whom you live and go to school. Because we live with many people there are rules, rules become laws and laws become government." (Comment: I really like the simplicity in which we encourage students to realize that rules, laws and government come from sharing space with others).

Teachable Moment:

Discuss with your students that because we live among other people we have to have rules, laws and government. What would it be like if we did not have these? (When appropriate you may want to introduce vocabulary such as: social, values, morals, culture, traditions, etc.)

Third part of the story:

"Imagine there are eight students who want to play softball, but there is one boy who does not want to play softball. That boy wants to fly his kite. The boy's name is 'Just ME' and he goes and flies his kite by himself because that is what he wants to do." (Comment: It is important to note that 'Just ME' never looks happy, even when he gets to do just what he wants.) "What should the other kids do? They should not watch the boy fly his kite because they might get bored. They should play softball and just let the boy fly his kite by himself. One day 'Just ME' wants a drink from the water fountain so he barges into the line and takes a drink, pushing people out of his way. When the other kids want a drink from the water fountain they wait in line for all the people who were in front of them."

Teachable Moment:

Discuss with the group what 'Just ME' is thinking about when he is flying his kite and drinking from the fountain. Is he trying to make the other kids feel good, or is he just thinking about what makes HIM feel good?

Lesson 12: Good Thoughts / Weird Thoughts

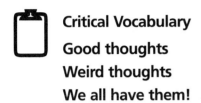

Critical Vocabulary
Good thoughts
Weird thoughts
We all have them!

Each of us has many thoughts about the different people at school, in the community and even at home. This means we all have to be aware that others have thoughts about us as well, even when we are not talking to them! Many of the thoughts people have about us are appropriate thoughts or good thought. But all of us, at times, can cause other people to have weird thoughts about us.

What is critical in this lesson is that you do NOT call the students or yourself "weird." We simply want the students to realize that people can have a weird thought about each other based on their social behavior.

Our students are often very quick to label another child as "weird," identify behaviors that other children are doing as wrong, or at least be aware of what behaviors people think are weird. What they lack is awareness that others hold them accountable to this same set of social expectations. For example, they don't like it when others yell and they get upset about this, but then our students yell at others as well!

Have your students observe some other students at school. Who did they have "good thoughts" about? Why were their thoughts good (e.g. kids were following directions, sharing, etc)? Who did they think was not being part of the group, who wasn't doing the work, who wasn't being nice?

Encourage the students to discuss what behaviors and language cause us or others to have a "weird thought."

How to use this lesson in the classroom:

1. First, review this important concept with students: Each one of us can make people have good thoughts and weird thoughts about us by the way we behave. But when others have too many weird thoughts about us they may think that we are not fun, safe or easy to play or work with.

2. Visually demonstrate to students how their behaviors generate different types of thoughts in others (weird thoughts/good thoughts). Demonstrate this through the use of two different colored popsicle sticks, paper clips, or any other small colored objects you have.

   a. Provide each student with a set of objects that are two different colors (for example, blue popsicle sticks and red popsicle sticks). You can use any two colors you choose; just try and keep your colors consistent over time.

   b. Give a transparent cup to each child in the group. Reserve one for yourself. The cups sit in front of each child.

   c. The sticks (or other items) represent what you, the educator, think about the student's behavior. A blue stick represents a "good thought" you are having about the child and a red stick represents a "weird thought" you are having about the child.

   d. When a child is working as part of the group and he is doing expected behaviors that are generating good thoughts about him (e.g. waiting for others to speak, sitting patiently at the table, and establishing good physical presence) put a blue stick into his cup. Initially tell him the blue sticks are for good thoughts I am having about you.

e. Once you have established the purpose of the blue stick, then you can silently acknowledge a person's good behavior by dropping a blue stick into his cup without having to say anything to the student. If it is not disruptive to the child, occasionally tell him what social behavior you observed that merits the student receiving another blue stick. It is especially important to acknowledge new emerging skills.

f. When the child exhibits a "negative" behavior, give him a red stick. Describe the behavior and let him know his behavior made other people have a weird thought (e.g. "your eyes were not thinking about the people in the group," "your body was not in the group," "you said words that caused others to feel sad"). Again, minimize the language associated with placing the stick in the cup once students understand the meaning of the sticks.

g. Avoid giving only red sticks to a child. It is important to realize that the red sticks are ONLY significant if the child has accumulated a series of blue sticks! Most students, even difficult ones, exhibit many "blue stick" behaviors, but we often forget to give them credit for doing what we expect them to do. We pay more attention to their "red stick" behaviors. For the lesson to succeed, you must actively pay attention to the "blue stick" behavior and give selective attention to the "red stick" behavior.

 You must find the opportunity to give students plenty of blue sticks to motivate them to reduce their "red stick" behaviors.

4. Make a list of expected behaviors that earn blue sticks. The opposite – or absence – of blue stick behaviors is what constitutes red sticks behaviors. Add new behaviors to the blue stick list as your group learns new social thinking behaviors during future lessons.

5. You can use the visual information represented by the sticks to help students understand why other students choose to work with some kids and not others. The students with too many red sticks may not be seen as "safe" (fun, easy, etc.) to be with because their behavior is less predictable. The sticks also motivate students to monitor their social behavior more closely as they serve as a mild reward system.

6. Students will ask to have you remove their red sticks once they repair their behavior. DO NOT remove a student's red stick yourself. Instead, explain that the student can take the red stick out of the cup, he can even break it, but what he can't do is take it out of my memory. The sticks in the cup represent my thoughts and my thoughts help to form my memory.

7. However, the student CAN make the red sticks appear to go away by earning more blue sticks. This makes it difficult to even see the red sticks in the cup, thus visually underscoring the idea that good thoughts overtake any weird thoughts that might be in my memory. This is an important behavioral concept we need to introduce and then reinforce; behavior can be modified and plenty of good thoughts help to minimize the power of weird thoughts we have about people.

 The use of a visual object makes this social concept more understandable for students.

RUBBER CHICKEN MOMENTS

The rubber chicken, or some other similar, soft toy, can be an effective tool for reinforcing the concept that we all behave in ways that can cause people to have weird thoughts about us. We use the rubber chicken in the group as follows: we let the student who causes others to have weird thoughts – because of what he said or did – lightly tap himself on the head to acknowledge he made an error. Kids love this slapstick humor.

To avoid injury, make sure you teach the "rubber chicken holding rule": the student grips the chicken between the wings (rather than by the feet).

At some point everyone in the group has a "rubber chicken moment" since we all (teachers included) make communication errors on a fairly regular basis (calling someone by their wrong name, interrupting someone who is talking, not keeping our body in the group). This is not a bad thing. It is just a reminder that we have to monitor how our behavior impacts the way other people think about us.

The rubber chicken becomes a welcome part of the therapy/educational group for many students. They really like the humor of having a rubber chicken around, especially when they catch someone else in a rubber chicken moment or, very often, when they catch themselves. In our clinic we use the term "rubber chicken moment" so often that we can talk about it even when we don't have a rubber chicken around, or when it would not be appropriate to use it (for instance, in the cafeteria or during a quiet moment).

Read more about the rubber chicken in *Thinking About YOU Thinking About ME, 2nd Ed.* (2007).

Lesson 13: I've Got a Secret!

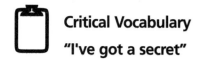 **Critical Vocabulary**
"I've got a secret"

This lesson helps students increase self-awareness and the ability to self-monitor very specific social behaviors. To teach this lesson you must choose, from all that you have observed, one target behavior each student needs to closely self-monitor. This targeted social behavior will help develop stronger self-awareness and self-monitoring skills.

How to use this lesson in the classroom:

1. Write the student's name and target behavior on a small strip of paper. For example: "Kevin: Think with your eyes to watch what other people are planning;" "Julianna: Keep your body and brain in the group."

2. At the start of a class or therapy session, announce to the group, "I've got a secret for each student."

3. Have the group of students partake in some fun activity like playing with play dough or Lego's, where they don't need strong supervision.

4. Take each student, one by one, to a corner of the room and whisper that you have a secret for him.

5. Present each student with the paper strip that has the target behavior written on it.

6. Remind the student this is the **secret** you shared with him. Take a moment to have the student describe what this behavior looks like and how he can pay attention more to this behavior when part of the group.

7. Let the student know you will remind him about this behavior when he is working in the group by saying to the student "remember our secret."

8. Have students put their strip of paper in their pockets (often this provides a visual support to refer to as needed).

9. Once this strategy is introduced, you can use it at different times, across the different lesson sections.

Lesson 14: Learning to Watch Ourselves on Video

Critical Vocabulary

Video Moments

Prepare to show the video taken the first day the students got together. Inform them they are going to watch videos to figure out how the students were participating on their very first day, before they started to learn about how their bodies helped them to be part of a group. Help the students verbally identify their own areas of progress as well as that of their peers in the group. Review the vocabulary concepts presented on the Video Moments checklist on the next page. Use pictures and words to help them review the vocabulary learned up to this point.

How to use this lesson in the classroom:

1. Review Video Moments Checklist on the next page.

    A. Who is listening with their whole body?

    B. Who is thinking about other people with their eyes?

    C. Whose body is in the group?

    D. Whose body is out of the group?

    E. Who is acting like a "Just ME"?

    F. Who is doing a good job "Thinking of You"?

    G. What things are happening that make people have good thoughts? What things are happening that make people have weird thoughts or **rubber chicken moments**?

---

2. Positively praise/encourage those students who were not doing things well when the video was made and are now showing some increasing self-awareness. Acknowledge improvements students have shown in each of these ways.

3. Make a new videotape of the students working well together using some of their new skills. You might consider videotaping them building a block tower together. Have them rate themselves using this same checklist as they improve their cooperative skills, whether building the block tower or doing any other task.

4. Do this on a regular basis, across time. Have them use the vocabulary concepts to talk about their own strengths.

Video Moments Self-Monitoring Checklist - Section 3

Self-awareness and Self-monitoring Our Behavior in a Group

Student's Name _____ **Date** _____

We are learning to watch people's social behavior and figure out how these behaviors are making other people feel.

Every once in a while you are going to be a "behavior checker," meaning you will be checking on someone's behavior in the group.

Sometimes the person you are going to check on is you, other times it is someone else in the group.

The person you are going to check on today is _____

Behavior to monitor or watch	Put a check here if the student is making others feel like he is doing a good job.	Put a check here if the student is not doing a good job.
Whole body listening.		
Keeping one's body in the group		
Keeping one's brain in the group		
Being a "Thinking of You" kid versus a "Just ME"		
Are you having mostly "good thoughts" about this person?		

Based on what you checked, do you think this person would be a good person to work with on a project?

Circle: YES or NO

If not, what is one behavior the student could try and think about more to help people want to work with him?

Review for Teachers & Parents
🔊 Section 3

Self-awareness and Self-monitoring
Our Behavior in a Group

Teaching social communication skills and behaviors is quite complicated. We can introduce these lessons in the therapy room, resource room, special needs classroom, and even the regular classroom, but to have the student really learn to grasp how these skills impact him all day, every day, we need educational professionals and paraprofessionals, along with family members, to become acquainted with how to break down the information, teach and reinforce these skills on a regular basis as the need comes up in the environment.

We have developed a set of lessons for the student to become more efficient at social thinking and understanding the related social skills. We need all persons who work or live with the student to also become familiar with the social thinking concepts and to use them during "teachable moments."

Please review the vocabulary terms and concepts on the other side of this sheet and use them with the student as they apply.

If you have any questions on how to use these terms please contact your child's teacher:
_____at (phone number) _____.

Thanks for helping _____ learn to use these skills throughout his/her day, at home and school!

Use these vocabulary concepts learned in previous lessons while teaching new concepts!

- Doing what is "expected" in the group.
- Doing what is "unexpected" in a group.
- "You can impact/affect my feelings."
- Observing others through imitation.
- Big problem - little problem.

- Three parts of play: set up, play and clean up.
- Whole body listening.
- Think and thinking with our brains.
- Thinking with our eyes.
- Thinking about what other people think.

VOCABULARY & CONCEPTS

Self-awareness and Self-monitoring
Our Behavior in a Group

We are currently exploring the following terms. Remember to use them with students now and over time to help them generalize the concepts beyond the room where the lesson was first taught.

Critical Vocabulary	Definitions
Your body is in the group/ Your body is out of the group	We notice when someone's body is turned into the group and they look like they are working as part of the group. We also notice when someone's body is not in the group or is turned out of the group.
Your brain is in the group/ Your brain is out of the group	We notice when someone's body is in the group and their brain is actively paying attention; we think that person is really doing a good job participating in the group. We also notice when someone's body is in the group but it does not appear that their mind is thinking about the same things as the rest of the group. When we see a student whose "brain is not in the group," then we don't think he is really paying attention.
Being a "Thinking of You" kid versus a "Just ME"	These are terms to define the difference between cooperating in a group versus focusing on one's own needs. A "Thinking of You" kid cooperates by considering what other people need or want in a group. A "Just ME" kid just thinks about and acts upon primarily what he or she wants to do.
Good thoughts / Weird thoughts	All people have thoughts about other people. Most thoughts are good or normal thoughts, but each of us may do things each day which can cause people to have "weird thoughts" about us. Creating a small number of weird thoughts each day in other people is totally acceptable, but when we create too many weird thoughts in others, they start to think we may not be nice or safe to be with or that we just don't seem to care about them.

Goal Suggestions - Section 3
Self-awareness and Self-monitoring Our Behavior in a Group

__Based on curriculum activities in Section 3 and the California Content standards__

Goal #	Goal Suggestions

3-1
The student will monitor other students as well as his/her own ability to stay central in a group of students by monitoring if their brains and body are in the group or out of the group, ____% of intervention session, and then using these concepts beyond the intervention room ____% of the time.

3-1a
When in a structured small group activity, _____ will monitor other students' as well as his/her own ability to stay central by determining if their brains/body are "in the group" or "out of the group" ____% of intervention session.

Take this skill beyond the intervention setting: There the student is expected to monitor if his mind/body is in the group discussion ____% of the time.

3-2
The student will be able to define and use the concepts of being a "Just ME" versus a "Thinking of You" kid, when considering if other people think the student is working as a member of the group or not appearing to be part of the group ____% of intervention session, and then using these concepts beyond the intervention room ____% of the time.

3-2a
While in a small group interaction and asked to assess his behaviors, _____ will use the concepts of being a "Just ME" versus a "Thinking of You" kid, to evaluate how other people think he is working as a group member (vs. not appearing to be part of the group) ____% of intervention session.

Take this skill beyond the intervention setting: There the student is expected to use the terms "Just ME" or "Thinking of You" to describe his behavior when interacting with others, when asked by teachers or parents, ____% of the time.

3-3
The student will monitor and modify his or her own behavior to keep his body and brain in the group, allowing him/her to be considered a "Thinking of You" kid by other people, ____% of intervention session, and then using these concepts beyond the intervention room ____% of the time.

3-3a
While in a small group interaction, _____ will monitor and modify his own behavior to 'keep his body and brain in the group', allowing him to be considered a "Thinking of You" kid by other people, ____% of intervention session.

Take this skill beyond the intervention setting: There the student is expected to monitor and modify his body and brain to be considered a "Thinking of You" kid while in a small group interaction with peers, teachers or family members ____% of the time.

Goal #	Goal Suggestions

3-4

The student will be able to use the concepts "good thoughts, weird thoughts" to describe his/her thoughts about other people's behavior and then to regulate how people are thinking about his/her behavior, ____% of intervention session, and then using these concepts beyond the intervention room ____% of the time.

3-4a   While in a structured small group activity, _____ will use the concepts "good thoughts, weird thoughts" to describe his thoughts about other people's behavior, ____% of the intervention session.

Take this skill beyond the intervention setting: There the student is expected to observe the behavior of others and determine his reactions using the concept of "good thoughts, weird thoughts" and share those thoughts when asked by others who want constructive feedback ____% of the time.

3-4b   When given feedback regarding his behavior (which may be generating "weird thoughts" from others), _____ will attempt to regulate his own behavior based on how people are thinking about him ____% of the intervention session.

Take this skill beyond the intervention setting: There the student is expected to modify his behavior so others have a more positive thought about him ____% of the time.

3-5

When reviewing videotaped footage of the social thinking group in which the student participates, the student will be able to identify the targeted behaviors first on other students and then on himself/herself, focusing on identifying when "expected behaviors" happened; ____% of the intervention session.

3-5a   When reviewing videotaped footage of the social thinking group in which _____ participates, _____ will be able to identify at least two - three targeted behaviors in other students, focusing on identifying when "expected" behaviors happened, ____% of the intervention session.

3-5b   When reviewing video taped footage of the social thinking group in which _____ participates, _____ will be able to identify at least two - three targeted behaviors in himself, focusing on identifying when "expected" behaviors happened, ____% of the intervention session.

California Content Standards - Section 3
Self-awareness and Self-monitoring Our Behavior in a Group

Grade	Area of the curriculum	California Content Standard
1	Listening and Speaking: Pragmatics	Listen attentively
2	Listening and Speaking: Pragmatics	Determine purpose for listening/ Problem solve/ enjoyment

Bibliography and References - Section 3:
Self-awareness and Self-monitoring Our Behavior in a Group

Leaf, M. (1939). *Fair Play*. Frederick A. Stokes Company: New York.

Winner, M. (2007). *Thinking About YOU Thinking About ME, 2nd Ed.:* Think Social Publishing: San Jose, CA. www.socialthinking.com

Section 4

Starting the Detective Agency: Learning More About Observing Others

In this section we will provide more sophisticated information regarding being part of a group. These lessons help students with their academic curriculum by teaching them explicitly about making educated or "smart guesses."

We are also working on observation skills by learning how to "think with our eyes" and make predictions, as well as beginning to explore how emotions are a very real part of relating to and understanding others.

How do these lessons relate to classroom participation?

As children develop literacy and written expression, it is critical not only that they be able to interpret people's thinking but also that they can predict what might happen next based on information learned from context. In the lesson below, we encourage students to think like a detective in order to develop critical thinking skills needed for both reading comprehension and expressing themselves through writing.

A Range of Ages

The lessons in this section are good for students of all ages; in fact they are good for adults as well. However, when working with the older student (middle school and beyond), **do not** use the detective agency concept. Instead just talk about how each of us really is a "social spy" or "social observer" when sharing space in any environment.

Remember, do not assume your students know how to observe social information just because they are older.

You may also want to refer to Dr. Mel Levine's book *Jarvis Clutch: Social Spy* for more lessons for older kids.

Tools & Materials

- Movie or TV clips that show clearly animated faces in scenes (recommended: "Toy Story 1" or "Toy Story 2," or soap opera type shows shown without the sound)

- Building blocks, Lego toys or a puzzle to be used within a group activity

- Books, pictures and other published curriculums to explore feelings and emotions

- Book: *Thinking About YOU - Thinking About ME*: Social Behavior Mapping

- Book: *The Incredible 5 Point Scale*

Critical Vocabulary & Concepts

- Be a detective: watching people/observing

- Making a guess: prediction

- Figuring out people's plans from observing

- Smart guess - Wacky guess

- Identify feelings

Lesson 15: Becoming a Detective

Critical Vocabulary
- **Be a detective**
- **Become a better observer and figure out people's plans**
- **Motives, intentions**

This lesson, "Detective Agency," teaches students to develop better skills in observing social behavior. This includes observing not only what people are doing in the moment, but also predicting what they might be planning to do next, based on their body and eye movements. We begin our "detective work" by observing nonverbal cues provided through the environment and people's bodies. Eventually a student can generalize these skills to help with reading comprehension.

How to use this lesson in the classroom:

1. Define what detectives do.

    A. Brainstorm with your students the role and purpose of a "detective" or "spy." Write the information on your white board/chart paper.

    B. Explain to your students that a good detective observes people to try and figure out what they are presently doing, how they are feeling, and what they may plan to do next. Through this discussion you are encouraging students to think about people's motives/intentions. However, the students do not need to learn these more abstract vocabulary concepts.

    C. Use the more simple social thinking vocabulary: **"reading people's plans"** by observing their actions. We will help students understand this concept more deeply in the next lesson.

2. Discuss the strategies of making guesses and predictions through observation of visual information.

A. Tell the students we are now going to take the activity of "thinking with your eyes" and use it to "figure out someone's plan" or "read people's plans" based on observing what people are doing with their bodies and eye-gaze direction.

 Note: These simple concepts are crucial to learning more advanced lessons later in the curriculum and should be infused as "teachable moments" across all future sessions. For example, when a student has successfully figured out what someone was going to do next, praise him by saying, "nice job figuring out that person's plan!"

3. Have the students watch clips from an animated movie such as "Toy Story" or one of the "Wallace and Gromit" series. (Animated movies are good since the characters' eyes and facial expressions are exaggerated to help the viewer think that the characters are real).

A. Play a short clip of the movie where characters are talking to or interacting with each other.

B. Pause the movie on clips that clearly show what a character is looking at or moving towards. This helps us figure out what the character plans to do next (e.g. when a character bursts into the room to look for one of the other characters).

C. Ask the students to figure out what the character is planning to do next.

D. When your students do this, tell them they have done a good job reading the character's plan!

E. You should start with animated movies, but you can graduate to movie clips from movies with human characters. Use the same set of skills as listed above, but recognize that reading people's faces is harder since they are not as exaggerated as animated characters.

F. Avoid clips from students' favorite shows; students can get carried away focusing on their favorite details, rather than paying attention to the social thinking lesson.

4. Play the game, "Can you read my plan?"

A. Explain to the students they are now "detectives" and their job is to try and figure out what you are going to do next.

B. Teach the students when they are "thinking with their eyes" they can start to figure out someone else's plan, which is the same as figuring out what someone is planning to do next.

C. You should reach for objects or walk towards people or doors, etc. but you should stop just short of actually touching the object or talking to the person you are approaching. (You may have to go slowly and exaggerate your actions at first. As the students improve, your actions can become more subtle.)

D. The students are then asked to make a guess about what you are going to reach for, who you are going to talk to, where you are going to go, etc.

E. Now allow each of the students to take the lead role in performing an action that shows what they are planning to do next, having each one stop just short of touching the object, talking to the person, etc. At first encourage them to do very simple activities like reaching for a pen, the door handle, or throwing something in the trash can. The tricky part here is helping students understand that they are not supposed to try and trick the other students. Instead they are engaging in "teamwork" where they are actively paying attention to what others are doing or thinking.

F. Encourage the students by coaching them with our social thinking vocabulary concepts: "think with your eyes" and then make a "smart guess" about "figuring out someone's plan."

G. Provide verbal praise when you see them doing this well. The students' behavior is also naturally reinforced when they see that others are able to figure out their own plans.

H. Once students get the idea, try a more advanced game using the same social concept. Have the students play together with building blocks, Lego toys, puzzle pieces and videotape them while they are playing.

5. Expand on the concept of "figuring out people's plans."

A. Talk to the students about "figuring out other people's plans" being a useful strategy even while playing with toys. In play, just like in any other social activity, we are supposed to keep an eye on—and have thoughts about—what other people around us are planning to do. For example, if Jaime sees Amy reaching for a toy, then Jaime should be able to predict that Amy wants the toy. Given this knowledge, Jaime, the detective, should NOT reach for that toy. If Jaime **does** reach for it, she will be seen as "stealing" the toy and this makes Amy feel frustrated or sad. Amy expects other people to read her plan. If Jaime is a good social thinker, she would have read Amy's plan and taken a different toy instead.

B. You can purposefully model the WRONG behavior by having another adult (or one of your more flexible thinking students) play with some Lego toys with you.

i. Whisper to the person that you are going to grab any object for which he reaches in order to show what it looks like when we don't think about what people's actions mean, or when we don't take the time to read people's plans.

ii. Ask your students to observe you and think about what each person in the example is doing. When your partner reaches for a Lego, you should then start to grab it as well.

C. Monitor the reactions of your observing students. Have the students talk about whether you are doing it right (thinking about the other person's plan and then making a different choice), or doing it wrong (not thinking about the other person's plan and just doing whatever you want.) You will find that many of your students clearly identify the mistake you made.

D. Talk about how people feel when someone takes something from them they were planning to use.

E. Discuss how they feel when they play with a person who does not take toys from them.

F. Discuss how to "repair" the situation when a student takes something away from a person because he did not read their plans. Assure students that we all do this sometimes, even adults! Problem solve how to help other people feel better once it has been acknowledged that a mistake has been made. For example, they can say, "Sorry! I didn't realize you were using that!" Help them figure out why this is a better response than, "I want it now!"

G. Explain that this behavior is what is meant by **cooperation** (being able to read another person's plan and not interrupting it!) and **sharing** (letting others have a turn or get the things they want, etc.). Use age appropriate vocabulary.

H. This activity is difficult for students. It requires students to self-regulate their behavior while they play with toys or objects they enjoy. Plan to review this lesson and concept many, many times over the coming years. Each year the sophistication of the concept and vocabulary increases a bit, but the fundamental lesson is the same.

6. **Help students explore how to decipher the plans of the characters they are reading about in books.**

   A. Copy a passage from their literature curriculum.

   B. Have the children use a highlighter to color words that indicate what a character is planning to do, or what a character is thinking about.

   C. Have the student make a guess about what might happen next in the story based on figuring out the character's plans.

   D. Have the students write their guess in the margin of the book, or state their guess aloud if they don't want to write.

    Remember this exercise can be very hard for these students. Reading at a more critical level (rather than at the level of understanding facts), making predictions, and writing their ideas on paper can be quite challenging. To be effective as a teacher, appreciate their struggle and pick one hard skill to work on at a time. If you push them to do it all, you will kill their motivation to try. As they become more confident, they can then be guided towards writing and predicting, etc.

Lesson 16: Video Moment for Exploring Being a Detective

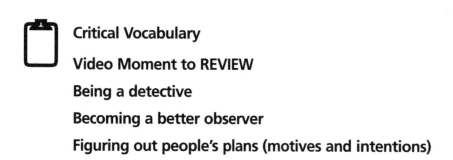

Critical Vocabulary

Video Moment to REVIEW

Being a detective

Becoming a better observer

Figuring out people's plans (motives and intentions)

How to use this lesson in the classroom:

1. Videotape the children playing. (Note: Be sure to obtain any necessary parental consent).

2. Tell the students they are now going to practice being a detective by watching the video of their play and figuring out who did a good job "reading the plans of other people."

3. If the detectives notice a student who has NOT done it well, reassure the student that we all make mistakes at this sometimes. Use humor to explain how hard this is for all people, including adults. For example, at a baseball stadium, adults routinely fight over who actually caught the ball that was hit into the stands. Even if one person is holding it, adults may argue that another person actually caught it, but the other person stole it out of their hands. We don't expect people to accurately read people's plans all of

the time but students should be aware of the "expected behavior," because it helps keep other people calm.

4. The video moment helps students see how their behaviors look to other people and to themselves. Use video moments with caution. If you have one student who makes constant mistakes, but the other students are doing well all the time, do NOT use the video to constantly point out that individual student's mistakes. Try to find a video clip that shows each student doing well. Then, on occasion, when students point out what is "unexpected" you can explore how that behavior makes the observers feel. When the students observe what they or someone else did not do as well, have them discuss how they—or the other student—could do it better next time. Showing children what they do well on video is a type of intervention technique called "video modeling."

5. See the Video Moment Sheet at the end of this section.

Lesson 17: Smart Guess – Wacky Guess

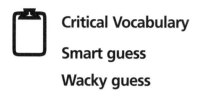 **Critical Vocabulary**

Smart guess

Wacky guess

Being a **social thinker** means you have to be a **flexible thinker.** Part of thinking socially is being able to make smart or educated guesses about what people are thinking, what they may be about to do, what you should do given the situation, etc.

At the same time, the academic curriculum demands that we also begin to make guesses by predicting outcomes in literature and social studies, schedules and mathematical word problems.

Many of our students with social thinking challenges do not know it is expected that they should actively be making guesses about the world around them and about the school work they are doing. While they may make excellent guesses about their own areas of interest, it is surprising how hard it is for them to apply this same set of skills to information they do not find intrinsically interesting.

This set of lessons familiarizes students with the process of making smart guesses, and reinforces smart guessing as an important part of being with others and learning information beyond the facts in school.

Videotape some of your lessons to use in the "video moment" activity at the end of this section.

How to use this lesson in the classroom:

1. Compare the difference between a "smart guess" and a "wacky guess." At this point, keep the majority of the smart and/or wacky guessing tied directly to what is happening in the environment and to the people in the environment (concrete actions and objects). This set of lessons is NOT about investigating what people mean by what they say.

2. Teach students a "smart guess" is when we make a small guess based on some information we have already learned or know. (These are also called inferences, predictions and educated guesses.). An example of a smart guess is when the teacher says to think about what a character is going to do next as the character is walking into a grocery store. The student predicts he is going shopping for food.

3. A "wacky guess" is when we do not have any good information and we make a guess with no real solid clues. An example of a wacky guess is when we ask a student, "Guess what color I am going to wear to school tomorrow?" and he guesses "blue" without having any real information to base his guess on.

4. Explain to students that teachers usually want students to make smart guesses based on what they have taught their students. (As students get older, with each passing year, the curriculum requires them to make more and more smart guesses. This is also referred to as "critical thinking.")

5. Explore with students that when they think with their eyes, they can make smart guesses about what someone else is going to do, or how they might be feeling. Remind them what a good job they did making smart guesses when they were reading people's plans in the movie clips and when they were practicing with the other students.

6. Use the worksheet on the following page to have students make various smart guesses or wacky guesses. For example, "What happens when the session is over?" would be a "smart guess." "What will the teacher eat for lunch tomorrow?" would be a "wacky guess." If your students are not cognitively able to fill out the worksheet, modify the activity to encourage the students to discuss the information as a group.

→ *Teachers - what other activities can you think of to promote students' confidence in their ability to make guesses about people and curriculum?*

Smart Guess - Wacky Guess
Student Worksheet

Name _____ Date _____

Smart Guesses are guesses you make based on some information you have already learned. When you make this type of guess you try and figure out the next logical piece of information based on what you already know.

Wacky Guesses are guesses you make when you do not have enough information. Wacky guesses are when people try and make you guess something you have no information about. Teachers do not usually ask you to make these guesses in your school work.

List 3 Smart Guesses You Can Make	List 3 Wacky Guesses You Can Make
Make one smart guess about what your mom will do tonight when she is home.	Make a wacky guess about what is going on in a kindergarten class right now.
Make a smart guess about what your teacher is going to teach in your next Math class.	Make a wacky guess about what your teacher is having for dinner tonight.
Make a smart guess about what you have to do as soon as you get to your class in the morning.	Make a wacky guess about who the principal will be talking to at 3 p.m.

Lesson 18: Reading People's Emotions

📋 **Critical Vocabulary**

Reading people's emotions

In this lesson you will help students explore **feelings** and **emotions** as part of understanding ourselves and others.

Students need to recognize (decode) and produce (encode) an array of different spoken messages, facial expressions, gestures and body language to accurately gauge emotions conveyed during a conversation.

Many professional resources now exist that can help you teach students to read and decode facial and body language to understand emotion. Drs. Duke and Nowicke use the term "dyssemia" to describe people who do not intuitively read face, voice and body cues. Please refer to their books, *Teaching Your Child the Language of Social Success* and *Will I Ever Fit In?* (a book focused on these issues in adults).

Rather than re-create the wheel in this curriculum, I encourage educators to seek out these lessons about reading faces, tone of voice, body language and gestures. A list of specific books and manuals is referenced in the bibliography at the end of this book.

Suggestions for Expanding on Lessons

One of the more complicated aspects of teaching students to read emotions, which then leads to the development of empathy, is the understanding that emotions can ONLY be interpreted within their appropriate context.

We need to teach students that "reading" other people's emotions is not just based on listening and looking at their bodies and faces, but also on being able to read the environment and situations around them. For example, a bride who is crying at her wedding is showing tears of happiness, even though we often teach students when people cry it means they are sad!

How to use this lesson in the classroom:

1. To teach students how to identify emotions in context, start with still photos/pictures of social scenarios.

    A. Use pictures of people interacting in different contexts. There are a number of boxed sets available for this purpose. Preferred products include:

        i. Emotion and Expression Cards: (PRO-ED, Inc.). Find these in their "speech and language materials" section. For more information, please see the bibliography at the end of the book.

        ii. Color cards: (Speech Mark). Boxed sets for "Emotions" and "Daily Activities." For more information please see the bibliography at the end of the book.

    B. Select single pictures (even if they are part of pictured sequences; just use one of these pictures for now).

    C. Ask the students to explain how the environment/context helps you understand how someone is feeling. Students will know how to do this based on their own recollection of what they have experienced about the world. For example, when they explain that the girl feels sad because her mom is leaving the house, the students understand the girl better because they remember how they have felt when a loved one left. Praise the students for making this "smart guess" based on what they know about the world.

    D. You may notice that this is a difficult activity for some students since their eyes don't naturally seek information from people's faces to find out how they feel. If this happens, explain that most people look at people's faces first to try and figure out how people feel, before they start looking around at the environment the person is in. Work with students to develop logical steps that help them evaluate people in situations.

Step 1: Look at people's faces, what type of facial expression do they have?

Step 2: Look to where people are looking to figure out what they are thinking about.

Step 3: Look for environmental clues that tell the student more about why this person feels the way he does.

Step 4: Have them make some smart guesses based on their own life experiences or from things they have learned about the world, even if they have not experienced it themselves. For example, kids usually know people are sad at funerals even if they have never been to one.

2. **Use movie clips as we did in Lesson 16,** but this time, encourage students to do more than read a character's plan. This time we also want students to try and figure out how the characters are feeling based on the situation in the movie, and what they think will happen later in the movie, not just in the next scene. Suggest that they can:

A. Make a smart guess about what the character is looking at.

B. Make a smart guess about how a character may be feeling based on how they look.

C. Try and figure out if the character is "bad" or "good." Have them use this information to try and figure out if the character is going to make things worse for other people in the movie, or better for them.

D. Make a smart guess about what might happen by the end of the movie based on what they are learning the characters know or don't know.

Tip on Reading Comprehension: This same type of social information is required for comprehending literature or for understanding the thinking behind notable people in history or social studies. If the children cannot do this activity when supplied with rich visual information—such as the information shown in a movie—it is very unlikely they will be able to interpret this social information when decoding text in a book. Remember, words on a page look like zebra stripes to a person who cannot interpret information from social scenarios.

3. **Videotape some of your lessons to use in the "video moment" section.** These basic lessons need to be taught to students over time. However, these lessons can be taught slowly, over and over again across the years, and across all the sections in this curriculum. Remember, none of us stops learning about interpreting our own and other's emotions, so it makes sense that as kids age and the lessons are re-explored, students can grasp them in more mature and meaningful ways. There is a huge difference in a 12-year-old's and a 16-year-old's grasp of emotions, even when they both are on the autism spectrum.

   A. What are feelings? How do you see them on people (faces, bodies)?

   B. How do you hear what someone's feelings are (tone of voice)?

   C. Do we all have feelings?

   D. Is there ever a time when we are awake that we are without feelings?

   E. Is it common for people experiencing the same event to share the same set of feelings? For example, how do most people feel when school is out for the day? How do most people feel when they experience an earthquake, tornado or hurricane? We can use smart guesses to figure out other people's emotions at times.

F. Practice identifying feelings from pictures.

G. Practice identifying feelings from situations. This includes reading emotions in the real environment.

H. Practice identifying feelings from people's tone of voice.

I. Explore how emotions/feelings have to be quickly determined by looking at the context of the situation.

    i. If Amy is smiling after she has just been yelled at, how does she really feel?

    ii. If Sally is crying when she just received really good news, how do you think she feels?

    iii. If Jack is looking surprised on his birthday, how does he feel?

    iv. If Mark is looking surprised when someone plays a mean trick on him, how does he feel?

    v. What other examples can you or your students think of?

J. Reiterate that the behavior of people around you can change how you feel and how others feel.

K. Discuss the importance of taking the time to read the cues on people's faces, bodies, and in their tone of voice.

4. Go on detective field trips around the school campus:

A. Walk around the school and peek in on secretaries, librarians, custodians, and P.E. classes.

B. Have students make smart guesses about what the different people are doing, what they might be feeling, and what they might be doing later in the day depending on who they are (secretary, custodian, parent, student, etc.)

C. Once you have worked through "Social Behavior Mapping" (SBM), discussed in the next Activity, you can also observe whether people are doing the expected or unexpected behavior and how their behavior is making other people feel.

Lesson 19: Our Behavior Impacts How People React and Respond to Us:
An Exploration of Thinking Through Behavior

Critical Vocabulary

Social Behavior Mapping (SBM)

How our behaviors affect others' emotions and actions toward us, which affects how we feel about ourselves

Social Behavior Mapping (SBM) was developed to teach students how to think through emotional and behavioral reactions when sharing space with other people. While we often teach students that we expect them to behave correctly in a given situation, and at times we reward them with artificial consequences for doing so, we often don't teach students why their behavior is important in the first place. We just assume students understand the impact of their behavior on others around them.

SBM is a common sense approach to teach all students that how we treat people around us affects how these people feel about each of us; how they feel about us, in turn, affects how they respond to us. How people respond to us has a lot to do with how we feel about ourselves. SBMs also explore how behavioral expectations vary from situation to situation.

Social behavior mapping is not a panacea. It is a concrete lesson to help simplify the abstract nature of co-existing with other people in the same environment. It is good to remind students that when we share space in a common environment, people will ultimately have thoughts and feelings (even if they are at the subconscious level) about each of us, whether or not they are interacting with us.

Social Behavior Mapping is described in great detail in my books, *Thinking about YOU Thinking about ME, 2nd Ed.* (2007) and *Social Behavior Mapping* (2007). I have also attached a more succinct review of these concepts and procedures in Appendix 4-1. Please review this material and make it available as a handout for parents and other school professionals.

Social Behavior Maps are VERY appropriate for students and poster-size maps are available for use in the classroom from our web site (**www.socialthinking.com**). Two SBMs are available: one explains the hidden rules and reactions to working in the classroom; the other poster is blank with a dry erase surface, for the educator to use and reuse with students to explore behavioral expectations and predicted responses in different contexts. (Sample social behavior maps are posted at **www.socialthinking.com**, under "Products.") In my book, *Worksheets! for Teaching Social Thinking and Related Skills* (2005), the last section provides information on the binder-paper-sized posters for students to use at their tables.

How to use this lesson in the classroom:

1. Create an SBM for a specific setting in which the students in your group need to further explore social rules and reactions.

2. Review with the students the different parts of the SBM and how they relate to each other.

   A. Define the environment or context that is the focus of the SBM.

   B. Define the **expected/unexpected** behavior.

   C. Make smart guesses about what other people feel when the **expected** versus the **unexpected** behaviors occur.

   D. Make smart guesses about how people naturally respond to another person's behavior based on how they feel about that person's behavior. For example, when we are happy or calm, we often use a calm voice, may use praise or talk about positive topics. When we are mad or worried, we often use a more upset tone of voice. We often nag the person who has upset us by telling them what they should have done, or what they should do next.

   E. Have the student define how he feels about himself based on how people are treating him.

   F. Use the language of the SBM to talk about student behaviors that are expected, how they make others feel, and then how they are treated. Always focus MOSTLY on the positive. To a lesser extent, also point out when someone is doing something unexpected and how teachers or students may treat him. The key is to use the map to "catch the student in the act of doing what is expected" to keep the student recognizing the positive result of that behavior.

G. Post the Social Behavior Map in the classroom and use it on a regular basis with ALL students to reinforce that their own behavior affects how people treat them. For egocentric students use the map to spotlight how their own behavior impacts how they end up feeling about themselves. Some of our students really struggle to find meaning in other people's emotions. Begin by teaching them that their expected behavior helps them be more satisfied. The idea of being more satisfied is a great motivator for them when first using this tool.

H. If using binder-paper-sized SBMs at student desks or at home, draw circles around the key concepts in each column to help students visually connect these concepts: your behavior affects people's emotions, which impacts how people treat you, which impacts how you feel about yourself.

I. Draw a line to visually connect each set of circles. By drawing these circles and lines, you show students how behavior creates a chain reaction.

J. You can use the same map (expected behaviors on one side of the paper, and unexpected behaviors on the other side of the paper) over and over again. Circles and lines will eventually collide after repeated use, but the students still understand the concepts.

K. You can use an SBM for each student at the table, but generally when we work in groups we refer to one overall map (student-sized or poster-sized) for the whole group.

Lesson 20: The Incredible 5-Point Scale: Learning to Gauge our own Response to our Inner Feelings

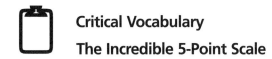

Critical Vocabulary

The Incredible 5-Point Scale

The book, *The Incredible 5 Point Scale* (Dunn Buron & Curtis, 2004) is a terrific adjunct lesson to Social Behavior Mapping. The authors provide a template for a "five-point scale" to help students understand the range of their own behaviors and feelings, and the impressions their behaviors create in others.

On their scale, points 1 - 3 represent behaviors that are within an acceptable standard in a given environment. Points 4 and 5 indicate a person is no longer in control of his behavior. The authors provide strategies and suggestions so that educators can help students learn how to keep their behaviors in the 1 - 3 range by being aware of their own feelings, body regulation and mood.

The Incredible 5-Point Scale helps students recognize and regulate their behaviors. It also helps them avoid letting their behaviors escalate into the 4th and 5th point of disaster and momentary doom! This is an excellent tool for developing self-awareness and self-calming strategies to help students regulate their own behavior.

Please review this useful book and incorporate lessons from it into your therapy sessions. See the bibliography to learn where to obtain it.

Lesson 21: Video Moment: Exploring Lessons in this Section

Critical Vocabulary

Video moment to review the concepts in this lesson section

After you have videotaped students across a variety of social contexts, ask the students to take on the role of social detectives in reviewing it. Have them observe, for example:

• Who is making a smart guess?

• How are people feeling?

• Does the teacher feel good about students' behavior or if she is worried?

Use the Video Moments Checklist on the following page.

Video Moments Self-Monitoring Checklist - Section 4

Learning More About Observing Others

Student's Name _____ Date _____

We are learning to watch people's social behavior and figure out how these behaviors are making other people feel.

Every once in a while you are going to be a "behavior checker," meaning you will be checking on someone's behavior in the group.

Sometimes the person you are going to check on is you, other times it is someone else in the group.

The person you are going to check on today is _____

Behavior to monitor or watch	Put a check here if the student is making others feel like he is doing a good job.	Put a check here if the student is not doing a good job.
Reading other people's plans.		
Making a smart guess/wacky guess. Being able to tell the difference.		
Thinking about what other people are feeling.		
Using the expected side of the Social Behavior Map.		

Based on what you checked, do you think this person would be a good person to work with on a project?

Circle: YES or NO

If not, what is one behavior the student could try and think about more to help people want to work with him?

Review for Teachers & Parents
🔊 Section 4

Learning More About Observing Others

Teaching social communication skills and behaviors is quite complicated. We can introduce these lessons in the therapy room, resource room, special needs classroom, and even the regular classroom, but to have the student really learn to grasp how these skills impact him all day, every day, we need educational professionals and paraprofessionals, along with family members, to become acquainted with how to break down the information, teach and reinforce these skills on a regular basis as the need comes up in the environment.

We have developed a set of lessons for the student to become more efficient at social thinking and understanding the related social skills. We need all persons who work or live with the student to also become familiar with the social thinking concepts and to use them during "teachable moments."

Please review the vocabulary terms and concepts on the other side of this sheet and use them with the student as they apply.

If you have any questions on how to use these terms please contact your child's teacher:
_____

at (phone number) _____.

Thanks for helping _____ learn to use these skills throughout his/her day, at home and school!

Remember the concepts we have introduced in previous lessons:

Section 1: Doing what is "expected" in the group; doing what is "unexpected" in a group; "You can change my feelings"; observing others through imitation; big problem - little problem; three parts of play: set up, play and clean up.

Section 2: Whole body listening; think and thinking with our brains; thinking with your eyes; thinking about what other people think.

Section 3: Your body is in the group; your body is out of the group! Your brain is in the group; your brain is out of the group!; Just ME/Thinking about You; good thoughts/weird thoughts; "I've got a secret"; video moment to watch what other people are doing.

VOCABULARY & CONCEPTS

Learning More About Observing Others

We are currently exploring the following terms. Remember to use them with students now and over time to help them generalize the concepts beyond the room where the lesson was first taught.

Critical Vocabulary		Definitions
Figuring out other people's plans		Observing other students in order to figure out what they are planning to do next based on the actions of their body (e.g. walking towards the pencil sharpener means the person is likely to sharpen his pencil).
Smart guess - Wacky guess		Guessing is an important part of participating in school lessons and communicating with others. There are two major types of guesses. "Smart guesses" (same as educated guess) are guesses you make based on a fact or some information you have learned about a topic. A "wacky guess" is a guess you may be asked to make when you have not been given any (or enough) information. For example, asking someone who has never been to my house to guess what color it is. In school, teachers ask students to make "smart guesses."
Identifying one's own feelings		Helping our students identify that they have feelings and helping students communicate these feelings more clearly. Also helping students understand that we can share feelings about the same event (earthquakes, hurricanes, etc.).
Social Behavior Mapping		This is a technique to help students understand that their behaviors impact how people feel about them and the natural consequences that arise due to people's feelings or response to such behaviors. A student's feelings about the people around him are often based on how people are treating him. Please ask for the handout that explains this process in more detail.

Goal Suggestions - Section 4
Starting the Detective Agency: Learning More About Observing Others

Based on curriculum activities in Section 4 and the California Content Standards

Goal #   **Goal Suggestions**

4-1   The student will be able to reliably "read someone's plan" or report how someone is feeling based on observing their body language in the environmental context, ____% of intervention session, and then using these concepts beyond the intervention room ____% of the time.

4-1a   While in a small group activity and asked to assess the situation, _____ will be able to reliably "read someone's plan" and then report how someone is feeling based his observation of that person's body language (and using the environmental context) ____% of the intervention session.

Take this skill beyond the intervention setting: There the student is expected to assess others' intents & plans of actions by observing their body language ____% of the time.

4-2   The student will be able to modify his or her own actions based on what he/she determines someone else is doing or going to do, ____% of intervention session and then using these concepts beyond the intervention room ____% of the time.

4-2a   When in a brief social interaction that involves movement, _____ will modify his own actions based on what he determines someone else is doing or going to do ____% of the intervention session.

Take this skill beyond the intervention setting: There the student is expected to modify his actions in anticipation of what he thinks another peer, teacher or family member is doing ____% of the time.

4-3   The student will be able to distinguish between a smart guess and a wacky guess, and then be able to attempt to make a smart guess, ____% of intervention session and then using these concepts beyond the therapy room ____% of the time.

4-3a   After gathering information in the intervention room, followed by a request to make a guess, _____ will distinguish between a "smart guess" and a "wacky guess" ____% of the intervention session.

Take this skill beyond the intervention setting: There the student is expected to assess whether his guess was a "smart guess" based on the information he or she was considering ____% of the time.

Goal #	Goal Suggestions
4-4	The student will define what it means to be a flexible thinker; he/she will then be willing to make choices, once they are presented to the student by the teacher, ____% of intervention session and then using these concepts beyond the therapy room ____% of the time.
📂	
4-4a	When asked, _____ will define what it means to be a flexible thinker and identify times during the social thinking groups when we use this skill ____% of the intervention session.
4-4b	When asked to make a choice, _____ will indicate his preference once they are presented to the student by the teacher ____% of intervention session.
	Take this skill beyond the intervention setting: There the student is expected to show his ability to be a "flexible thinker" by making a choice or considering options presented to him by peers, teachers or parents____% of the time.

Goal #	Goal Suggestions
4-5	The student will define what it means to be a flexible thinker and will then be willing to make self-generated choices, ___% of intervention session and then using these concepts beyond the therapy room ____% of the time.
📂	
4-5a	Using the concepts of being a "flexible thinker" _____ will make 2 -3 **self-generated** choices in a small group interaction ____% of intervention session.
	Take this skill beyond the intervention setting: There the student is expected to make self-generated choices that indicate his ability to be a "flexible thinker"____% of the time.

Goal #	Goal Suggestions
4-6	The student will use what he knows about the person or character's emotions and actions in specific contexts to predict what the person/character will do next, or to predict if his motives are just or questionable, ____% of intervention session and then using these concepts beyond the therapy room ____% of the time.
📂	
4-6a	Using what is known about the person/character's emotions and actions in specific contexts, _____ will predict what that person/character will do next, ____% of the intervention session.
	Take this skill beyond the intervention setting: There the student is expected to read a short passage and predict (make a smart guess) about what the character will do next with ____% accuracy.
4-6b	Using what is known about the person/character's emotions and actions in specific contexts, _____ will predict if their motives are just or questionable ____% of intervention session.
	Take this skill beyond the intervention setting: There the student is expected to read a short passage and predict if the characters motives are just or questionable with ____% accuracy.

Goal #	Goal Suggestions

4-7

The student will be able to note people's facial expressions, body language, tone of voice within specific contexts to determine how that person is feeling, ____% of intervention session and then using these concepts beyond the therapy room ____% of the time.

4-7a   After watching a brief video involving a social interaction, _____ will identify a selected person's facial expressions, body language, and tone of voice, within specific contexts, to determine how that person is feeling, ____% of intervention session.

4-7b   While in a social interaction with at least three people, _____ will identify a selected person's facial expression, body language and tone of voice, within specific contexts, to determine how that person is feeling, ____% of the intervention session.

Take this skill beyond the intervention setting: There the student is expected to utilize the nonverbal and verbal cues of others to determine how persons may be feeling____% of the time.

4-8

The student will define what it means to be a "social detective" and then observe people in his/her therapy room, school or home to identify how they feel and what they need from others, ____% of intervention session and then using these concepts beyond the therapy room ____% of the time.

4-8a   When asked by the instructor, _____ will define what it means to be a "social detective" and providing ____(# of) examples about this concept taught within the social thinking sessions with ____% accuracy.

4-8b   After an observation of ____ (# of) people in his therapy room, school or home, _____ will identify how each person may feel, using at least ____ (# of) vocabulary words taught in the social thinking sessions, with ____% accuracy.

Based on what _____ has observed and stated as the feelings of others, _____ will make a "smart" guess as to what that person(s) may need from others with ____% accuracy.

Take this skill beyond the intervention setting: There the student is expected to use "social detective" skills to observe others and determine how they may be feeling and what they may need from others during a brief social interaction ____% of the time.

4-9

The student will explain how the four columns of a Social Behavior Map are related to each other, and then complete his or her own Social Behavior Map for a specific environmental context with ____% accuracy.

4-9a   Given a visual model of the Social Behavior Map, _____ will explain how the four columns of a Social Behavior Map are related to each other using at least two (or other #) concepts for each column with ____% accuracy.

4-9b   Given a visual model with a blank Social Behavior Map, _____ will complete his own SBM for a specific environmental context with ____% accuracy.

Goal #	Goal Suggestions

4-10

The student will monitor his/her own production of expected behaviors identified on the student's Social Behavior Map, ____% of intervention session and then using these concepts beyond the therapy room ____% of the time.

4-10a   Using his/her completed Social Behavior Map, _____ will monitor his own production of "expected" behaviors ____% of intervention session.

Take this skill beyond the intervention setting: There the student is expected to use his personal Social Behavior Map to monitor his "expected" behavior within a selected classroom or interaction at home ____% of the time.

4-11

The student will target two expected behaviors on the Social Behavior Map, keep his/her own data on the production of these behaviors and then chart the occurrence of these behaviors in the appropriate context, ____% of intervention session and then using these concepts beyond the therapy room ____% of the time.

4-11a   Using his/her completed Social Behavior Map, _____ will target two expected behaviors to use within the intervention session.

4-11b   Once target behaviors are selected, _____ will keep his/her own data on the production of these behaviors by charting their occurrence in the appropriate context, ____% of intervention session.

Take this skill beyond the intervention setting: There the student is expected to focus on the two selected expected behaviors in another classroom environment, using his established data tracking system ____% of the time.

4-12

When reviewing videotaped footage of the social thinking group in which the student participates, the student will be able to identify the targeted behaviors first in other students and then in himself/herself, focusing on identifying when "expected behaviors" happened; ____% during the intervention session.

4-12a   When reviewing videotaped footage of the social thinking group in which he participates, _____ will identify the targeted behaviors of _____ in other student(s), with ____% accuracy.

4-12b   When reviewing videotaped footage of the social thinking group in which he participates, _____ will identify the targeted behaviors in himself, focusing on identifying when "expected behaviors" happen, with ____% accuracy.

California Content Standards - Section 4
Starting the Detective Agency: Learning More About Observing Others

Grade	Area of the curriculum	Essential Intervention California State Standard
K	Reading	Predictions with pictures and context
3	Reading	Connect/relate prior experience/insights/ideas to the speaker
4	Reading	Make and confirm predictions about the text by using prior knowledge and ideas presented in the text itself, including illustrations, titles, topic sentences, important words and foreshadowing clues
4	Reading	Distinguish between cause and effect and between fact and opinion
4	Reading	Use knowledge of situations, settings and character traits/motivations to determine cause for character's actions
5	Listening and Speaking: Pragmatics	Engage audience with appropriate facial/tone/gestures
5	Listening and Speaking: Pragmatics	Interpret speaker's verbal/nonverbal message/purpose/perspective
6	Listening and Speaking: Pragmatics	Identify tone/mood/emotion conveyed
6	Listening and Speaking: Pragmatics	Relate the speaker's verbal to the nonverbal communication
6	Reading	Analyze effect of the qualities of the character (courage/coward) on the plot and resolution of conflict
6	Reading	Critique the credibility of characterization and degree to which plot is contrived/realistic (compare use of fact/fantasy in historical fiction)
7	Listening and Speaking: Pragmatics	Determine speaker's attitude toward subject
8	Listening and Speaking: Pragmatics	Paraphrase a speaker's purpose/point of view and ask related questions
8	Reading	Interpret and evaluate the various ways in which visual image makers (e.g. graphic artists, illustrators, new photographers) communicate information and affect impressions and opinions.
9	Reading	Analyze interactions between main and subordinate characters in text (conflicts, motivations, relationships, influences) and explain why these affect plot
9	Reading	Determine character's traits by seeing what characters say about themselves in narrative, dialogue, drama, monologue, soliloquy
9	Listening and Speaking: Pragmatics	Formulate judgments about ideas discussed

Bibliography and References - Section 4
Starting the Detective Agency: Learning More About Observing Others

Agassi, M. (2000). *Hands Are Not For Hitting.* Free Spirit Publishing Inc.: Minneapolis, MN.

Berry, Joy Wilt (2000). Book Series: *Let's Talk About Feeling Frustrated; Let's Talk About Feeling Disappointed; Let's Talk About Feeling Embarrassed; Let's Talk About Feeling Inferior; Let's Talk About Feeling Cheated; Let's Talk About Feeling Jealous; Let's Talk About Feeling Rejected;* Gold Star Publishing: Scottsdale, AZ.

Brown, L. and Brown, M. (1998). *How To Be A Friend: A Guide to Making Friends and Keeping Them.* Little, Brown and Company: Boston, MA.

Cardon, T. (2004). *Let's Talk: Emotions.* Autism Asperger Publishing Company: Shawnee Mission, KS. www.asperger.net

Curtis, Jamie Lee (1998). *Today I Feel Silly & Other MOODS That Make My Day.* Scholastic: New York, NY.

Duke, M.; Nowicki, S.; Martin, E. (1996). *Teaching Your Child the Language of Social Success.* Peachtree Publishers: Atlanta, GA.

Duke, M.; Nowicki, S.; Martin, E. (2002). *Will I Ever Fit In?* The Free Press: New York, NY.

Dunn Buron, K. & Curtis, M. (2004). *Incredible 5-Point Scale: Assisting Students with Autism Spectrum Disorders in Understanding Social Interactions and Controlling Their Emotional Responses.* Autism Asperger Publishing Company: Shawnee Mission, KS. www.asperger.net

Emberley, E. & Miranda, A. (1997). *Glad Monster, Sad Monster.* Little, Brown and Company: Boston, MA.

Everly, N. (2005). *Can You Tell How Someone Feels.* Linguisystems: East Moline, IL. www.linguisystems.com

Koenig,T. & Meyer, B. (1999). *Caring Kids: Social Skills & Character Education Lessons for Grades 1-3.* Thinking Publications: Eau Claire, WI. www.thinkingpublications.com

Levine, M. & Clutch, J. (2001). *Jarvis Clutch: Social Spy,* Educators Publishing Service, Inc.: Cambridge, MA.

Madison, L. (2002). *The Feelings Book: The Care and Keeping of Your Emotions.* American Girl Library. Pleasant Company Publications: Middleton, WI. www.americangirl.com

McAfee, J. (2002). *Navigating the Social World.* Future Horizons, Inc.: Arlington, TX. www.futurehorizons-autism.com

Pro-Ed (1990s). **Emotions and Expressions:** Photographs. Imaginart: AZ. www.proedinc.com (ask for these in the speech and language materials section of their product line).

Speech Mark (1990s). *Color cards - Different boxes: Daily Activities; Emotions; Daily Living Cards.* www.speechmark.net

Stallard, P. (2002). *Think Good-Feel Good: A Cognitive Behavior Therapy Workbook for Children and Young People.* John Wiley and Sons, LTD.: West Sussex, England.

Winner, M. (2007). *Thinking About YOU Thinking About ME, 2nd Ed.* Think Social Publishing, Inc.: San Jose, CA. www.socialthinking.com

Winner, M. (2005). *Worksheets! for Teaching Social Thinking and Related Skills.* Think Social Publishing, Inc.: San Jose, CA. www.socialthinking.com.

Winner, M. (2005). *Social Thinking Posters: Social Behavior Map Dry Erase surface, Social Behavior Map for the Classroom, The Boring Moment, Being Part of A Group.* Think Social Publishing, Inc.: San Jose, CA. (www.socialthinking.com)

Videos:

Park, N. (1993). "The Wrong Trousers." Wallace & Gromit Video Series. CBS-Fox.

"Toy Story" (1995). Pixar Films.

"Toy Story 2" (1999). Pixar Films.

Social Behavior Mapping

Students with Asperger Syndrome or related disabilities have difficulty seeing the "gestalt," the whole. Therefore, any behavioral system built for them needs to provide extra information about context and generalization. It cannot be assumed that a student understands how his behavior is linked to its consequences or that he understands how his behavior affects the perspective of fellow students or educators.

Expected Behaviors

I believe it is also important to teach students about sets of behaviors rather than simply point out each singular behavior being done inappropriately. For example, students in classrooms who have difficulty staying on task and learning as part of a group need to actively learn about "behaviors for learning". Depending on the student, these might include:

A Stay in your chair

B. Sit up straight in your chair

C. Keep you feet on the floor

D. Look at the teacher when she is talking

E. Keep your voice quiet except to speak when the teacher has called on you

F. Raise your hand when you need help

These are the behavioral sets we expect students to perform to be ready to learn as part of a group.

Unexpected Behaviors

To further break this down, we need to explore with a student what behaviors are expected versus unexpected. In general, expected behaviors are those that help a child learn and be perceived in a positive light by his peers and educators. It is the unexpected behaviors that cause a child to be perceived as "weird" by peers and may cause frustration in those trying to support him. In contrast to expected behaviors for learning, unexpected behaviors include:

A. Falling out of your chair

B. Wandering around the class

C. Making noises or talking to classmates

D. Saying things unrelated to what the teacher is discussing

E. Not paying attention to the teacher or what she is referencing

F. Yelling out answers in class or never raising your hand to give answers

A number of different behavioral sets exist at school and at home:

  A. Expected/unexpected behaviors for learning

  B. Expected/unexpected behaviors for friendship

  C. Expected/unexpected behaviors on the playground

  D. Expected/unexpected behaviors when using humor

  E. Expected/unexpected behaviors for eating food in the company of others

  F. Expected/unexpected behaviors for being part of a family

The education team and the parents should determine the behavioral sets relevant to work on with any given student.

Perspective Taking and How it Links to Behavior

Once we have determined what behaviors are expected or unexpected, we then need to explain to students how these behaviors affect people's perspectives. Students with Asperger Syndrome or related disabilities often fail to fully account for the emotional context that surrounds them. They don't realize that a behavior they are exhibiting is inappropriate and further, don't understand how the inappropriateness of their behavior impacts how others feel about them. We, as educators, can help them make this connection by mapping out how people feel when they observe students acting in expected ways, versus how they feel when the unexpected happens. Please see the template, "Social Behavior Mapping," which follows.

For example: When a student is sitting up in his chair and watching the teacher, she feels proud of him, she is happy he is learning, and other students may also notice that he is doing a good job. However, if a student falls out of his chair or makes "monkey" sounds, the teacher may feel frustrated and worried that he is not learning, and that he is impeding other student's learning as well.

Educators have commented that they feel uncomfortable telling a student that his particular behavior affects the feelings of an adult or a peer. The important point to consider is that our reluctance to verbally acknowledge our feelings to others is based on the idea that typical people can "read" our feelings intuitively and thus can regulate their behavior according to their intuition. The reality for many of our kids is that they have true social-cognitive deficits impacting their ability to "read" how emotional states are connected to behavioral actions. There are times when one of our students chooses to do a malicious behavior, with full awareness of how he is impacting others even after he has learned these lessons. I have observed students purposely misbehaving, but then I have observed those same students doing an unintentional unexpected behavior with no awareness of how it was impacting others in their environment.

Connecting Expectations and Perspective to Consequences

The final step in using the map is to make the association to the related consequences. Students need help understanding that consequences are often tied to the emotional states of the people around them. If they are doing what is expected, people feel good and they will get some type of acknowledgement (verbal praise) and perhaps even a reward (a star on a chart that eventually earns something for the student). If the student demonstrates unexpected behaviors, others in the environment may notice and react to such behaviors by giving a less desirable consequence. For example, if a student is being highly distractable to himself and others, he may get three opportunities to pull it together before he is removed from the classroom to calm down. There may also be a decision to remove earned points from a chart thereby reducing the student's potential rewards.

While I realize we try to be extremely positive when working with behavioral teaching plans, it is my opinion that students with social processing deficits have a difficult time knowing when they have acted in an "unexpected" manner. If we pay attention only to their positive behavior, we may not be giving them all the information they need to recognize both expected and unexpected behaviors and appreciate the relationship between them.

Using the SBM

Start by completing the "expected" behaviors map (this has the smiley face on it).

1. List at the top of the map the behavioral set you are describing, e.g. "behaviors for learning."

2. List the "expected" set of behaviors.

3. List how expected behaviors make other people feel (i.e. their perspective). Use emotion words or phrases such as "pleased," "proud," "happy Paul is working as part of the group."

4. List any consequences (these are generally the more positive ones) that result from exhibiting expected behaviors.

5. Go through the same process on the "unexpected" page:

   A. List how these unexpected behaviors affect someone else's perspective by listing emotion words such as "frustrated," "annoyed," "worried that Paul is not learning."

   B. Next, list the related consequences, e.g. "Paul's teacher has a strict tone of voice when she tells him what he needs to do;" "Paul may need to leave the group or the room;" "Paul loses a point on his earning chart;" "Paul feels frustrated."

Introducing the SBM to Students

1. Educators should review the maps as a team before the maps are introduced to the student. It is also important that parents see these ahead of time and accept the language and consequences.

2. Once approved, make several copies to use throughout the day in the class or in whatever setting they are needed.

3. These maps are then used to explain to the student what is happening with the people around him when he shows different behaviors. The team sets a schedule for how often the aide should fill out a map for him. Filling out a map means observing the student's behaviors and then circling which behavior he was exhibiting, how it made others feel, and the related consequence. How frequently a map is used depends on how often you need to map out the student's behavior in order to consistently catch him in the act of doing what is "expected." If a student consistently receives positive comments for "doing what is expected," he or she will likely be more willing to adjust when his "unexpected" behavior is pointed out.

4. Keep a simple graph in the **ME Binder*** that charts how many times each day the student was "caught in the act of doing something expected" versus "caught in the act of doing something unexpected." Encourage the student to monitor his own behavior by looking at the graph. Set goals to decrease the number of unexpected behaviors or increase the number of expected behaviors, eventually using a token system so the student earns a larger predetermined reward.

    * For information on the **ME Binder**, refer to *Thinking About YOU Thinking About ME, 2nd Ed.* (Winner, 2007) and *Social Behavior Mapping* (Winner, 2007).

In Summary

Social Behavior Maps give more information to the student and his team of educators about his behavior. They also provide vocabulary for discussing behavior with the student. It is an easy and effective tool to help students recognize their own actions, their effect on others, and the indirect effect back on themselves. I discourage a lot of talking while the maps are being filled out since I don't want to encourage students to be argumentative or thrown off task.

A behavioral system is just one element among many the student needs in his day. Equally important is making sure he has accommodations in his classroom experiences to foster success, which then will encourage him to stay behaviorally on track.

Appendix 4.2: Social Behavior Map

Behaviors That Are EXPECTED For Learning as Part of a Group in the Classroom

Expected Behaviors	How They Make Others Feel	Consequences You Experience	How You Feel About Yourself
Sit where the group is sitting.	Happy	Calm voices	Good
Keep your eyes on the teacher or what she is talking about.		Pleased look on peoples' faces	Calm
Work on tasks the teacher assigns during work time.	Proud	People compliment or praise your behavior.	
Ask for help.		People may just let you work quietly so that you can work.	Happy
Touch only your own materials.	Calm	People might give you special opportunities or special tasks.	
Use fidgets to help keep your body calm.			
Keep your comments and questions focused on the class topic.	Pleased	Students want to work with you.	Relieved
Take out your book, pencil, and paper at the start of class.		Students may want to hang out or play with you during non-work times.	
Write down your homework assignment.	Successful	You earn a break time for concentrating well.	Included
Put materials away at the end of class.			
Monitor your talking time so that you participate as a member of the group; not too much nor too little.			

Behaviors That Are UNEXPECTED For Learning as Part of a Group in the Classroom

Unexpected Behaviors	How They Make Others Feel	Consequences You Experience	How You Feel About Yourself
Your body does not look like it is part of the group (e.g. wandering, body turned away from the group).	Frustrated	Tense faces	Sad
		Angry or solemn sounding voices	Anxious
Your eyes are not focused on the teacher or what she is doing.	Annoyed	People tell you what you should be doing (they nag you).	
Refusing to work; including sleeping.	Irritated	Students may not want to work with you.	Mad
NOT asking for help.			
Body is not calm and you are doing things that distract yourself or others.	Worried you are not learning as part of the group.	Students may not choose to hang out or play with you.	
Smelling or touching people.		You are sent out of the classroom.	Not included
Talking about things of interest to you, but your comments do not add to the class topic.	Tense	You do not get any special rewards.	
Not getting materials out at the start of class.		People laugh at something you say or do but they do not want to hang out with you.	
Not writing down your homework assignment.			
Not putting materials where they belong at the end of class.			

Social Behavior Map

Behaviors That Are EXPECTED

Place: _____

Expected Behaviors	How They Make Others Feel	Positive Consequences You Experience	How You Feel About Yourself
1.	1.	1.	1.
2.	2.	2.	2.
3.	3.	3.	3.
4.	4.	4.	4.
5.	5.	5.	5.
6.		6.	
7.		7.	

Social Behavior Map

Behaviors That Are UNEXPECTED

Place: _____

Unexpected Behaviors	How They Make Others Feel	Negative Consequences You Experience	How You Feel About Yourself
1.	1.	1.	1.
2.	2.	2.	2.
3.	3.	3.	3.
4.	4.	4.	4.
5.	5.	5.	5.
6.		6.	
7.		7.	

Section 5

The Super Detective Agency: Figuring Out What People Mean by What They Say

The concepts that follow help our students better interpret what they hear, as well as learn how to code their own spoken messages more abstractly. Educators will have to keenly observe what they see and hear from their students to determine what contextual information to provide during "teachable moments." They will also need to provide more specific lessons in structured teaching situations. It is important to realize the information in this set of lessons may literally span a lifetime for many of our students.

How do these lessons relate to classroom participation?

Obviously, language meaning and use are very important to interpreting and producing relevant information in class discussions and coursework (literature, history, social studies, written expression and even science) across the school day.

Interpreting increasingly abstract language is a necessary part of each verbal student's school and life experience. Our students with social cognitive deficits tend to be overly literal and miss many cues that might help them interpret indirect messages. For this reason, our students need to have language nuances taught more explicitly.

Any lesson about the interpretation of abstract language might be helpful to our students. However, it must be presented at a level they can understand. It will likely be necessary to teach them the information in specialized ways so that they can grasp the same social concepts that come more naturally to their neurotypical peers.

 Students with very sluggish perspective-taking ability will have great difficulty acquiring the mental flexibility to interpret different types of social language. I strongly believe, even if research has not definitively proven it yet, that these skills are directly linked!

Tools & Materials

- Any movie clip that shows someone trying to convince someone else to do something. (For example, the scene in *The Princess Diaries* where the Queen of Genovia and her granddaughter crash their car into a trolley car. The queen convinces the people that she is bestowing upon the police an honor from her country of Genovia. However, the queen's real intention was to get her granddaughter freed from a possible traffic ticket and a probable trip to the police station).

- Any book that provides lessons or exploration into idiomatic language, the double meaning of language or the fact that language has to be interpreted in the context (indirect language). The bulk of these books will be found in materials created for speech and language specialists. One example that is ideal for this set of lessons is *Saying One Thing, Meaning Another,* published by www.thinkingpublications.com.

- Books and stories that teach idiomatic language. A good story book is Amelia Bedelia. However, there are many other children's books that "play" with language to explore the difference between the literal and figurative expressions. Any of these books can be useful, provided they are appropriate to the child's age and developmental levels.

- Sequence picture cards and/or wordless picture books

- Small rubber brains for the flexible brain lesson (optional)

Critical Vocabulary & Concepts

- Body language

- Spoken language

- Literal language

- Figurative language

- Indirect language, idioms

- Four groups of clues to decipher language

- Flexible Brain

- Reading people's spoken or unspoken plans (motives/intentions)

- Predicting what people might say next

Lesson 22: Comparing Body Language and Spoken Language

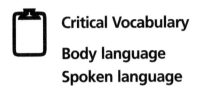 **Critical Vocabulary**

Body language
Spoken language

How to use this lesson in the classroom:

1. Compare body language to spoken language. Have students contrast how they communicate the same message verbally with language and non-verbally through their gestures, facial expression and body language.

   a. Make a list of nouns, actions or concepts that students will have fun acting out. (e.g. alligator, cat, using a house key, drinking from a glass, driving a car, buying something at a counter, putting on a pair of shoes, etc.) You can add many of your own words/concepts to this list.

   b. Cut the list up so that each strip of paper has one concept or word written or drawn on it. Put these strips in a jar or cup for the student to pull out one at a time.

   c. Take turns having the students either physically act out the word/concept or explain the word/concept without using the actual words. The students are not permitted to use any non-verbal messages while they are talking. There are board games on the market that can be used to help teach this concept such as games of charades or "Taboo." What other games can you think of?

   d. After finishing with the strips of words/concepts, ask students to describe the differences between acting with their bodies and faces versus using words to describe the word/concept to others. Encourage the students to notice the difference in the speed of the message; point out how spoken language is much faster.

e. Define "body language" as ways we use our body to send nonverbal messages. Define "spoken language" as using a verbal message. Define the term "communication" as a combination of nonverbal and verbal language. Discuss that the best and quickest method for conveying a message combines body language and spoken language together.

☼

2. Combine body language and spoken language together. The goal of this lesson is to have students pay attention to cues from both body language and spoken language to figure out what people really mean.

A. On strips of paper, present the students with words or concepts that are vague in meaning until paired with body language and/or facial expression that clarify the meaning. Concepts on paper strips can include:

   i.   "Look" (the child needs to point at what he wants someone to look at)

   ii. "Do you want a drink?" (The student has to look at the person to whom he is talking.)

   iii. "I like these" (the student has to indicate what he likes)

   iv. "Don't go in there" (the student has to point somewhere)

   v.   "That's gross"

   vi. "Wow, that's cool"

vii. "I don't want to do that"

viii. "Open this"

ix. "Don't drop that"

x. "Here, eat this"

What other lessons can you think of to help our students explore ways we communicate in two different systems, verbal and nonverbal, simultaneously?

Lesson 23: Comparing Literal and Figurative Language

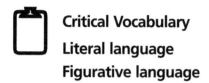 **Critical Vocabulary**
Literal language
Figurative language

Spoken communication generally falls into one of two categories: **literal** and **figurative language.**

1. Teach that **literal** language is like **cement** or **concrete.** You can discuss that concrete is hard and immovable. It stays in the same state all the time. Draw a sidewalk on the board. Talk about how it never changes shape, even when we all jump on it at the same time.

2. Teach that **figurative** language means **your brain has to figure out what is meant.** We can discuss that language meaning is flexible or figurative depending on what is happening in the context. See Activity 1 below to help teach this idea.

Figurative language does NOT mean exactly what it says. To interpret figurative language, we have to figure out the implied meaning of the word or phrase. We make a "smart guess" based on the person and the situation that existed when the language was being used.

How to use this lesson in the classroom:

The goal of this activity is to "play" with simple language concepts and then slowly use more complicated words and concepts to explore figurative language. This lesson spans time. You can build a literal/figurative language game into each one of your social thinking group sessions to continually expose students to the abstractness of language and how it changes with age.

1. Read one of the Amelia Bedelia books (see bibliography) or a similar book that contains words and phrases used out of context, creating humor and misunderstanding.

2. Make a list of words that have multiple meanings. For example:

   A.   Ball (We are having a ball vs. I play with a ball.)

   B.   Hot (That is so hot! vs. It is a hot day.)

   C.   Fly (There is a fly on the wall vs. The plane can fly vs. Your fly is down.)

   D.   Chill (There is a chill in the air outside vs. Chill dude, calm down.)

   E.   Cool (She is cool (awesome) vs. She is cool (cold).)

   F.   Flower/flour

   G.   To, too, two

   H.   Punch (He drank punch vs. He received a punch.)

   I.   Feet (He has two feet vs. It is two feet long)

   J.   Pop (Her dad is her pop vs. She heard a pop vs. She drank a pop.)

   K.   Concrete (The sidewalk is concrete vs. the schedule is set in concrete.)

3. Have the students, with your help, discuss the various meanings of each of the words.

4. Have the students pick out a word and then have them use the word in a larger context. For example, "my pop took me to a baseball game, where we kept hearing this pop, and when we looked around we saw all these people opening a can of pop." The student does not have to create the same setting for the different words in context; however, it may be fun for them to try.

5. Have other students identify what each use of the word means.

6. Then have the students figure out how they knew which version of the word had meaning in the context of the situation.

7. Encourage students to explore the fact that language, just like emotions, only makes sense by looking at what is happening in the environment, or in the sentence, to figure out what the words mean.

Lesson 24: Learning About Idioms

Critical Vocabulary

Idioms

Idioms are phrases we use in our language where the meaning is definitely NOT literal. In fact, if we try to figure out what an idiomatic phrase means by literally interpreting each word, we are not accurately figuring out what people mean by using it.

For example, if you are trying to figure something out but are going about it the wrong way, we can use the idiom "you are barking up the wrong tree" to describe this type of action.

The concept of idioms is often taught to children around third grade. However, students usually learn idioms just by hearing them enough times, which can be a frustrating way for our literal-minded students to try and learn. The activities that follow provide opportunity for more explicit practice. Expect this lesson to span years!

Avoid teaching this lesson to younger children, for whom it is too abstract.

How to use this lesson in the classroom:

1. Using the worksheet on the following page, complete each of these activities:

   A. Act out or describe what each idiom literally means.

   B. Describe what each idiom means, figuratively, after making some smart guesses and/or discussing it with your teacher.

   C. Draw a line from the idiom to its intended figurative meaning.

Idioms
Student Worksheet

Draw a line from the idiom to its meaning.

The Idiom	The Meaning
1. Shake a leg.	A. Have you been in a bad mood all day?
2. Has the cat got your tongue?	B. What is new in your life?
3. 24-7	C. Get started with your work.
4. He is cool.	D. Time to stop doing what you are doing.
5. Put your nose to the grindstone.	E. He is a good person.
6. Get a jump on it.	F. Why aren't you speaking?
7. Let's wind it up.	G. Hurry up!
8. Chill out.	H. Time to get to work.
9. What's up?	I. It happens all the time.
10. Get up on the wrong side of the bed?	J. Stop acting so upset.

2. What other idioms can you add that are commonly used in your region of the country or at your school? Idiom use is cultural and regional, even within the same country such as the United States.

Have your students determine what each idiom would mean if taken literally. Then have them try and guess the figurative meanings of the idioms. Enjoy making up reasons for how these phrases developed into their figurative meanings.

3. A wide variety of sources are available for exploring idioms. Entire web sites exist that define idioms and document their origins. Interesting and fun books explore the meaning of idiomatic expressions. Some of these include:

   A. Idioms Fun Deck

   B. Who Put the Butter in Butterfly

   C. You Can't Judge a Book by Its Cover

   D. Idiom dictionaries

4. Using an idioms dictionary, write three to five idioms on the board each week when your group meets.

  A. Decipher and discuss the literal versus the figurative meaning of these idioms as part of a warm-up lesson in your class.

  B. Have the students practice using all of the idioms in one paragraph they create to demonstrate their figurative meaning. For example, if the three idioms listed are…

    i. The cat's got your tongue.

    ii. Hold your horses.

    iii. You are off your rocker!

  …then a sample paragraph can be something like: *I told my mom to hold her horses; she was acting like she was off her rocker. Finally, I didn't say anything and then my mom asked me if the cat's got my tongue. I can't win for losing!*

  C. Post a list of all the idioms learned across the sessions as the year progresses. Students really enjoy referring to the list.

  D. Challenge students to bring in new idioms they have heard at home or at school to try and stump the group.

 What other lessons can you think of to help our students explore that we communicate with both literal and figurative language?

Lesson 25: Deciphering Language Meaning – The Four Clues

Critical Vocabulary

Indirect language, Four groups of clues, "Flexible brain"

Indirect language is language used to allude to a message not directly stated. It is broader than idiomatic language, since the meaning is not only transferred through predictable phrases as is the case with idioms. Instead, the meaning is often conveyed through what is not stated but is apparent given the environment. Indirect language is highly context driven. The only way to interpret it is for the listener to try and determine the speaker's motive at the time the message is stated by using clues from the specific environment.

In an earlier section, we worked with students to read people's (physical) plans. By watching people's actions we could figure out what people were planning to do next which also gave us insight to what they were thinking.

With indirect language, we try and read people's intentions without depending on their physical movement. An example of indirect language is when one person says to another, "would you like the window open to cool off?" When we hear people say this, we either determine this was said because the speaker noticed the listener was very hot (because of an action such as fan-

ning herself), or because the speaker was getting hot and wanted to allude to her own discomfort without directly stating it.

Strangely, in our culture, we have a "hidden rule" that we should not speak too directly about our wants, needs or discomforts, so we state them indirectly. Interestingly, it appears women use this language form even more than do men. This is likely because women are not supposed to be seen as "pushy" or "direct" in stating their needs. Direct language is like literal language; it means exactly what it sounds like it should mean.

This is interesting on a couple of levels, one being that our students may not easily intuit what is being said to them or asked of them. Second, the majority of teachers are women. Female educators need to be aware of their own indirect use of language when working with students or they may accidentally add to their confusion!

It should also be pointed out that one of the few times we use direct language is when we are angry. In those instances we often tell people exactly what we think or what we want.

Interpreting indirect language can be confusing. Help get your students to focus by teaching them to think about the following four clues:

1. What the person might be thinking

2. Spoken language

3. Body language

4. The environment/situation where the communication happens

Indirect language requires the listener to be a "social spy" or detective, figuring out the speaker's intentions. It is important to discuss with your students that all communication has a purpose and that all speakers have intentions. When we talk to people we need to figure out what their intentions might be. In doing so, we can then adapt our response as we see fit.

Figuring out people's intentions is a more sophisticated way of "reading people's plans." It usually involves nuances of language as well as nonverbal communication.

How to use this lesson in the classroom:

1. Discuss with students that the only way to figure out what is being said is to take into consideration the Four Clues: 1) what the person might be thinking; 2) their spoken language; 3) their body language; and 4) the environment in which they said it. For example, if someone says to a student, "do you want some water?" it could mean that the person asking is truly worried that the student is thirsty or it could mean that the speaker is thirsty and is trying to explain why he or she is now walking away from the student in the direction of the water fountain. To decipher this meaning students have to consider:

    A. What is the setting or situation?

    B. What are people thinking in this setting?

    C. What spoken language did they use?

    D. How did their body language/facial expression add to the overall meaning?

2. Create four columns on a white board to explore how we interpret word or phrase meaning. Incorporate words from Lesson 23 into the table below. Decipher the cues that lead to the meaning of the word in each context.

What Were People Thinking?	Words Said	Body language that helps to explain	Setting that Gives Information about What is Happening
People are thinking about a dance they are organizing.	We are having a ball.	Serious facial expressions, calm body, calm tone of voice.	Sitting in a meeting room with other people while trying to draft details for the dance.
People are thinking that it is fun to be together.	We are having a ball.	Happy faces, excited bodies, high or louder tone of voice.	Doing a fun activity together.
People are thinking that they are frustrated or bored.	We are having a ball. (Sarcasm)	Unhappy faces, tired or bored looking bodies, soft or bored tone of voice.	Doing a work project or a chore that people don't really like to have to do.

3. In order to interpret indirect meaning we have to use our "flexible brains." A flexible brain means the student can consider that there is more than one choice to make. The smart choice is the one that makes logical sense or the one that keeps the majority of the people calm and satisfied. At our clinic we have miniature rubber brains with "flexible thinking is social thinking" imprinted on them. We have these available on our website, www.social-thinking.com. Every time a student does a good job interpreting the literal and figurative meanings in the appropriate context, verbally reinforce that "you are doing a good job using your flexible brain!"

   A. To help introduce the concept of the "flexible brain" more concretely, you can show your clients a miniature rubber "flexible brain" and then compare that to what a "rock brain" would feel like. DO NOT bring rocks into your group (since this could be danger-ous), but do pretend that the table is a rock and knock on it to show it is firm and inflexible.

   B. Compare how a rock brain would have just one way to give meaning to something, while a flexible brain thinks about many different meanings.

4. What examples can the students think of? Look for examples that happen right in your class-room, therapy room, in the literature students are reading in class, or on TV sitcoms. (It is interesting to note how this type of language play – using indirect language – is common in sitcom humor.) Increase your own attention on how teachers use A LOT of confusing phrases that "neurotypical" students figure out quickly. We have to pay attention to the language used in our own rooms, not only to help clarify what we are trying to convey to our stu-dents, but also to capture further examples to be used in activities that promote students' awareness of these concepts. The handout on the following page can get the group started. This handout was created for high school aged kids.

 To help our students better understand the concept we are teaching, you should keep an active eye on the student's learning environment and create a list of examples of indirect lan-guage that have been used in the classroom or on the playground.

5. Using the whiteboard, brainstorm with the students a list of things that have been said at school and are indirect in meaning.

   A. Anyone cold in here?

   B. What time is lunch?

   C. Do you know how to do the math?

   D. It would be nice if you sat down.

   E. Why doesn't everyone line up at the door?

   F. What are you looking at? (Either curious about what you are looking at, or the person is asking you why you keep staring at him.)

   G. Did you want to go to the movie? (Perhaps you had discussed it earlier, or perhaps this person is suggesting you go to a movie with him or her.)

   H. Boy, my mom is going to be mad. Did you think the test was hard? (The speaker clearly thought the test was hard and he is worried about how his parents would feel if he got a low grade.)

   I. I am so hungry and I forgot my lunch. (The speaker is asking you to either share your food, loan him money, or suggest ideas on how he can get some food.)

   ⟿ *Plan to do this type of lesson many, many times across a variety of days, months and years.*

Lesson 26: Indirect Language —
What is the Motive Behind the Words?

Critical Vocabulary

Motive

Intention

All people have a "motive" or "intention" (conscious or unconscious) when they talk, and often when they move their bodies. A motive is simply a plan someone has that is not directly stated.

Social thinking includes being constantly aware of people's motives/intentions and interpreting what they mean by what they say. People often do not tell others exactly what they are thinking. Rather, they imply it by asking questions or stating information indirectly. Your job is to figure out what they really mean.

Often people's motives/intentions are fine...but sometimes people will try and bait you into doing something you may not want to do. You have to be aware that people can attempt to use you to achieve their own wants and needs. This is not necessarily bad, as long as their intention is not evil. For example, if someone finds out you are going to a movie they are planning on seeing, they may say, "do you have room in your car?" This helps them out but also allows for a social outing.

How to use this lesson in the classroom:

1. Discuss the motives the person speaking in the following situations and how you should respond.

   A. You are in a food line with a person you know and they ask, "How much money do you have?"

   B. You are playing on the computer and your parent asks "How long will your home-work take to do?"

C. A person you don't know calls on the phone and says they are from your bank and they need your social security number.

D. A friend asks, "Do you have a car with you today?"

E. A teacher asks you to stop burping.

F. It is evening at your home. Just through this setting, what do people need from everyone else in the house? How are people feeling? Why?

G. After you have finished your class project, the teacher asks, "Do you have something else you can work on?"

H. You are at a job and the boss sees you surfing the internet. She asks you how your work load is.

I. You are at a mall and a girl says she really likes a shirt but she doesn't have any money.

J. You have finished your assignment for a class and the teacher asks you to "get to work."

K. A teacher says, "I have a headache."

L. Your parents tell you to come out of your room.

M. You are at your job and you need to speak to someone who is in a room talking to other people. Another person comes along and sees you standing outside the door. He says, "you can go in there."

N. On a weekend day your mom says, "I have so much to do tonight I don't know how I will get it all done."

O. A counselor says, "How do you think people feel about your behavior?"

P. Your parents or friends say, "What did you do to yourself?"

Q. What are some examples your students can think of?

 What other lessons can you think of to help our students explore how we decipher the meaning of language?

How this lesson concept interfaces with reading comprehension

A critical aspect of reading comprehension is determining the character's motives. Helping students evaluate the setting of a story defines the parameters in which the characters express themselves as well as the overall mood. All of these factors, in addition to dialogue and accounting for character's inner thoughts, help the reader identify with the character's personality, motive, ensuing problems, etc. The student can use the Four Clues to explore the character(s) to better grasp the overall meaning of the story. Work with your students to evaluate reading based on what the character might be thinking, the written dialogue, and cues about body language, facial expressions and mood/emotions. All of these factors should be interpreted within the context of the setting. Since many of our clients struggle to interpret so many clues simultaneously, they get easily overwhelmed by reading comprehension, even if they read the text fluently. For more information on reading comprehension, you might enjoy:

I Read It But I Don't Get It by Cris Tovani.

Lesson 27: Predicting What People will Say Next

Critical Vocabulary

Prediction

When communicating with others, we try to stay actively involved in the process by not only speaking and listening, but also by trying to predict how people are going to react and/or respond to what has been said.

We often predict what people might say based on what we know of the people or characters, what people may be thinking, their emotions, the situation (environment or context) and what we have learned from past experiences.

We want students to become more efficient at predicting communicative and emotional responses by reading cues from people and their environment.

How does this assist with reading comprehension?

A strategy regularly used by the active reader is to make smart guesses about what the character may do next. However, this strategy is not just reserved for reading literature. We also use it when reading about history or even when reading the morning newspaper.

By helping our students make predictions based on the total communication being used in specific contexts, we help them become more actively involved in the reading and communicative process.

How to use this lesson in the classroom:

1. Use sequence picture cards or wordless picture books to teach this lesson. An example of a wordless picture book for an older student is *The Further Adventures of the Little Mouse Trapped in the Book*. For younger students, try *The Snowman, Carl Goes Shopping, Carl's Afternoon in the Park* and *Carl's Christmas* (see bibliography for details).

    A. Encourage students to anticipate what might happen on the next page. We want them to practice making "smart guesses" even if their guess is wrong. By making the guess they are staying actively involved in the process.

2. Use sequenced picture cards. Some examples of these include sequenced pictures by "Color Cards" which are manufactured in the U.K. There are many different boxed sets of Color Cards, but the ones I regularly use are "Social Situations" and "Daily Activities."

   A. Have students put the sequence picture cards in order to tell a specific story.

   B. Have them tell the story aloud.

   C. Next, have them go through each picture and describe what the people in the pictured scenario might be thinking and what they might be saying to each other based on the situation.

   D. Assist the students, as needed, by pointing out important nonverbal social cues or cues from the environment that help to clarify the situation. For example, in one picture, I often point out that a mom is looking, with a worried or sad look on her face, at her daughter. My students often tell me it looks like the mom is crying, but then when you look at the fact that the mom is looking towards her daughter who is sad and the mom's arms are reaching out to her daughter, you can then see that her face represents worry about how her daughter feels and that the mom is just trying to make her daughter feel better. This is a very different interpretation than "the mom is crying." These are the subtle cues our students often miss.

3. Teach this in real time: Use teachable moments to work with students to predict what someone else might be thinking, feeling, and what they might say next. This is not only important for the very anxious, non-initiating child, but also for the child who does not appear to be sensitive to other's feelings or needs in the classroom or on the playground.

4. What other lessons can you think of to help our students explore how they can sometimes predict what people might say next?

Video Moments Self-Monitoring Checklist - Section 5

Figuring Out What People Mean by What They Say

Student's Name _____ **Date** _____

We are learning to watch people's social behavior and figure out how these behaviors are making other people feel.

Use your observational skills to see how a person in your group is doing during this video-moment on the new skills you and they have been learning.

The person you are going to check on today is _____

Behavior to monitor or watch:	Put a check here if the student is making others feel like he is doing a good job.	Put a check here if the student is not doing a good job.
Flexible brains		
Literal language		
Figurative language		
Idioms		
Figuring out people's plans based on what they say		
Indirect language: figuring out what people mean based on what is going on in the room		

Based on what you checked, do you think this person would be a good person to work with on a project?

Circle: YES or NO

If not, what is one behavior the student could try and think about more to help people want to work with him?

Review for Teachers & Parents
🔊 Section 5

Figuring Out What People Mean by What They Say

Teaching social communication skills and behaviors is quite complicated. We can introduce these lessons in the therapy room, resource room, special needs classroom, and even the regular classroom, but to have the student really learn to grasp how these skills impact him all day, every day, we need educational professionals and paraprofessionals, along with family members, to become acquainted with how to break down the information, teach and reinforce these skills on a regular basis as the need comes up in the environment.

We have developed a set of lessons for the student to become more efficient at social thinking and understanding the related social skills. We need all persons who work or live with the student to also become familiar with the social thinking concepts and to use them during "teachable moments."

Please review the vocabulary terms and concepts on the other side of this sheet and use them with the student as they apply.

If you have any questions on how to use these terms please contact your child's teacher:
_____

at (phone number) _____.

Thanks for helping _____ learn to use these skills
throughout his/her day, at home and school!

Remember the concepts we have introduced in previous lessons:

Section 1: Doing what is "expected" in the group; doing what is "unexpected" in a group; "You can change my feelings"; observing others through imitation; big problem - little problem; three parts of play: set up, play and clean up.

Section 2: Whole body listening; think and thinking with our brains; thinking with your eyes; thinking about what other people think.

Section 3: Your body is in the group; your body is out of the group! Your brain is in the group; your brain is out of the group!; Just ME/ Thinking about You; good thoughts/weird thoughts; "I've got a secret"; video moment to watch what other people are doing.

Section 4: Figuring out other people's plans; smart guess/wacky guess; identifying one's own feelings; Social Behavior Mapping.

VOCABULARY & CONCEPTS

Figuring Out What People Mean by What They Say

We are currently exploring the following terms. Remember to use them with the student now and over time to help them generalize the concepts beyond the room where the lesson was first taught.

Critical Vocabulary		Definitions
Body language and spoken language		Exploring how we communicate using these two systems. For younger students we call it "spoken language" rather than verbal language.
Literal language and figurative language		We describe "literal" language as being like concrete, never changing. We describe "figurative" language as being something that your brain has to figure out.
Indirect language		Exploring how we may state what we want by alluding to it rather than directly stating it. For example, a person who says "do you understand the math?" may actually be asking for help.
Figure out meanings using four clues		We try and figure out the hidden meaning in what people say by considering: what they were thinking; the words said; body language/facial expression; and the environment/context in which it was said. These four clues help define the meaning or relevance of the statement.
Figuring out people's intentions		All communication has a purpose. When we are talking to people we often try and figure out what their intentions are when they are talking to us. Once we figure out their intentions, we can then adapt our response accordingly
Flexible brains		We talk about using our "flexible brains" when we recognize that a student has some choices to make or has different ways in which he can interpret the situation. We have a saying that "flexible thinking is social thinking."

Goal Suggestions - Section 5
Figuring Out What People Mean by What They Say

 Based on curriculum activities in Section 5 and the California Content Standards

Goal #	Goal Suggestions

5.1   The student will define how spoken language and body language help to convey a larger meaning and then use this knowledge to interpret meaning of spoken phrases ____% of intervention session and then using these concepts beyond the therapy room ____% of the time.

5-1a   When asked to define how spoken language and body language help to convey a larger communicative meaning, _____ will give at least _____ (# of) examples explored in the social thinking sessions, with _____% accuracy.

5-1b   Utilizing the concepts of understanding verbal and nonverbal language, _____ will accurately interpret meaning of spoken phrases within a brief social exchange _____% of the intervention session.

Take this skill beyond the intervention setting: There the student is expected to utilize the concepts of understanding verbal and nonverbal language, _____ will accurately interpret the meaning of spoken phrases within a selected classroom, during a ____ minute interaction ___% of the time.

5-2   The student will define and give examples of the difference between literal language and figurative language, then make "smart guesses" to determine language meaning in context, _____% of intervention session and then using these concepts beyond the therapy room ____% of the time.

5-2a   When given (# ___) words/phrases, _____ will state the difference between literal language and figurative language in each with _____% accuracy.

5-2b   Using the selected list of words/phrases _____ will make "smart guesses" to determine language meaning in each context; with _____% accuracy within the intervention session.

Take this skill beyond the intervention setting: There the student is expected to demonstrate an understanding of figurative language contained in an academic context with ____% accuracy.

Goal #	Goal Suggestions
5.3	The student will define the Four Clues we use to interpret language meaning and then make smart guesses to determine language meaning in context, ____% of intervention session and then using these concepts beyond the therapy room ____% of the time.
5-3a	When asked, _____ will define the Four Clues used to interpret language meaning with ____% accuracy.
5-3b	While in the social thinking session, _____ will make smart guesses to determine language meaning in context with ____% accuracy.
	Take this skill beyond the intervention setting: There the student is expected to make "smart guesses" when interpreting language meaning in a selected reading context with ____% accuracy.
5-4	The student will define and give examples of indirect language and how they interpret indirect language by determining people's motives; they will then interpret indirect language meaning in context, ____% of intervention session and then using these concepts beyond the intervention room ____% of the time.
5-4a	When asked, _____ will define and give at least ____# examples of indirect language and how they interpret indirect language by determining people's motives with ____% accuracy.
5-4b	When provided with a short passage to read, _____ will interpret the indirect language meaning in context with ____% accuracy within the intervention session.
	Take this skill beyond the intervention setting: There the student is expected to demonstrate his understanding of indirect language meaning within the context of a selected academic assignment with ____% accuracy.
5-5	The student will try to predict what people will say next based on their behavior (emotions, body language, previous spoken language) in a specific context, ____% of the time in the intervention session. *Take this skill beyond the intervention setting: There the student will try to predict what people will say next, based upon their behavior (emotions, body language, previous spoken language) in a specific context with ____% accuracy.*
5-6	When reviewing videotaped footage of the social group thinking group in which the student participates, the student will be able to identify the targeted behaviors first in other students and then in himself/herself, focusing on identifying when people need to interpret language meaning, ____% of the time during the intervention session.

California Content Standards - Section 5
Figuring Out What People Mean by What They Say

Grade	Area of the curriculum	Essential Intervention California State Standard
K	Reading	Predictions with pictures and context
K	Reading	Retell familiar stories
4	Reading	Distinguish and interpret words with multiple meanings
4	Reading	Define figurative language and identify its use in literary works
6	Reading	Identify and interpret figurative language and words with multiple meanings
6	Reading	Understand and explain the shades of meanings in words
7	Reading	Identify idioms/analogies, metaphors in prose/poetry *Also: 8 (to infer literal figurative meaning), 9-10*

Briggs, R. (1978). *The Snowman.* Random House, Inc.: New York, NY.

Day, A. (1990s). Book series: *Carl Goes Shopping, Carl's Afternoon in the Park; Carl's Christmas.* Farrar Straus Giroux: New York, NY.

Feldman, David (1989). *Who Put the Butter in Butterfly…and Other Fearless Investigations Into our Illogical Language.* Harper & Row Publishers: New York, NY.

Felix, M. (1983). *The Further Adventures of the Little Mouse Trapped in the Book.* Green Tiger Press: La Jolla, CA.

Idioms Fun Deck, Super Duper publications. Greenville, SC. www.superduperinc.com

Parish, P. or Parish, H. (1990s). Book series: *Amelia Bedelia 4 Mayor; Amelia Bedelia and the Baby; Amelia Bedelia Goes Camping; Amelia Bedelia Helps Out; Amelia Bedelia's Family Album; Good Work, Amelia Bedelia; Merry Christmas, Amelia Bedelia; Teach Us, Amelia Bedelia; Bravo, Amelia Bedelia; Good Driving, Amelia Bedelia.* Harper Trophy: New York, NY.

Sheindlin, Judge Judy. (2001). *You Can't Judge a Book By Its Cover: Cool Rules for School.* Cliff Street Books. www.harperchildrens.com

Spector, Cecile. (1997). *Saying One Thing, Meaning Another: Activities for Clarifying Ambiguous Language.* Thinking Publications: Eau Claire, WI. www.thinkingpublications.com

Speech Mark (1990s). *Color Cards - Different boxes: Daily Activities; Emotions; Daily Living Cards.* www.speechmark.net

Taboo: The game of unspeakable fun. Milton Bradley.

Toomey, Marilyn (2002). *The Language of Perspective Taking.* Circuit Publications: Marblehead, MA.

Tovani, C. (2000). *I Read It, But I Don't Get It: Comprehension Strategies for Adolescent Readers.* Stenhouse Publishers: Portland, ME.

Section 6

Adjusting our Participation and Language Based on What Other People are Thinking, Imagining or Wondering

In this section, we will explore the abstract notion that others have independent thoughts from ours and how we might connect to their ideas, feelings and intentions through our own imagination and wonder. We will encourage students with social thinking deficits to explore other people's thoughts and actions through verbal and nonverbal activities. Through these experiences and gained knowledge, they will attempt to modify their participation in the social interactions based on what they think others in the group might be thinking or wondering.

Our active imaginations and sense of wonder about others are essential elements of social communication and conversational language. These lessons help individuals explore how conversational language springs forth from this.

 The reader may want to review ideas related to theory of mind or perspective taking to better understand the genesis of these concepts. These ideas are discussed in my book **Thinking About YOU Thinking About ME,** *as well as in some other resources included in the bibliography.*

 ### Tools & Materials

- Video camera
- *Comic Strip Conversations* (Gray, C. ,1994)

 ### Critical Vocabulary & Concepts

- Thinking about what others are thinking
- Synchronizing our movements - moving in relationship to another person's actions
- Imagination
- Wonder
- World Wonder
- Social Wonder
- Wonder Bubble

Lesson 28: Observing Student's Own Play and Activities

Critical Vocabulary:

Thinking About What Others Are Thinking

The purpose of this section is to encourage students to observe each other while interacting or playing within a group. You can develop any game that requires students to observe others while participating in the activity themselves, without talking. Initially the games have to be fairly simple in nature. The students are encouraged *not* to talk, because once our students rely on talking to interact, they often have a much harder time observing critical details in others. Non-verbal activities force students to watch and respond to others through non-verbal communication, which is typically a weak mode for students with social cognitive deficits.

How to use this lesson in the classroom:

1. As the students come into the room, whisper to them they will not be using their voices today. You model this by pretending to pull your voice out of your mouth as if you are removing a piece of chewing gum and putting it into a cup. Continue to pass the cup around asking students to put their voices into the empty cup. Encourage them to "put their voice" in the cup at the very start of the lesson.

   Note: If needed, have a visual cue card, e.g. a picture of a closed mouth with a finger lifted to the lips indicating "shh" or a note stating "No Voices Now."

2. Now the students are expected to be quiet. Explain that you are the only one allowed to turn your voice on and off during the activity. Demonstrate this by pretending to turn on an on/off switch on your throat. Explain you will only use your voice to help explain the day's activities or to provide some special help; otherwise you will not use your voice to engage in the activities.

3. Have a list of games/activities written on the board in your room. Explain to the students that they will be doing different actions as part of each game, and all activities will be done within a group. The list can include games/activities such as:

   A. Play follow-the-leader

   B. Get a drink of water at the water fountain

   C. Build a block tower at the table

   ♫

4. Explain when the game begins you will also turn off your voice. Remind them you have the option of turning it back on briefly just to explain something.

   ♫

5. Be sure to check the students' understanding of nonverbal gestures and body language gestures such as:

   • the gesture representing "OK"

   • thumbs up for "good job"

   • shoulder shrug for "I don't know"

- a guiding touch on the child's back/shoulder to guide him to the correct place in the group

- using two fingers, the index and middle fingers held up to create a "V" to direct the student's eyes to where he is supposed to be looking, etc.)

6. Once the guidelines are established, you will then turn off your voice and continue to prompt students nonverbally.

Activity 28a

Sample Nonverbal Game 1
Follow the Leader

A. Position the students in a line.

Use body language/gestures to communicate nonverbally where they are to stand.

B. Model a behavior the children are to imitate as part of playing "follow the leader."

Keep an eye on the students and redirect them to model the behavior (nonverbally, through body language/gestures).

NOTE: Be careful initially NOT to choose complex body motions for their imitation. Many of our students have real difficulties with motor planning. Do activities such as tapping your head; waving hello; bending at your knees; wiggling your fingers, etc.

C. After you have modeled how to lead so they could "follow the leader," select a student to lead the next game.

Nonverbally direct this student to the front of the line, and without using words, communicate it is his turn to select a body movement for the others to imitate. You can prompt the student to make a choice by making an exaggerated shoulder shrug (indicating "What are you going to do?" or "Now what?") to suggest he needs to make a choice.

D. Monitor the group and prompt the other students to pay attention and imitate the activities of the "leader."

Give a "thumbs up" or other positive signal as praise for students who are doing this activity well. Try to budget your time to allow each student to have a turn being leader.

E. Videotape this activity to show the students towards the end of the therapy session or on a different day.

When you review the videotape, encourage the students to observe who was doing a good job thinking about what other people were planning, doing, and thinking.

Activity 28b

Sample Nonverbal Game 2
Getting a Drink from the Water Fountain

A. Have the group line up quietly at your door.

You choose who will go first, second, last, etc. Remind the students to use their flexible brains when it comes to lining up.

NOTE: Avoid having students push to get to the front of the line. Make your choice as to who is the line leader in advance, based on who has done the best job thinking about other people in the earlier activity. However, over time, you will want to give all the students a chance to be a line leader, even when they may not be the best at social thinking.

B. Have the students walk in a line, quietly and with self control, to the water fountain.

This may be difficult for some in the group; they may push each other trying to be the first one to arrive at the fountain. If so, practice walking as a group back and forth in your therapy room or the hall, prior to heading to the water fountain. You may need to turn your voice on to remind them we can "think with our eyes" even when we are walking. When walking together, send the message that those who "win" are the ones who are still part of the group. The winner is NOT the first person to the water fountain.

You can also prompt them to think about how they are perceived by asking, "Whose body is in the group, whose body is out of the group?" Once the students appear to be aware they have to be social thinkers even when walking or just standing within a group, it is a good time to take them to the destination.

NOTE: Students may need to repeat this part of the lesson frequently to learn to walk as a group; for example, walking down the hallway to the office or library. The trick will be getting students to regulate their speed and awareness of others so the group stays together while the students walk. In order to do this, they have to actively think about those around them. While they walk, say aloud, "social thinking, in this case, is simply walking together as a group!"

C. Once you get to the water fountain, videotape the students waiting in line and taking their turn.

Show the video at the end of this session or at the start of the next session. Review the video to see if they are doing a good job "reading people's plans" and "thinking about what people are thinking."

Activity 28b

continued

Sample Non-Verbal Game 2
Getting a Drink from the Water Fountain

D. Actively praise those who are doing a good job being a social thinker.

You can give "rubber chicken kisses" to those who do well, versus "rubber chicken taps" to those who need to keep thinking. Use humor when analyzing both mistakes and progress. Most students will more readily accept constructive criticism when they can laugh a bit about their errors.

E. As you review the videotape, suggest strategies to help them know what to do when they are in that situation.

For example, if a student gets to the water fountain and takes a really long drink or pauses to take multiple drinks while everyone else is waiting for one drink, was he really thinking about the people behind him, who are also thirsty and waiting?

Ask the students how that person could change what he was doing so that others in the line believed he was thinking about each of them, but at the same time got his thirst quenched.

Possible strategies include:

• Taking a drink and then go to the end of the line.

• Telling those waiting, "I am really thirsty but I will hurry as fast as I can."

• Letting the next person go after two or three sips.

Explain that by using one of these strategies, others are alerted to the student taking a longer drink while showing he is aware of those around him.

AVOID telling a student he did something wrong or was not a good member of the group. Your teaching is effective when you provide them new ways to think about what they should do.

F. Once the students feel they have some new strategies, do this type of activity many times across a year.

Videotape intermittently throughout the year. Review the videotape each time with the group and hopefully they will be able to see when they are using more strategies and can note their progress!

Activity 28c

Sample Nonverbal Game 3
Building a Block Tower

1. Before doing this activity, look at the block shapes in your box of blocks. If there are many odd shaped blocks which are not easy to build upon (e.g. triangles), remove most of these prior to the task. Some students gravitate towards odd shaped blocks which may stunt the tower's ultimate growth.

2. You must "turn on" your voice to provide the initial instructions.

3. Let the students know they are going to build one block tower or block building, as a group. Explain all of them are going to help direct each other to build the tower, but they are going to do this without using words.

4. Emphasize an important rule: a student CANNOT move any block once it is placed on the tower (unless it is about to fall and it is just being re-adjusted).

5. Start by taking five blocks and nonverbally and dramatically counting them to get the student's attention. You then encourage the students to take their own five blocks.

6. Congratulate (nonverbally) all the students who took five blocks. Then instruct or re-adjust (also nonverbally) the students who took more or less.

7. Encourage them to build a tower by taking turns, the same way it is described above in Section 2. However, this time the students are going to instruct each other on where each should place his/her block. The following steps further define this task.

8. Once a student (Student A) looks at another student (Student B) to indicate it is their turn, Student A also points, with his/her index finger, to a specific block that is Student B's. This gesture will indicate which block Student B is to use.

9. Student A is to now point from Student B's block to the block tower, being built in the middle of the table, to instruct Student B exactly where he should place the block on the tower. Student A can also instruct, through gestures, which way the block should align with the tower (lie flat, or stand up tall, etc.). Many of our students do not easily read

continued...

Activity 28c (continued)

Sample Nonverbal Game 3
Building a Block Tower

these smaller more subtle gestures and you may have to turn your voice back on to explain the meaning of specific hand gestures. While challenging, students seem to enjoy this lesson as they get to control the movements of others. The more carefully they communicate non-verbally, the more control they have in the precarious outcome of how the tower is built.

10. At this point, Student B, who is placing the block on the tower, has no real say in where his block goes, so he has to use his flexible brain to allow another student to direct the block placement.

11. However, once Student B places his block, it then becomes Student B's turn to take control. This student now gets to select whose turn it will be by directing eye contact at the other student, and then pointing or gesturing which block is to be used, where it will be placed, and how it should sit on the tower.

12. Encourage the students to give non-verbal compliments to each other for

following their directions. This is as simple as having the student who directed the behavior hold up his fingers to gesture "ok" or "good job" when the task is successfully completed. Remember, you may need to check the knowledge of your group to make sure all know a range of nonverbal gestures which indicate a positive compliment.

13. Continue to have students select who they will give a turn to until all the blocks are gone. You should monitor that the students are allowing all students to participate equally.

14. Work closely with students who are struggling to keep their attention on the group. Create success by helping them be attentive during their turn and provide close support to help them figure out what other people are thinking. Different students will have different levels in which they can successfully participate. Make this task successful for everyone who is trying hard but just can't do as well due to their own attention or cognitive limitations.

continued...

15. The exception to this positive support is with a belligerent student. If he is trying to mess up the tower on purpose, give him a warning and then remove him from the group.

16. The game is completed when each student's blocks have been used, or when the tower tumbles over. Continue to have the students' voices turned off while you all celebrate the creative tower that the students built.

17. Turn your voice on and ask the students to evaluate nonverbally how the group did together on this task. For example, ask them questions such as:

   • How many people followed all the rules? (e.g. have them hold up fingers to show how many participated well.)

   • How did you feel when the students followed the rules? (e.g. have them respond with facial expressions.)

   • How did you feel when someone didn't want to follow the rules or wasn't paying attention?

18. You can remark on how "cool" it was that the students figured out so much about each other even without using any words.

19. One by one, direct the students to turn on their voices. Explore how they felt when they were not allowed to talk. Encourage them to describe how they understood what other people were thinking or feeling. Verbally praise students for trying to explain their emotional reactions and responses.

20. What other games can you create to add to the above sample?

Problem solving some of the difficulties or glitches that can arise during the block building task

Problems with paying attention to each other's eyes:

You must actively help students who do not easily pay attention with their eyes. This is particularly important when they are to participate during the selection of who gets the next turn. You may have to physically, or even verbally, cue the student who is at risk for not being selected, due to their inattention.

However, if a student is fairly attentive, but is not paying attention at that moment and missed being selected (in other words, Student A tried to look at Student B to get his attention, yet Student B was not thinking with his eyes about Student A, so Student A moved on to someone else), allow Student B to have his chance missed or skipped.

When this happens, you should immediately comment, "Wow, (student's name), you just missed your turn because you were not thinking about who (name of student in charge) was going to pick! You need to think with your eyes in order to make sure you get your turn!"

Problems with mental flexibility: The student gets mad that the tower is not being built the way HE wanted it built!

If a student (e.g. Student B) does not want to put his block where Student A directs him because Student B thinks he has a better idea, indicate (nonverbally if possible) that Student B either has to skip his turn, or do as he was directed.

Remember, with our students we are working on observing other people's intentions (following other people's plans), following through and working as part of a group. This often means we do not always get to make the choices we would like!

If you see the lesson breaking down for some students, what do you do next?

You should observe the students' abilities to follow nonverbal instructions, recognize when it is their turn, and be able use their index finger to point and direct others. Create further opportunities to develop these skills by providing similar lessons for continued practice. Do NOT assume that all students understand what an index finger point means, how to follow a point or how to create a point for others to read (ability to encode and decode a pointing gesture). A number of our students have developed index finger points that look more like "flashes." They do not realize that other people need time to focus on where someone is pointing. We need to practice effective pointing skills. You may be surprised to find that some of your very bright and verbal students cannot read or encode index finger points well.

I have had to do many explicit lessons with students of all ages, including college educated adults, on the importance of an index finger point. Surprisingly, a number of my clients have not learned to read a person's pointing gestures. If this is the case, create lessons where you discuss and practice pointing skills.

Tip: quick instructions on reading people's index finger points

1. Allow the students to turn their voices back on to discuss the meaning of "pointing."

2. Have the student look at the pointer's eye gaze direction and related finger point direction. Follow both their gaze and their extended arm and index finger like you are following an arrow.

3. The student should check back to make sure he is accurately reading the direction of the other person's point.

4. The "reader" should make a comment to the person who was pointing to confirm that he understands the pointer's reference. The reader can also let the pointer know that he is not sure what is being pointed to. The pointer should then make it more explicit by describing what he is thinking about while still pointing.

What to do if a child refuses to engage in the nonverbal task:

If a student refuses to cooperate in the task, pull out a chair and nonverbally direct the child to sit down and stay in the chair. Continue working with the rest of the students. You can use some humor by exaggerating your body language, conveying to the child that he is to sit in the chair until they are ready to join the activity of the group.

Avoid being strongly punitive or harsh in your redirection; try to keep it somewhat lighthearted. Help the student understand that a different choice, to participate, puts him right back into being an effective and active member of the group. If the student tries to actively seek negative attention while he is sitting out, ignore him unless there is a safety issue.

Return to the student after a short time and ask (nonverbally) if he is ready to participate. If he refuses, direct him to stay in the chair and go back to the group. When you get to the next activity, he will most likely want to re-enter the group. Verbally reinforce the idea: in order to play or work within a group, we have to think about what everyone is doing in the group. Throughout your activity, nonverbally praise students for working cooperatively by thinking with their eyes and adjusting their bodies around other people's plans.

An important message we are consistently sending the students is they have to work to be part of a group and that not all this work or play makes us happy. However, it does keep us actively part of the group. Students who are not willing to work cooperatively then have to sit outside of the group! This avoids falsely reinforcing a child's defiance by allowing him to stay in the group and get attention for not cooperating or actively participating.

Redirect the child, yet avoid talking to him, even if he is talking to you. If you cannot ignore, you will need to stop the activity. However, before the other children turn their voices back on, have them indicate how many people in the group followed the rules by holding up their fingers to show their count. When they point out how many children did not follow the rules, congratulate them for being such good social thinkers that they could figure this out with their eyes. Hopefully, this will not be the case and the activity can progress.

Lesson 29: Building a SHARED Imagination Through Shared Structured Imaginary Sequences

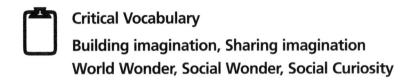

Critical Vocabulary

Building imagination, Sharing imagination
World Wonder, Social Wonder, Social Curiosity

Many students with social cognitive deficits have a good imagination for things they find interesting. However, the majority of our students are weak at sharing other people's imagination in a flexible manner. The impact of failing to share in imagination with others is HUGE.

When we engage in creative and interactive play, we often imagine what others may be thinking. This process allows us to share an idea of the play, in our heads, so we can create and sustain play with contributions and ideas from all the play partners. For example, when children play "house" they share an image/concept of a house, a social order and imagined tasks/activities they are creating through their play. The richer their imaginations are and their ability to share their imagination with each other both through action and language, the richer their play. While children are given the opportunity to practice sharing ideas and imagination through play, it is these same skills that are crucial for more sophisticated social interactions and conversation as they age. (More on this will be discussed later.)

When communicative partners are not willing or able to share and explore imagination with others, limitations occur. For example, some of our four-year-old students have a very clear, imagined play routine established and will want others to play with them. Because of their social cognitive deficit, however, these students may then insist that the play partners play the game exactly the way they imagined it. They may get very angry or frustrated if their peers want to explore their own imaginative way to play through the activity. Our students are perceived as rigid players who are unfriendly. In reality, they are not able to incorporate others' ideas into their play.

Our shared imagination is not only a tool for use in play and conversation; it also is used to interpret the teacher's discussions and assignments. It is crucial for understanding someone else's perspective or opinion. A student can't just listen to the teacher talk; he must imagine what the teacher is trying to convey, then consider the teacher's intentions, then interpret what the teacher wants from him on a given homework assignment.

It is important to recognize that building imagination is not an easy skill to teach. The following strategies will get you started teaching students how to engage with others through a shared imagination. Plan to repeat these types of activities many times over the course of years with a student while adding your own set of creative tasks to the list.

As you work on these concepts, keep in mind that many of our students have difficulty interpreting the imaginary play plans of others. Because of their deficits in reading other student's intentions they do not anticipate how play will evolve.

In addition, they often lack the ability to develop synchronicity in their play, meaning they often prefer to play on their own in a group rather than watch other people's body movements to anticipate how to move their body in sync with the activity. For example, we had our students engage in pretend play in an imaginary grocery store. Our "shopper" did not pass his food items to the cashier, rather he required adult cues to help him synchronize his movements with the physical needs of "cashier" (who needs groceries put near him to process the order). The cashier didn't think to push the scanned groceries over to the bagger who needed them close by in order to bag them.

In order to synchronize play, partners have to anticipate people's needs and intentions, and then match their actions with the perceived needs of the play partners. Instead, our students got caught imagining how they wanted to play in the grocery store, giving little attention to their fellow players' needs or play roles. Furthermore, the students often tried to dictate others' actions and force a play scenario they had already defined, rather than allow the scenario to emerge from shared ideas.

We use a variety of language concepts to explore how we share our imagination, including a study of "wonder," and for our older students, investigating "social curiosity." We try to move the students from using their own imaginations to a adopting a shared sense of imagination, wonder or social curiosity, which will further support social thinking across play, communication and other social interactions.

Actually, an active imagination, wonder and social curiosity are required components of reading comprehension. However, you are left to imagine on your own how the information in these lessons can be applied to reading!

How to use this lesson in the classroom:

To begin, we will explore imagination within a very structured activity, where each child has a defined role. He is asked to perform this role within an imaginary play scheme. This helps children develop the idea of synchronizing their movements around other people's imaginary actions.

1. Give students a choice of different imaginary activities that require the students to move through a pre-established sequence. If you think your group is not ready to make a group choice then don't initially provide that option!

   An example of some activities that would be appropriate include making a peanut butter and jelly sandwich; writing a letter, putting it in an envelope and taking it to the mailbox; making cookies, etc. What other activities can you think of that require a clear and familiar sequence? Try those as well! One of my groups chose to make guacamole!

2. Using the example of making a peanut butter and jelly sandwich, have four students in the group brainstorm the necessary steps for making the sandwich.

   A. Undo the tie on the bread bag and remove two slices of bread.

   B. Put the two pieces of bread on a cutting board or plate.

   C. Take out the peanut butter and jelly jars.

   D. Unscrew the lids.

   E. Get out a butter knife (not a sharp knife).

F. Dip the knife into the peanut butter, then spread the peanut butter on the bread.

G. Use the knife to scoop out jelly and then spread that on the bread.

H. Put the two slices of bread together.

I. Cut the bread into four pieces.

J. Each child gets a piece of the sandwich; everyone eats it together.

K. Each child can comment on how good the sandwich tastes and how well it was made.

3. Remember, the above steps are all IMAGINED while performed in sequence. Assign your group members specific jobs to help with the construction of the sandwich. To begin, assign each child one of the following roles:

A. Bread Distributor: Takes two slices of bread out of the bag, puts them on a plate and passes the plate to the peanut butter spreader. The bread distributor can also pass out the peanut butter and jelly jars, the plate to make the sandwich on, as well as the knife.

B. Peanut Butter Spreader: The peanut butter spreader receives the plate. He then dips his knife into the peanut butter jar and spreads it on the bread. This student now passes the whole plate to the jelly spreader. If the spreader does not unscrew the top of the jar, you should playfully exclaim that his knife keeps crashing into the top of the lid!

C. Jelly Spreader: The jelly spreader unscrews the jar lid, dips the knife in the jar and then adds the jelly to either piece of bread (or both, if the child prefers). He then passes the plate to the sandwich cutter.

D. Sandwich Cutter: This person puts the two pieces of the bread together and then cuts the sandwich into four pieces. He then passes the plate to each child to take a piece of the sandwich so they can all enjoy it together.

E. All the children become sandwich eaters! Encourage them to comment on how much they are enjoying the sandwich they all made together.

F. Videotape the whole process! If you try this activity a second time, try making the sandwich without dropping or smearing the food (read below). Show the students both sets of videos to let them see the difference between little attention to what they are doing and improved attention.

♬

4. Peanut Butter and Jelly Pitfalls: Think this task sounds simple? Lots can go wrong and you may want to work on these corrections in another session. Use exaggerated expressions, invoking humor, as you encourage the students to work through their challenges in this task:

A. The students seldom put the bread onto the plate since they do not do a great job imagining the bread and the plate together; at times they just drop it on the floor.

B. The spreaders rarely unscrew the lids to their jars.

C. They may spread peanut butter and jelly on the table, their hands, the plate itself, etc.

D. The students may not be thinking with their eyes when they are passing the imagined objects. The peanut butter, jelly, knife, or plate often drop off the table. You should react with "Oh my gosh, you just dropped the sandwich on the floor!"; "Yuck, now we have to clean it up!"; "Oh, we better throw it away. No one wants to eat that." or "We better start again!". Obviously, part of the fun of this exercise is your dramatic expression when they fail to synchronize their movements with each other because they do not watch the pass-off or pay attention to what they are doing.

E. They only put one lump of peanut butter or jelly right in the middle of the bread and do not spread it around. You will also see a lack of coordination in many of our students with motor planning problems. Do not call negative attention to poor coordination if they cannot help it! However, if they are only using one hand (the other one is dropped at their side), encourage them to use two hands so the sandwich doesn't fall on the floor.

 NOTE: The lack of using two hands simultaneously is a frequent problem of students with social cognitive deficits. Occupational therapists help students learn to have fuller awareness of their bodies and to cross midline to help their hands work together. You will notice similar difficulties when you observe our students writing with pens or pencils.

F. The students get upset when asked to eat the sandwich because they don't like peanut butter and jelly or they are allergic to it! (Remember, you are just imagining the sandwich, so you always have the option of changing the type of sandwich you are making, if you know this ahead of time). When a child refuses to eat it, teach him how to politely refuse ("No, thank you"), while he is playing. Or, work with the student to imagine that his allergy has gone away and he can eat it an imaginary sandwich even if he cannot eat it in real life.

G. As you will experience, there are many more challenges in this "simple" lesson. Remember to have fun with the task of sharing an imagination while actively encouraging and rewarding students for participating successfully in this task.

H. I have had groups try and do the imagined sequence in the right way, but then decide they enjoy throwing the food at each other. So look out...an imaginary food fight can get messy! It does, however, provide an opportunity for the group to work together to clean it up.

 NOTE: While this activity seems suited for very young students, it is also fun to do with high school kids. Be sure to keep it fun by using humor. On my birthday, my high school students had to make me an ice cream sundae which we all ended up sharing. But somehow it got out of control, and they had a mess to clean up.

Activity 29a

Sharing an imagination in a less defined pretend play setting.
(For younger students through fifth grade)

You will be developing "group imaginary play" where the students interact within a theme that is less structured than the previous task. Themes can include, but are not limited to, working in a hospital, grocery shopping, teaching school, etc.

1. Tell the students we are going on an imaginary trip to a place in the community, you can give them a choice as to the place. (Note: Allowing our students to constantly deal with group choices helps them work on flexible thinking.) Explain, as we all imagine this group trip, we must continue to pay attention to what other people are planning to do. They will need to pay attention to each person's actions and try and connect their own actions to the others in the group.

2. Determine the play theme and then briefly discuss the different roles students can be assigned in the play. Use the example of "shopping at a grocery store." Different roles for grocery shopping include:

   • Shoppers who are using shopping carts

   • Cashier

   • Bagger

2. Allow students to choose the roles they want in this activity; if multiple people want the same role, then review with them the earlier lesson about the "three stages of play" and also offer that they can go shopping many different times today so each person can experience having a different role. Remind them that this is the very fun part of imaginary play; they can make it work for everyone!

3. Have the students engage in this shared imaginary play verbally and at times, nonverbally. When you have asked them to "turn off their voices," remind them being silent helps improve their ability to observe what other people are doing. At times you may be a verbal "narrator" to help explain what each person is doing (e.g. "I like how Ben is looking at Dan, the shopper, and is ready to have Dan come to his counter!")

4. Prompt the students to create nonverbal social interactions with each other. For example, if a shopper gets stuck shopping, another player (the cashier) may signal for the shopper to come to his counter; or if the play is verbal, allow the cashier to suggest to the shopper that his bag is too full and he should come purchase his goods.

5. Tip: What if...the shopper is having fun letting his imaginary groceries fall on the floor? Facilitate an interaction that will bring the bagger over to direct the shopper to keep the floor area clean. The bagger can also ask for assistance cleaning up the mess. If the shopper contin-

Sharing an imagination in a less defined pretend play setting.
(For younger students through fifth grade)

ues, the cashier or the bagger can choose to close the aisle because the mess was made. Hopefully this won't happen but be prepared to stay flexible to students' imaginations. This would be an opportunity for the group to work on problem solving or negotiating the more troublesome activities of play.

6. When the shopper goes to the cashier, he now has to synchronize his movements to empty his cart so that the cashier can reach the groceries to scan them.

7. The cashier then has to pass the scanned groceries down to the bagger, who puts them in a bag and then transfers the bag back into the grocery cart before passing the cart back to the shopper. The bagger can also ask if the shopper would like the bagger to take the groceries out to the shopper's car.

8. Just like the PBJ sandwich sequence, watch for all the ways students may be forgetting to pay attention to each other. Again you may dramatically discuss the impending problems ("Oh dear, the cashier is dropping the groceries on the floor"; "Oh no, the bagger just dropped the meat on top of the eggs!"). At the same time, be sure to compliment the students on the good, cooperative work you have observed.

9. If you need to temporarily stop play to help the children get better organized, announce "pause." Then explain specifically what you want the child to think about (e.g. "I need my bagger to think with his eyes about what the cashier is doing" or "I see my bagger is looking at the ceiling, so I think she is thinking about the ceiling, rather than us. What should my bagger be thinking about?"). You can re-engage play by announcing "OK" or "end-pause."

10. You can do the same activity again. If you played it with verbal interaction the first time, try it nonverbally the second time or vice-versa. Or elaborate on the verbal language used by encouraging more social interactions (e.g. have the cashier make friendly comments to the shopper, have the shopper see a friend in the store, have the bagger ask the shopper if he wants plastic or paper bags, etc.).

11. Be prepared for a lot of humor as students imagine and share imaginations together.

12. Videotape, if possible, to review how the students participated together in each imagined role and how well they anticipated or imagined what someone else was thinking. Did they watch for other people's plans?

Activity 29b

Sharing an imagination during shared charades.
(For older students; sixth grade and older.)

For older students we do the same type of scenario; however, we encourage more age appropriate activities such as: going to a pizza parlor, playing a simple card game together, going bowling, etc. Have students break into teams of two. One team has to act out (pantomime) group interaction (e.g. working together at a pizza parlor; driving in busy traffic; taking a test in a class) and the other team has to guess what they are doing. These are generally nonverbal activities, but if the audience is having difficulty guessing, the actors can then provide a couple of well placed statements (e.g. if at a pizza parlor, the actor who is throwing the pizza dough can ask "what size, small, medium or large?" Or the actor putting the pizza together can say "do you want pepperoni?"). The teams take turns, either acting or being members of the guessing audience. This task not only encourages a shared imagination, but it also requires both the actors and the audience to make a series of smart guesses based on their ability to predict the shared knowledge of all participants.

If the audience is not able to guess, the actors may need to clarify or adjust their actions to help the other students more accurately determine what actions they are performing. For example, if someone is throwing the pizza dough and the audience cannot figure out what the actor is doing, he needs to consider what other gestures or key phrases may help the audience make a smart guess based on their shared knowledge of the event. While this may seem obvious, it is not uncommon for our students to come up with one way to convey the concept and just repeat the same action over and over given their limited mental flexibility. You can prompt them to perform a different action. This helps students learn how to convey more elaborate messages using their body.

Lesson 30: Moving from Imagination to Wonder –
World Wonder versus Social Wonder

Critical Vocabulary

Imagination

Wonder

Define the difference between imagination and wonder. The definitions used in the curriculum take a bit of liberty with the standard dictionary definitions . Both are listed below. Before engaging the students in this lesson take some time to consider these meanings. Consider the meaning of curiosity and its relationship to asking questions for the purpose of seeking information.

How to use this lesson in the classroom:

1. Define Imagination and Wonder

    A. "IMAGINATION" is being able to try and see, or pretend to do, something that is not right in front of you.

    (Definition: 1a) the act or power of forming mental images of what is not present, b) the act and power to create new ideas by combining previous experiences, 2) the ability to understand the imaginative creations of others. 3) resourcefulness

    Resource: Webster's New World Dictionary and Thesaurus - 2002

    B. "WONDER" requires one to imagine while posing verbal and/or nonverbal questions (curiosity). (In the following tasks we are going to encourage the students to think their questions out loud, to each other.)

    (Definition: 1a) the feeling aroused by something strange, unexpected, etc. to be filled with wonder; marvel, 2a) to have curiosity, sometimes mingled with doubt (he wondered what happened)

    Resource: Webster's New World Dictionary and Thesaurus - 2002

2. Introduce the idea there are two types of wonders: world wonders and social wonders.

    A. World wonders relate to factual information about the world we are curious about (e.g. "How tall is the Empire State Building?", "Why does moss grow on the north side of a tree?").

    B. Social wonders (e.g. "social curiosity") involve our wanting to know how people think or feel (e.g. "What do you like to do?", "Why are you so sad?").

3. Discuss students' world wonders and with whom they might share this information. Explore how they gain access to this information and how it helps them in school and in their life.

4. Explore with the group the concept of social wonder.

    A. Ask the students what they wonder about their parents, their teachers or other students. Discuss why we wonder about people. How does this information help us in school, friendship and at home?

    B. Create a list of events that are social and emotional in nature. Have the students share their social wonder. (This list will be cut up later on in the lesson, so leave room between events.) For example, the list can include:

       • The student goes to the ice cream store but they were out of the flavor he wanted.

       • Your parent is mad at you because you won't get off the computer.

       • You just got an award at school for being very helpful to others.

- It is your birthday and you are in Disneyland but it is really crowded and hot.

- You got an A on a test but you know that most other students did not do as well.

- You don't have anyone to play with or hang out with, but all the other children look like they are having fun.

- You are excited to get presents during the holidays.

- You are bored sitting at Thanksgiving dinner.

 NOTE: Can you think of other items for the list that are more relevant based on your students' experiences? You may want to discuss this with your students in more detail to solicit additional ideas of times when they have felt more positive or negative.

C. Cut up the list so each slip of paper contains one of these items.

D. Put the slips in a bag, so the students cannot see them.

E. Select one student to be the activity leader. Have the leader pick an item out of the bag. It is acceptable for the student to choose his own scenario.

F. The leader describes the situation to the others so all can imagine the social experience.

G. The leader then imagines this scenario is happening currently to him. The other students then wonder how the leader feels and should ask related questions to learn more about that person's experience.

H. You, the teacher, should continue to explore with the students, across this task, how this information helps them think about each other which, in turn, shows that we are interested in the feelings and thoughts of the people around us.

Lesson 31: You Know More Than you Realize...
What Type of Animal can you Imagine?

Critical Idea

Students' knowledge about the world helps them understand other people or stories in books

This activity teaches students that their experiences in the world help them to imagine and wonder what others' experiences are like, even if the student will never experience it themselves.

How to use this lesson in the classroom:

1. Have your students imagine what it would be like to be an animal. You can provide them a list of animal choices or animals doing certain activities. They can choose from your list or they can make up some of these choices themselves. Some ideas include:

   - A cat lounging in the sun

   - A horse romping through a field

   - A dog who wants his owners to walk him

   - A bee looking for pollen

   - A fly stuck in a house, trying to get out through a closed window

   - A chicken laying an egg

   - A bird sitting on a telephone line with a bunch of other birds

   - A turtle in a turtle tank

   - A snail in your garden

   - A squirrel being chased by a dog

2. Ask your students to answer the following questions about their animal assignments:

- How would this animal feel in this situation? Name some emotions.

- How would he sound?

- What would this animal want from other animals or people around him?

3. Encourage students to take turns moving around while acting out their animal.

4. While they are going through this task, encourage them to see how "neat" (fun/exciting/cool) it is for them to imagine and act out an experience they have never had before! Have fun commenting on their creative imaginations!

5. Remind them that their ability to imagine things they have not directly experienced, such as imagining to be these animals, will help them imagine what people are talking about and what they are reading about in their school books. Discuss that when they are reading about things they have not experienced, or when they are listening to people talk about unfamiliar things, they can imagine what that experience is like based on what they know about the world!

Lesson 32: You Know More Than you Realize...
What Type of People can you Imagine?

Critical Idea

This activity teaches students that their experiences in the world help them imagine and wonder what others' experiences are like, even if the student will never experience it personally.

How to use this lesson in the classroom:

1. This time your group will imagine other people's experiences. It is important for these situations to be something they most likely have never experienced. (One common reason for the lack of experience is gender differences.) There is a lot of humor and playfulness generated with these ideas, so have fun!!!

Some ideas include:

- A boy in a girls locker room, or a girl in a boys locker room.

- A boy pretending to buy a dress for himself.

- A driver who needs to stop and fill the car up with gas.

- A quarterback on a professional football team.

- A catcher on a professional baseball team.

- An Olympic ice skater.

- A boy putting make-up on in the mirror.

- A dad or mom trying to get the kids ready for bed.

- A person in a wheelchair.

- A teacher whose students won't follow directions.

- A baby who cannot yet talk but wants food.

- A person moving away from home into an apartment for the first time.

- A cashier at a supermarket.

- A vendor selling hot dogs at a carnival.

2. As you start this task, encourage your students to realize how much they already know about the person in each of these situations even though they have never experienced these situations directly. For example, when asking a boy to imagine being in a girls locker room, have the boy think about: "What do you know about girls?" "How would your sister, or mom behave when they are getting dressed that is different from how a guy would behave?" "What do you see on TV or in the movies that gives you clues as to how girls would behave?"

3. As the teacher, you may have to loosen the group up by acting out what it would be like to be the opposite gender.

4. Ask your students to answer the following questions about being this other type of person:

   • What would he or she feel like in this situation? Name some emotions.

   • What would he or she likely say? What would he or she want from the people around them?

   • What would he or she likely do? (Act it out.)

5. Encourage your students to get up from their chairs and move around while acting out being this person.

6. As in the previous activities, encourage them to see how neat (fun/exciting/cool) it is for them to imagine and act out an experience they have never had before. Have fun commenting and laughing with them about their creative imaginations.

7. Once again, remind students that their ability to imagine and wonder about these people's thoughts and actions will help them in many ways, such as having to write a paper from another person's point of view and when interacting with people. Point out when they are reading about things they have not experienced or when they are listening to people talk about unfamiliar things, they can imagine what that experience is like.

Lesson 33: You Know More Than You Realize...
Taking Our Imagination to Different Places

Critical Vocabulary

World Wonder

Social Wonder

Wonder bubble

This lesson continues to explore imagining about the experiences of others, this time related to different environments or locales.

How to use this lesson in the classroom:

1. The group is going to share an imagination about different places. The students are to imagine going to a certain place or destination. As a group, they can compare their visions to explore similarities and differences. You, the teacher, should encourage all students to learn that each individual's imagination is valid and valuable, reinforcing that different people can have and express different points of view about the world.

   Some ideas include:

   - A baseball stadium

   - Beaches of Hawaii

   - New York subway station

   - Dining on a cruise ship

   - Staying at a hospital overnight

   - Staying at your grandparent's house

- Your house in China

- Going to Disneyworld

- Riding a horse through a meadow

- Your school cafeteria

 NOTE: If the place is too broad...narrow it down; a beach in Hawaii or a particular spot in Disneyland like Space Mountain.

2. When you start this task, encourage the students to think about the place, based on their own experience. Encourage them to make smart guesses.

3. Ask them to consider the following questions:

   a. Who are you with?

   b. What does it look like?

   c. What is your favorite thing to do there?

   d. What are other people enjoying?

   e. Is there something about it that you don't like?

   f. How do you feel when you are there?

   g. What other questions can you think to ask the students based on what they chose?

4. Have them ask these same questions to the others in the group and then compare their answers. When they are trying to figure out what people like or don't like about a similar experience, they are experiencing SOCIAL WONDER!

5. As they compare their answers, encourage them to imagine what the other person's experience is like, using their own thoughts. Encourage them to recognize that even though we don't necessarily agree with other people's imaginations, we can consider them.

6. What other questions can the students ask now that they are imagining and wondering about the other person?

7. When a student is imagining and wondering about another person's experiences we say they are sharing someone's "wonder bubble"! Wonder bubble can be defined as the result of sharing an imagination and world wonder simultaneously.

You can visually demonstrate this to students using comic strip type characters. Show a simple Comic Strip Conversation (Gray, 1994) when students are thinking about their own thoughts. This means they are NOT sharing their imagination and wonder bubble.

Compare this to a comic strip conversation that demonstrates what it looks like when students are mutually engaged with their imaginations and questions around the same topic (sharing a wonder bubble/world wonder/shared imagination).

Example A: demonstrates a comic strip conversation where students are engaged in their own, unshared thought. We can use the previously taught vocabulary of "Just Me" to further explain this concept.

Example B: demonstrates a comic strip conversation when students are engaged in sharing an imagination/world wonder/wonder bubble. We can use the previously learned vocabulary, "thinking of you" to discuss what the students are doing when they share an imagination and wonder.

8. Encourage your students to explore how example B is better than example A when you want to build a friendship or just get along with people at school or at home.

Lesson 34: Building Language-Relatedness Skills

Critical Idea

Using language (comments and questions) to further explore imagination

In this lesson, students will use language to describe something a student has experienced and then others in the group will imagine the experience and ask questions to show their wonder, interest or curiosity towards the speaker.

Our students often have a difficult time sustaining attention when others are talking about their own personal experiences, as they may be different or unfamiliar from the listening student. This set of activities will help to develop students' imaginations during this type of social communication. (For example, Sam is talking to Judy about his trip to Sea World. Judy has never been to Sea World but has gone to the beach. How can Judy use her imagination and sense of wonder to stay "engaged" in Sam's discussion?)

We encourage them to wonder, by asking questions or making comments, to explore what they don't know about someone else or that situation. (For example, Judy may say to Sam, "Did you see lots of sharks at Sea World? I heard there are sharks there just like at some beaches. I went to a beach once.") We establish world wonder by realizing what we might do or experience in that same situation (how can we relate to it?) and then asking questions to find out if their experiences were the same or different from what we imagined or thought. Sounds easy? It is NOT!

How to use this lesson in the classroom:

1. In previous lessons in this section, your students explored using their imagination and wonder from many different angles. Now we want them to use their imagination and wonder around someone else's topic. Start by having each student think of a place he likes to visit, or something he likes to do after school or on a family vacation.

   Use the following questions to help them organize their thinking:

• Where is this place? How do you get there?

• When do you get to do this activity?

• Why do you get to do it?

• Who do you do it with?

• What is it that you like to do? Why do you like this activity?

• How does this place or activity make you feel?

• What are the other people around you doing?

2. Tell each student our job is to climb inside the "wonder bubble" of the person we are talking to and imagine the activity that he enjoys and is describing.

Remind students when they are imagining they have to:

a. Try and see a picture of the place in each of their heads (imagine). Directly ask the students if they can imagine (see in their mind) what the other person is talking about. (For older students adjust the vocabulary: "Do you have a mental image?"; "Can you see with your mind's eye?").

b. Compare the speaker's experience to a similar experience another student had or compare it to what the student imagined it would be like even if he has not experienced it (e.g. Judy can imagine some things about Sam's trip to Sea World from her time at the beach and what she has seen about it on TV). Encourage the students to think about what they would have done or seen in the same situation or experience.

c. Ask questions, to either compare someone else's experience to their own experience or to find out something else they do not know about the person.

Some questions may be:

- What else did you get to do?

- What did you like about it?

- What else do you wish you could have done?

- What did it look like?

- When do you get to do it again?

3. Provide verbal praise for your students' improved ability to be "hanging out" and "sharing" conversation and ideas with the other kids based on what they were imagining about each other. Explain this is what people do when they are hanging out together; they imagine and wonder about other people by connecting their own experiences and thoughts to other people's lives!

4. Discuss how they can use this same skill with people at home, in the classroom and during free time at school.

5. Remember, you are going to practice this with them in many different ways across the years! This is such a hard lesson for them to incorporate!

Lesson 35: Using one's Imagination and Sense of Wonder with Reading Comprehension

Critical Idea

Wonder and imagination are a required part of reading comprehension

Reading comprehension requires each of us to use our active imagination to explore the experiences of the character(s), setting(s) and the situation(s) being described. We wonder or try to predict what the character(s) may do next by asking ourselves questions or having inner thoughts about the character's plans. The only real difference between what our students do while reading versus what they do while relating to other people is while reading, they wonder in their head, and while relating to others, they wonder by speaking out loud.

There are many connections between understanding and participating in the social world and being successful in reading comprehension. The exercise that follows helps students be more "active" in comprehending stories about people's experiences, whether they are fiction or nonfiction.

How to use this lesson in the classroom:

1. After reviewing the previous lessons on imagination and wonder, select some current literature from the students' language arts/reading curriculum. Have them read a passage aloud, as part of a group.

2. Ask the students to imagine the setting and the characters in their mind. Discuss what the setting looks like based on their imagination. Discuss how they would feel if they were in that setting or with those story characters.

3. As they read, ask them to keep their imagination pictures moving in their minds. Encourage them to describe what they saw at the start of the passage and how their pictures changed as they read on.

4. Encourage them to compare their imagined pictures from paragraph to paragraph.

5. Inspire them to keep imagining based on what they know about the world, even if they have never personally experienced what they are reading!

6. Encourage them to continue to wonder about the characters. What are some questions they can ask about the characters (i.e. what are the people in the story feeling, planning or doing?). Encourage them to generate a list of questions. (Again, this sounds easy but is so difficult for many of our folks!)

Lesson 36: Moving Beyond this Curriculum:
Other Areas we are Exploring at the Clinic

Nothing in this curriculum is an end point. Rather, these lessons are all launching points to create new examples to share with students.

As you move onto other lessons keep in mind:

1. Our shared imagination, social wonder (our social curiosity) and sharing our wonder bubble keep us actively connected to other people, not only in conversation, but when playing and reading as well.

2. Encourage students to not only share an imagination, but to monitor what other people are planning to do around them by thinking with their eyes.

3. Use language to find out more about what others are thinking; ask questions.

4. Use language to show we are connecting to other people's thoughts by adding our own thoughts through comments.

5. Practice using language simply to show someone we are paying attention. (Silent, non-responsive listening can be interpreted as being a judgmental listener.)

We use all of these skills in our play, in our classrooms and while sharing space or hanging out. We must work to get general education teachers, resource teachers, and parents connected to this vocabulary. The more often students are exposed to these concepts the better they will be at incorporating them into their base of knowledge.

Video Moments Self-Monitoring Checklist - Section 6
Adjusting Our Participation and Language Based on What Other People are Thinking, Imagining or Wondering

Student's Name _____ Date _____

We are learning to watch people's social behavior and figure out how these behaviors are making other people feel.

Use your observational skills to see how a person in your group is doing during this video-moment on the new skills you and they have been learning.

The person you are going to check on today is _____

Behavior to monitor or watch for	Put a check here if the student is making others feel like he is doing a good job.	Put a check here if the student is not doing a good job.
Thinking about what others are thinking while playing		
Reading people's plans		
Responding to people's plans/actions		
Keeping track of what makes others feel good and bad in play		
Asking questions when people are imagining other's experiences		

Based on what you checked, do you think this person would be a good person to work with on a project?

Circle: YES or NO

If not, what is one behavior the student could try and think about more to help people want to work with him?

Review for Teachers & Parents
🔊 Section 6

Adjusting Our Participation and Language Based on What Other People are Thinking, Imagining or Wondering

Teaching social communication skills and behaviors is quite complicated. We can introduce these lessons in the therapy room, resource room, special needs classroom, and even the regular classroom, but to have the student really learn to grasp how these skills impact him all day, every day, we need educational professionals and paraprofessionals, along with family members, to become acquainted with how to break down the information, teach and reinforce these skills on a regular basis as the need comes up in the environment.

We have developed a set of lessons for the student to become more efficient at social thinking and understanding the related social skills. We need all persons who work or live with the student to also become familiar with the social thinking concepts and to use them during "teachable moments."

Please review the vocabulary terms and concepts on the other side of this sheet and use them with the student as they apply.

If you have any questions on how to use these terms please contact your child's teacher:

_____

at (phone number) _____.

Thanks for helping _____ learn to use these skills
throughout his/her day, at home and school!

Remember the concepts we have introduced in previous sections:

Section 1: Doing what is "expected" in the group; doing what is "unexpected" in a group; "You can change my feelings"; observing others through imitation; big problem - little problem; three parts of play: set up, play and clean up.

Section 2: Whole body listening; think and thinking with our brains; thinking with your eyes; thinking about what other people think.

Section 3: Your body is in the group; your body is out of the group! Your brain is in the group; your brain is out of the group!; Just ME/Thinking about You; good thoughts/weird thoughts; "I've got a secret"; video moment to watch what other people are doing.

Section 4: Figuring out other people's plans; smart guess/wacky guess; identifying one's own feelings; Social Behavior Mapping.

Section 5: Body language and spoken language (verbal and nonverbal); literal and figurative language; indirect language; figuring out meaning using four clues; figuring out people's intentions; flexible brain.

VOCABULARY & CONCEPTS

Adjusting Our Participation and Language Based on What Other People are Thinking, Imagining or Wondering

---

We are currently exploring the following terms. Remember to use them with the students now and over time to help them generalize the concepts beyond the room where the lesson was first taught.

Critical Vocabulary	Definitions
Thinking about what others are thinking	Making the effort to try and determine the thoughts in other people's minds by watching their body movements and trying to figure out what those movements are telling us.
Synchronizing our movements/responding to people's action plans	When playing or just walking with others we have to plan our movements based on reading the action plans or thoughts of others.
Imagination	"IMAGINATION" is being able to try and see, or pretend to do something that is not right in front of you.
Wonder	"WONDER" requires one to combine imagination with verbal or non-verbal questions (curiosity). (In these tasks we are going to encourage the students to think their questions out loud, asking them of each other.)
World Wonders and Social Wonders	**World Wonders** are factual wonders we each have about the world. Our own unique curiosity and individual interests. **Social Wonders** are about the thoughts, feelings and emotions of others. You show you are interested in them by asking about things that are interesting to them.
Asking social wonder questions	Once we start to more actively consider the wonders and experiences of others, we have to ask people questions to learn more information about them. The more we show interest in others, the more they show interest in us!
Sharing someone's Wonder Bubble	The result of sharing an imagination and world wonder simultaneously.

Goal Suggestions - Section 6
Adjusting Our Participation and Language Based on What Other People are Thinking, Imagining or Wondering

 Based on curriculum activities in Section 6 and the California Content Standards

Goal #	Goal Suggestions

6.1 The student will be able to monitor and adjust his/her physical presence, modifying their own behavior based on the activity of the entire group, ____% of intervention session and then using these concepts beyond the therapy room ____% of the time.

6-1a While in a social thinking group activity, _____ will monitor/adjust his physical presence (e.g. move closer, move more slowly or faster) which will facilitate social exchanges, based on the activity of the group members ____% of intervention session.

Take this skill beyond the intervention setting: There the student is expected to adjust his physical presence in order to be a member of a social interaction with peers, teacher or family members ____% of the time.

6-2 The student will be able to read the meaning of another's index finger points as well as use an index finger point to alert others to look in specific directions, ____% of intervention session and then using these concepts beyond the therapy room ____% of the time.

6-2a While observing others in a structured activity, _____ will follow the direction of another group member's pointing index finger to understand its meaning ____% of the time.

6-2b When in a small group situation, _____ will use an index finger point to alert others to look in specific/desired directions as needed with ____% accuracy within the intervention session.

Take this skill beyond the intervention setting: There the student is expected to use and understand the meaning of an index finger point when interacting with peers, teachers or family members ____% of the time.

6.3 While in a sequenced imaginary play activity (e.g. making a pretend sandwich together), _____ will share an "imagination" as demonstrated by taking turns ____% of the time during the intervention session.

Goal #	Goal Suggestions
6.4	During a structured activity that involves synchronizing movements based on the shared imagination of the group, _____ will perform those actions to demonstrate his ability to share an imagination with other students ____% of the time during the intervention session.
6.5	During a structured imaginative play activity _____ will make _____ (#) of related comments or ask questions to demonstrate his sharing an imagination when playing with others, ____% of the time during the intervention session.
6.6	The student will demonstrate the ability to follow the lead of another child in a shared imagination activity by synchronizing movements, making related comments and playing cooperatively, ____% during the intervention session.
6.6a	In a shared imagination activity that involves synchronizing movements, _____ will demonstrate the ability to follow the lead of another child by imitating at least _____(#) of the observed movements with ____% accuracy.
6.6b	In a shared imagination activity that involves synchronizing movements, _____ will make _____ (#) of related comments to indicate his active participation in the structured activity with ____% accuracy.
6.6c	In a shared imagination activity that involves synchronizing movements, _____ will play cooperatively as indicated by such actions as _____ _____ (list observable behaviors) ____% of the time during the intervention session.
6-7	During an imaginative play activity, _____ will allow other students to take the lead during play (use a flexible brain), ____% during the intervention session.
6.8	The student will define the difference between world wonder and social wonder questions, asking his/her peers social wonder questions, ____% of intervention session and then using these concepts beyond the therapy room ____% of the time.
6-8a	When asked, _____ will define and give at least ____(#) examples of indirect language and how he interprets indirect language by determining people's motives with ____% accuracy.
6-8b	When provided with a short passage to read, _____ will interpret the indirect language meaning in context with ____% accuracy in the session.
	Take this skill beyond the intervention setting: There the student is expected to demonstrate his understanding of indirect language meaning within the context of a selected academic assignment with ____% of accuracy.

Goal #	Goal Suggestions
6.9	When given an imaginary "job" _____ will act out _____(#) specific tasks/roles using his imagination (based on a "smart guess" about the world) with ____% accuracy during the intervention session.

6.10	When reading or relating to peers, the student will be able to imagine a person's/character's feelings, motives, actions in a specific context based on his own smart guesses about the world, even when he has not shared this same experience, ____% of intervention session and then using these concepts beyond the therapy room ____% of the time.
6.10a	After reading a short passage, _____ will describe a person's/character's feelings (motives or actions) in the specific context based on "smart guesses" about the world, even when he has not shared this same experience, with ____% accuracy.
6.10b	When relating to his peers within the familiar group, _____ will describe a person's feelings (motives or actions) in a specific context based on "smart guesses" about the world, even if he has not shared this same experience, with ____% accuracy.
	Take this skill beyond the intervention setting: There the student is expected to describe others' feelings (motive or actions) using a smart guess even if he has not has the similar experience ____% of the time.

6.11	When relating to peers, the student will share in another's wonder bubble and ask questions and make comments related directly to what they are imagining other's experiences to be; ____% of intervention session and then using these concepts beyond the therapy room ____% of the time.
6-11a	When relating to peers, _____ will share in another's "wonder bubble" by asking ____(#) questions related directly to what he is imagining others' experiences to be with ____% accuracy within the intervention session.
	Take this skill beyond the intervention setting: There the student is expected to ask questions using his perceptions of an unfamiliar experience of a peer, teacher or parent ____% of the time.
6.11b	When relating to peers, _____ will share in another's "wonder bubble" by making ____(#) comments related directly to what he is imagining others' experiences to be with ____% accuracy within the intervention session.
	Take this skill beyond the intervention setting: There the student is expected to make comments using his perceptions of an unfamiliar experience of a peer, teacher or parent ____% of the time.

6.12	When reviewing videotaped footage of the social group thinking group in which the student participates, the student will be able to identify examples of the student and others in the group using an imagination to synchronize movements, ask questions and make related comments, with ____ % accuracy.

California Content Standards - Section 6
Adjusting Our Participation and Language Based on What Other People are Thinking, Imagining or Wondering

Grade	Area of the curriculum	California Content Standards
K	Reading	Retell familiar stories
1	Reading	Retell central ideas of expository/narrative passage
3	Reading	Distinguish the main idea and supporting details in expository text
4	Reading	Make and confirm predictions about text by using prior knowledge and text ideas (illustrations, titles, topic sentences, important words, foreshadowing cues)
5	Reading	Discern main ideas and concepts in texts, identifying and assessing important evidence
6	Reading	Connect and clarify main ideas by identifying relationships to other sources/topics
8	Written Expression	Write responses to literature: careful interpretations/insight, connect student's own responses to writer's techniques, draw supported inferences, and support judgments.
9	Written Expression	Develop main ideas within body of composition through supporting evidence (scenarios, commonly held beliefs)

Bibliography and References - Section 6
Adjusting Our Participation and Language Based on What Other People are Thinking, Imagining or Wondering

Attwood, Tony (1998). *Asperger's Syndrome: A Guide for Parents and Professionals.* Jessica Kingsley Publishers: London and Philadelphia.

Baron-Cohen, S. (1995). *Mindblindness: An Essay on Autism and Theory of Mind.* The MIT Press: MA

Baron-Cohen, S.; Tager-Flusberg, H.; Cohen, D.; Eds. (2000). *Understanding Other Minds: Perspectives from Developmental Cognitive Neuroscience.* Oxford University Press, Great Britain.

Gray, C. (1994). *Comic Strip Conversations.* Future Horizons: Arlington, TX.
www.futurehorizons-autism.com

Webster's New World Dictionary and Thesaurus. (2002).

Section 7

Our Language Makes Others Have Different Thoughts and Feelings

Communication unfolds through a process I described in the Introduction as the "Four Steps of Communication." The first step is *thinking about what people are thinking;* the second step is *establishing a physical presence,* the third step is *using your eyes to more fully consider and evaluate the people and the context in which the communication occurs* and the fourth step is *using language to relate to others.*

It is virtually impossible to teach effective communication skills if we have not taught our clients to think more effectively about communication. Our clients need to understand the non-verbal components of communication prior to exploring the impact of spoken language. For these reasons, this section on language comes towards the end of this curriculum.

In this section we will explore how interactive language arises from the exchange of comments and questions. The way in which we use these seemingly simple language concepts, however, contributes to or distracts from the relationship itself. The nuances of language carry a significant communicative impact, ultimately affecting how people feel about their communicative partner.

In the previous lessons, we focused on the impact of students' presence, thoughts and imagination in the group. We now shift to how our language makes others react or feel emotionally. As the curriculum progresses, we will teach students different strategies they can employ to modify how people are reacting and responding to them. Ultimately we want the student to be able to self-adjust

his communicative style based on his own awareness of how his message is being interpreted by his communicative partners.

A series of lessons follows to introduce a variety of ways you can break down language concepts to help our students explore the nuances of language. I have found it is far more important to teach students the hows and whys of conversational language before we expect them to converse. Once you start to explore these lessons with your students, it will become clear how much repeated practice is needed on an ongoing basis. Use these lessons to ignite your own exploration into language use so you create avenues for further practice.

Remember, typical children begin to explore and use

many of these concepts by the time they are in preschool. When working with teenagers, I remind them they have not had the same amount of practice using these types of language structures as have other children, thus we need to take this time to practice. For example, I might say, "because of your learning disability, you did not get to play or talk as much with other kids when you were younger, so you benefit from the extra practice now."

Your challenge as the educator is to make the lessons intriguing and the experience relaxing and fun.

Please review Chapter 4 (Using Language to Develop and Sustain a Relationship) in my book *Thinking About YOU Thinking About ME,* to grasp the overall value of language as it contributes to the interpersonal nature of communication.

 Note: The vast majority of our highly verbal students are usually weak in their ability to use language functionally when relating to others. Don't assume that because your student has such a tremendous vocabulary, his interactive language interactive skills are fine.

Tools & Materials

- Flat thin foam paper (available at an arts and craft store) to make a "conversation tree," which is fully described in my book *Thinking About YOU Thinking About ME*
- Video camera to take clips
- Emotion cards or word list
- Chart paper or white board
- Poster paper
- Digital camera with printer (if available)
- Timer

Critical Vocabulary & Concepts

- **Social thinking:** Keeping in mind that people like others to be interested in what they have to say. Social thinking also happens whenever you are just sharing space

- **People files** kept in your brain to open each time you either communicate with a person or are thinking about them

- **Asking questions** to people about these other people

- **Social Curiosity: World Wonders and Social Wonders**

- People's attention and reaction to us causes different types of feelings within us

- Communicating to learn about other's thoughts and emotions for shared events

- **Add-a-Thought** ("bridging comments")

- **Whopping topic change**

- **Initial and follow-up questions**

- **Supporting comments/responses:** Answering questions and making comments to support others

- **Bridging/baiting questions:** Asking questions to try and make the communicative partner(s) talk about what you want to talk about

- **Conversation Tree** and **Conversation Street**

- Topics for initiating communication

- **Rude versus Acceptable Interruptions**

- **Conversation stoppers:** "Saying 'nothing' gives others nothing to think about or work with!"

- How long is too long to talk?

- Developing competency in discussing topics considered "boring" or "bizarre"

- Where to begin: what topics to initiate?

- Talking about what people think or feel with regards to events where they have had shared experiences and/or events for which they have not had shared experiences

- Being willing to talk about what you don't know!

- Moving our bodies while communicating

Lesson 37: How People's Feelings are Related to the Message

Critical Idea

People's feelings change based on how they interpret the message

People usually feel good about themselves and their interactive partner if they think their partner is interested in what they have to say.

One of the ways people demonstrate interest in their communicative partner is by talking about topics they know are of interest to their partner. People don't tend to feel very good about a communicative partner who talks only about his own interests.

How to use this lesson in the classroom:

1. Throughout this section, have students label how they feel when others show interest in them, talk to them, or hang out with them in close proximity. Provide emotion words to help students organize their thoughts and feelings. Use of visuals (pictures or written emotions words) may facilitate the discussion.

   A. Have students identify how they perceive someone is interested or not interested in them during an interaction.

   B. Have students identify their own emotions/feelings when others show interest in them (e.g. good, happy, calm, pleased, proud, etc.).

   C. Have students identify their own emotions/feelings when others show they are NOT interested in them (e.g. irritated, sad, annoyed, mad, frustrated, etc.).

2. Use this information as an incentive/motivator to help students work on changing some of their **language-based interaction strategies** (more examples of how to do this are in activities that follow). Help the students understand that these emotions are shared by others as well. For example, if other students feel like you are not interested in what they are talking about, they may feel irritated with you.

3. Contrast the following two examples of people who are talking to each other. **Example A** features a person who uses self-oriented language and does not show any real interest in the other person. **Example B** features a speaker who shows some interest in his communicative partner. After using these examples, you may want to create some of your own.

> **Example A.** Joe told Frank that he (Joe) "got a new computer game at the end of the summer." Frank responded by saying "I got a new rock cleaner for my rock collection and I have been collecting and cleaning rocks including volcanic and moon rocks." Frank was very happy to tell Joe about his rock collection.
>
> *In this example, Joe is appropriately initiating a topic by sharing one of his experiences with Frank. Frank, on the other hand, does not show any interest in Joe. Frank just talks about himself, possibly making Joe feel like Frank does not care about him. In this example, Joe was the better social thinker because at least he tried to engage Frank by initiating a topic for them to talk about.*

> **Example B.** Joe told Frank that he (Joe) "got a new computer game at the end of summer." Frank asked, "What game did you get?" Joe told him the name saying "I even beat the first level." Frank responded, "That's really cool but I do not know how to play the game. I spent the summer working on my rock collection." Joe responded, "That's cool, I didn't know that people collected rocks." Then Joe asked, "What type of rocks do you collect?"
>
> *In this example both Frank and Joe were good social thinkers since they both asked a question about the other's area of interest. They each responded positively to the other's area of interest even if each person could not really share in the fascination of it.*

4. Explore the problems posed by Example A:

   A. Ask how Joe might have been feeling when Frank talked for a long time about his topic of interest (rocks). Have an emotion chart nearby and ask students to pick out at least three or four different emotions that might best relate to how Joe felt.

   B. Facilitate the discussion, as needed, to clarify the following points: In the first interaction Joe told Frank about something that made him happy and Frank completely ignored it, speaking only about what was interesting to him. It is possible Joe would feel like Frank did not care too much about Joe's interests which can make Joe feel frustrated when he is with Frank. Since Frank went on and on about what he liked, Joe might likely have felt that Frank was being selfish and even stuck up.

   C. What emotions might Frank feel? Was Frank aware of how Joe was feeling? Why wasn't he? How can he become more aware? Did Frank intentionally cause Joe to have these negative feelings? What should Frank be more aware of? How can he learn to change the way he talks to people?

5. Explore with the students why Example B was more positive for both communicative partners.

   A. Ask students how Joe might have felt when Frank asked him a question about the type of game he got, even if Frank did not know much about the game. Provide at least two words from the "emotion chart."

B. Ask students how Frank might have felt when Joe asked questions about rocks, even if he didn't know very much about them. Provide two more positive words from the "emotion chart."

C. Ask the students how Joe and Frank might have felt when each of them told the other boy that his interest was "cool."

D. Facilitate the conversation to encourage students to explore how their own words can alter people's feelings. Discuss the benefits of using words and interactions that change how people feel when you are talking to them.

Lesson 38: More About Words and Feelings

📋 **Critical Idea**
People's feelings change based on how they interpret the message

---

How to use this lesson in the classroom:

Discuss these points and ideas with your students:

1. Your students may benefit from a lesson that ALL humans have thoughts and feelings ALL of the time. In fact, those students who have pets can also talk about how their cats and dogs show their feelings as well.

2. Boys and girls have feelings, even if they don't like to talk about them.

3. Everyone is having thoughts and feelings at this very moment (as you are speaking) and these might be very different feelings from those they had when they woke up this morning. Compare those early morning thoughts and feelings to their feelings when school first started and then compare those feelings to how they will feel when school is out or this session is over!

 Important: At various times discuss the notion of feelings, thus making them a known entity. We tend to talk about feelings only when things are really bad or really good. However it is those moment-to-moment feelings (calm, satisfied, fine, etc.) that keep us safe, comfortable, connected to others and satisfied. Those feelings, in fact, are quite important. The feelings generated from hanging out with a person who is nice can be very valuable even if we normally don't talk about them.

Lesson 39: Defining Social Interaction

Critical Vocabulary
Social thinking means sharing space

Teach students that social thinking happens whenever you are sharing space with another person. Social thinking happens when you are quietly in another's presence or when you are actively engaged with them. During both of these times you have to consider what others are thinking and how they are feeling. You also have to be willing to modify your own behavior to keep people thinking about you the way you want them to think about you.

How to use this lesson in the classroom:

1. Ask the students how social thinking takes place in the environments listed below. Have them consider the social thinking of various people in different environments (parents, teachers, students, etc.). Remember: social thinking is not only considering what people are thinking but also how they are feeling in these various places.

   A. On the playground – at recess or while kids are hanging out during free time.

   B. In the classroom – when the teacher is trying to explain the homework to the students.

   C. In the principal's office – when he is trying to talk to a student who is not following the rules.

   D. At home, at bedtime – when the parents and kids are all supposed to be getting ready for bed.

   E. At home, in the morning – when everyone needs to get ready to start their day.

F. At home – when you have a friend over and he or she is playing in your bedroom.

G. At the grocery store – when you are walking down the aisle with the cart, shopping with your parent.

H. In school – when walking down the hall.

2. Ask students to discuss when a person does not have to be a social thinker. Is it possible to not be a social thinker when you are at school? In the community? At home? If so, when? Why? For how long?

Lesson 40: People Files–Learning Our Brains Store Information About Other People as well as Ourselves.

Critical Vocabulary

People Files

Develop the concept that we keep "people files" in our brain about people we meet. These "files" contain memories and insights about other people's areas of interests, likes and dislikes, belief systems, emotional reactions, and facts about their families and friends, etc.

People files represent files we store in our brain about friends, acquaintences, and even people we dislike. We need to remember both good and bad thoughts to help us make better judgements about people with whom we interact, or people with whome we choose *not* to interact.

Recalling information from our people files helps us interpret the motives and intentions of people with whom we interact repeatedly.

Unfortunately, I do not know which professional to credit with developing the term "people files" or "friend files." The idea of teaching our students that our brain stores information in files has been discussed as a treatment in autism literature for a long time.

Tools & Materials

- Blank paper (at least letter size)
- Pencils or crayons
- Review brain/face drawing

How to use this lesson in the classroom:

1. Have students draw a picture of their brain/face.

2. Have them draw a vertical line down the middle of their face.

3. On the right side, have them draw lines out from the side of their face to describe some of the things they are interested in. Suggested questions for them to answer:

   A. What do you like to do?

   B. What do you like to eat?

   C. Where is one of your favorite places to go?

   D. Who is in your family?

   E. What is your favorite restaurant?

   F. What books do you like to read? Or TV shows to watch?

4. Encourage the students to "interview" each other. The students can generate their own questions if they like. See the People Files Interview Form at the end of this section (Appendix 7-1).

5. Have the students draw a horizontal line on the left side of their brain/face picture. Tell each student to write a friend's name on this line.

6. Draw three little lines and boxes, underneath the name, that connect to the left side of the brain/face picture, creating a "graphic organizer" or "mind map."

7. Have each student take the three pieces of information he is most interested in remembering about the other person and write these three special facts in each of the three boxes attached to the friend's name.

8. If you have more than two people in your group, have students individually share with each other what they have learned about the one student they interviewed. This prevents each student from having to interview every person in the group. If needed, create a new graphic organizer on the left side of your student's pictured brain to show another three facts he can remember about another student.

By the time the students have completed the task, they should have their brain/face drawn with the right side showing information they know about themselves, and the left side should demonstrate what they think is interesting/special about the other people in their social thinking group.

9. Save the brain drawings to use for the next lesson. You may need to pull them out many times in the future. The point of this lesson is to illustrate for students that their brains can recall many things about themselves but their brain can recall things about others as well. **See the visual example below:**

Show how each of our brains remembers facts about ourselves and others.

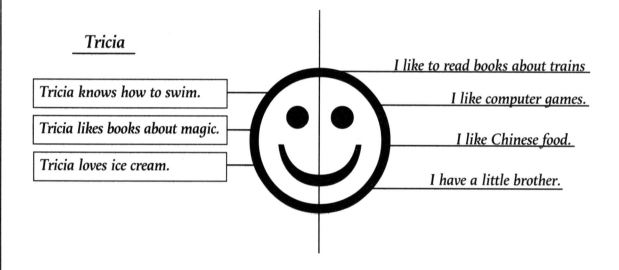

Tricia

Tricia knows how to swim.

Tricia likes books about magic.

Tricia loves ice cream.

I like to read books about trains

I like computer games.

I like Chinese food.

I have a little brother.

Lesson 41: Asking People Questions About Themselves

 Critical Idea

Asking people questions about their interests

It may come as a surprise to many parents and professionals that a vast majority of our highly verbal students with social cognitive deficits have great difficulty asking another person questions about himself. This skill is at the core of our ability to relate effectively through social language. For more information on assessing this skill, please review the last chapter in my book *Thinking About YOU Thinking About ME* (2002).

Tools & Materials

• Blank paper (at least letter size)

• Pencils or crayons

• Review brain/face drawing

How to use this lesson in the classroom:

1. Discuss how our communicative partners feel when a student uses language to show he remembers things about them.

    A. For older students, encourage them to base their discussions on their own life experiences.

    B. Would your students agree that people who are perceived as "friendly" are people who show interest in us/others?

    C. Would they agree that people we perceive as "unfriendly" are people we don't think are very interested in us/others?

2. Ask students to recall what they know about the other students in the group.

   A. Encourage them to practice asking others the more basic WH- questions. Copy the simple list of "Wh-"words at the end of this section to help students get started (Appendix 7-2). You may be surprised that many of our intelligent adolescents (even adults) will benefit from looking at these WH- words when first practicing with others.

   B. Have students practice asking each other questions based on what they know and remember about those other students.

3. Have students pass a small object to the person they are questioning. The object can be anything, but I prefer something humorous like a small rubber chicken or little troll doll. While some teachers may find the students are distracted by the object, the fact is, these odd objects add to the relaxed and humorous atmosphere in your group.

   While students may concentrate slightly better while passing a pencil, no student was ever happy to come to a group simply because he got to pass a pencil. However, most students enjoy attending a group where humor is used.

   A. Passing the object is a tangible, concrete way in which students can observe how their social language actually moves around the group.

   B. The student who receives the small object should answer the question asked of him, but then has the responsibility to ask a question of another person in order to pass the object on to that person.

      For example, Mary asked Sarah, "What movies do you like?" Mary then passes Sarah the little rubber chicken. Sarah receives the chicken and answers, "My favorite movie is Little Mermaid." Sarah now turns to Heidi and asks, "Where does your family like to go for pizza?" and at that point Sarah passes the little chicken to Heidi.

C. It is NOT important for the students to maintain the topic, nor is it even important that they maintain eye contact when first doing this exercise. What IS important is that students are getting practice learning the skill of asking other people questions. As the students become more skilled and confident, you can guide them to keep their topics related to the responses and/or questions made by other people in the group.

The students can also be guided, over time, to become more aware of their physical presence and eye-contact when they are sharing space with others. The reason I mention this is because it is easy to overwhelm our students with expecting overall effective communication skills, when in reality they have not even mastered one basic skill. Be careful what you ask of our students. Avoid wanting perfection too early in the process.

Lesson 42: The Basics of Maintaining a General Topic

📋 **Critical Vocabulary**
Topic coherence or Topic maintenance

At some point you will want to teach students to maintain a specific topic. Start by providing specific topics to them. You can either make up your own set of topics that may be relevant to the students or use the topics provided on the worksheet at the end of this section (Appendix 7-3).

How to use this lesson in the classroom:

1. Write or paste each of the topics onto an index card. We use these topic cards because it is truly difficult for our students to generate ideas while thinking about the people around them.

2. Using the same Wh-questions reviewed in the previous lessons, have the students practice asking each other questions about these topics. When using these cards, set a pile of them on the table and turn one over for the students to see. Ask the students to ask questions related to the suggested topic, while still passing the small object back and forth, to show movement of the interaction.

   ↪ *Remember to break it down. Know the targeted goal for each student. We are moving along one step at a time!*

Lesson 43: Social Curiosity: Wondering About the Person you are With by Asking Questions

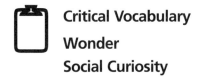

Critical Vocabulary

Wonder

Social Curiosity

This lesson reviews much of what was developed in Section 6. Encourage your students to explore their sense of wonder and to ask others questions to find out what they think, feel or know about a topic. Explore the idea of wonder by teaching that most people have wonders about the world (including facts and scientific information); and we will refer to this type of curiosity as "world wonders." When we are curious or wonder what other people experience, feel or think, we will call this "social wonders."

This activity is designed to teach students they may have a number of world wonders, which are really "cool," but to create a friendship or social interactions they will need to show they have some social wonders for other people as well.

Explore how our social wonders arise from our ability to sustain an imagination about other's thoughts and experiences. For example, when listening to friends talk about their trip to Europe, we can imagine being there. We then ask relevant social wonder questions to find out how our friends' perception of their trip to Europe matched our image of it.

You may observe it is often difficult for your students to generate social wonder questions and make spontaneous comments about other people's world wonders. Instead, they tend to get caught up in their own personal world wonders and have a difficult time inquiring about how others thought or felt. My therapists, Stephanie Madrigal and Randi Dodge, and I developed this next activity after realizing we can teach our students to ask others questions via language forms. Their questions often remain very stiff and impersonal unless we teach them to also engage their social imagination while talking.

Tools & Materials

• Blank paper (at least 11x14 or poster size), 1 sheet per 4 students

• Pencils or crayons

Social imagination breeds social wonder which breeds a social curiosity. These are all concepts we want to explore through this lesson.

How to use this lesson in the classroom:

1. Divide a piece of poster paper into four sections. You will need one section for each child in your social thinking group. You may need multiple pieces of poster paper.

2. Draw a large thought bubble in each section and assign one thought bubble to each student.

3. Have the students write inside their thought bubble things they like to think about or like to do. We can call these their World Wonders (e.g. fishing, computer games, gardening, black holes, how to do their math, etc.).

4. The students can now see that each person in the group has a different set of world wonders.

5. Cut out these squares of imagined world wonders.

6. Have the students stand in a circle facing each other.

7. Take turns having each child hold his thought bubble up over his head to show others what he likes to think about.

8. As members of the group focus on the thoughts of that student, they start to experience social wonder about some of the student's interests. To encourage wondering, it is important to let the students know this activity involves imagining! When a student is able to ask a question of a target student, about what the target student likes to think about or feels when he is involved in something on the list, then the student is asking a social wonder question.

 While this seems like a fairly simple concept, it is not easy for the majority of our students.

9. Facilitate students wondering about each other by encouraging the students to imagine they are doing the activity or studying a topic that another student is interested in. For example, if a student has listed that he likes to think about his vacation to Hawaii, then you can model your wonder by saying, "I am imagining Tom is in Hawaii and I am wondering about what part of Hawaii he went to" or "I am imagining that Tom got to do some neat things there and I am wondering about things he liked to do there." You can then say, "What questions would you ask based on what you are wondering or imagining about Tom's trip to Hawaii?"

10. An alternative to this lesson is to take digital pictures of all the students in your group.

   A. Print out each student picture on a separate piece of paper.

   B. Place the picture towards the bottom of a piece of paper and draw a thought bubble above the picture.

   C. Copy the picture for use in this lesson and future lessons.

   D. Have the students write their world wonders on the thought bubble. Then follow steps 8 - 9 above.

It is important for our students to learn each person has their own enjoyments about the world, and that each of us can share in each other's pleasures.

It is also important to be reminded how difficult these lessons are for our students. Repetition over time (on and off across years) is to their benefit.

Consider the following example:

John is holding a thought bubble that says: "I like to think about Legos and computer games."

John likes thinking about building with Legos and playing computer games; these are some of John's world wonders. Sue tries to imagine herself building with Lego toys and then she wonders about what John really likes to build with them, so she asks, "What do you build with your Legos?"

By Sue posing this question to John about his area of interest, Sue is demonstrating social wonder (another term for this is "social curiosity") about John. What is important to recognize is when Sue has social wonders about John, this actually makes John feel good because he feels like Sue is interested in what he likes. When people feel good about each other, they are more likely to want to be with each other. This is how friendships get started and then continue.

Lesson 44: Using "Follow-up" Questions, Once an Initial Question has been Asked

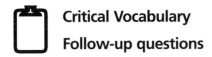

Critical Vocabulary

Follow-up questions

Another strategy students can utilize to show interest in another person's topic and to learn more information about them, is to ask additional questions in order to clarify information and seek new information. Students with social thinking deficits often lack extended reciprocity in their communication with others.

The following suggested ideas stimulate students to ask questions beyond the surface level. Your students need a lot of practice with this, because if they do ask a question to initiate a topic, they often don't use language to explore a person's topic much further. For example, a student may ask, "What are your hobbies?" and once a person tells them, they don't say anything else, or they may focus their response on describing their own area of interest.

Tools & Materials

• Friend file pictures

• Topic index cards

• Wh- questions: Appendix 7-2

• Ask a Question to a Person About That Person: Appendix 7-4

• Small (yet fun) object to pass

How to use this lesson in the classroom:

1. Discuss with students the difference between asking an initial question and then creating a follow-up question. Follow-up questions are those that seek more information about a specific topic that has already been introduced in order to keep the conversation going.

   For example, if I ask you, "What did you do this weekend?" (Initial question) you may respond by saying, "I played on the computer and went out to dinner." If I don't ask you anything else about your response, or I start talking about what I did this weekend, I am not "following up" to get into a deeper conversation with you. An example of a follow-up question to your response would be, "What computer game were you playing?" Or, "Where did you go to dinner?" When you answer those questions, I may have even more follow-up questions I can ask. This is one way a conversation unfolds.

A. Have students practice asking a question based on what they remember from their friend files about a student in the group. You may also pick topics from the previously developed topic index cards. Also provide the students with the list of "Wh-" questions found in Appendix 7-2. This helps students organize their question-asking skills.

   This strategy is often needed, even for students with very high technical language skills. They may lack the ability to initiate questions and sustain reciprocal conversations.

B. You can turn this activity into a game show format by giving one point for each follow-up question students ask. The students can work in teams or as individuals. However, be aware that some of your students are "hyper-verbal" and once you structure a task, they will talk a lot. Other students you have are "hypo-verbal"; they don't easily formulate language around their thoughts.

Tip: If needed, balance out the hyper and hypo-verbal students by telling each student his job is to earn eight points. This helps limit the questions of the hyper-verbal child and motivates the hypo-verbal child to participate more, even if this requires you to help him earn these points.

2. Encourage students to start talking about a topic and then have the other students generate as many follow-up questions as possible to find out more about the topic. Have students take turns suggesting the topic to be discussed. (Reminder: choose age appropriate topics!)

3. Use the handout "Ask a Question to a Person about That Person" - Appendix 7-4.

    A. Copy this form and cut out each box.

    B. Each time a student successfully uses a follow-up question, slip one of these messages in front of the student. The more times he uses this targeted language technique, the more slips of paper the student collects. This nonverbal technique affirms that they are doing the right thing.

Lesson 45: "Supporting comments": Showing you are Listening to What Someone has to Say

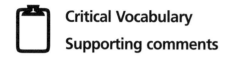

Critical Vocabulary

Supporting comments

Supporting comments are those little remarks and gestures we make in response to someone else's words. This type of comment shows we are paying attention to the speaker and have a thought or emotion in response to the speaker's message. Supporting comments can be as simple as: "wow," "cool," "sounds fun," "wish I was there," "yikes," "that doesn't sound good," etc.

At times we provide this type of response to make the speaker think we are paying attention, even though we really aren't. As long as the speaker thinks his communication partner is listening, then the comment has served its purpose.

Nonverbal supporting gestures can serve the same purpose. However, these are usually more subtle and fleeting. Students must use efficient eye contact or be "thinking with their eyes" about the other person for the body language or gestures to support the interactions. For example, while looking at a person, the student can nod his head in agreement to show he hears and understands what is being said.

Explain to students that supporting comments or responses should match the emotional tone of the speaker's message and should not be a "pat" or "rehearsed" response. For example, if someone says their "dog is sick," the supporting comment could be "bummer." Remind students, as they become more efficient through practice, their exchanges will become more "natural" or spontaneous.

Other reminders: Students need to keep their body turned toward the person speaking, even when giving simple supporting comment responses. Students also have to look in the general direction of the speaker while he is talking.

Tools & Materials

• Supporting Comments - Appendix 7-5.

How to use this lesson in the classroom:

1. Model supportive comments. Have the students tell you what they did last night and then say "wow", or "great" or "sounds nice", etc. You can also show video clips from favorite movies or TV shows and watch for supporting comments.

2. Role play NOT giving supportive comments after a student offers a comment about his life.

3. Invite students to compare how it felt when they received supporting comments, versus when they did not. Have students talk about how they feel personally when no one provides supportive comments about what they are saying.

4. Encourage students to understand they should produce these little comments for others, since they themselves prefer them.

5. Practice providing supporting comments.

   A. Use "Supporting Comment" sheet - Appendix 7-5.

   B. Copy this form and cut out individual boxes.

   C. Whenever you observe students using an appropriate verbal or nonverbal supporting comment, slip this comment paper in front of the student. The more times he uses this strategy, the more slips of paper the student amasses. This nonverbal reinforcement technique affirms they are doing the right thing.

Lesson 46: Add-A-Thought: Learning to use Language to Connect One's own Life Experiences to Those Described by Others

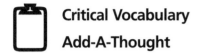

Critical Vocabulary
Add-A-Thought

We have spent a major portion of this section teaching students to ask questions. However, the fact is that social conversations and discussions often involve just sharing related comments. People often respond to others by simply adding their own thoughts and experiences to those of the communicative partner. In fact, most conversations are sustained by people adding their own thoughts onto what someone else has said.

It is also important to note, in contrast to popular thought, conversation topics are often not strongly maintained. In real life, conversations meander around a range of topics that connect loosely to another person's comment.

For example, if I say, "I had a great weekend; I got to go to a movie and out to dinner with my family," I have opened the door for communicative partners to provide their own com-

ments about a number of related topics. Based on my comment, it would be appropriate for a person to respond by talking about the type of weekend he had, what he did with his family, a good or bad movie he saw, a movie he wants to see, a place he went to dinner, or what he hopes to do related to any of those subtopics.

Thus, the key to teaching the concept of "add-a-thought" comments is to teach students to relate their own experience(s) directly to a comment made by a conversational partner. We are teaching students to "connect the conversation dots." We want them to recognize that other people's comments spur our own thoughts, and then stimulate us to connect one of our thoughts to the thoughts stated by others.

Some examples of "add-a-thought" conversations follow.

Add-A-Thought Conversation Examples

Conversation 1:

Michelle: I had a great weekend. I got to go to a movie and out to dinner with my family.

Mary: I didn't have much fun this weekend. I had to clean my house.

Sue: I have a woman who cleans so that I can try and relax on weekends. This weekend we went to the beach.

Joe: I love to sail. We went sailing in Hawaii last summer.

Michelle: My mom always used to sail but she never taught me.

Conversation 2:

Mark: Last weekend I just stayed in my house all day and played computer games.

Jaime: I didn't get to do anything I wanted to do. I had to go to a wedding and it was boring.

Mike: I went to my aunt's wedding and I had a lot of fun. It was in a big hotel and I got to go swimming at night.

Mark: My sister is on the swim team, but I hate swimming.

Mike: I am taking a karate class. It is really cool.

Jaime: I want to sign up for dance, but my mom says we don't have time.

In these examples, notice how the topic is established and maintained loosely by each person's life experiences and how each person's comment connects to a different person's prior comment. In making these "add-a-thought" comments, we relate our own topic by connecting it to the unfolding path of the discussion. We want to teach students to maintain the topic threads in conversation, rather than restrict conversation to a single topic.

It is important to make the distinction that in social language, the topic meanders as we continue to relate our life to the lives of our communicative partners. However, in more formal environments like classrooms or formal meetings, we actually need to sustain a fairly strong alliance to the topic being discussed.

With this "add-a-thought" activity, we are teaching students that social conversation can go in many directions, as long as the topic relates to some aspect of what was just said by other communicative partners. We need students to learn to make supporting or connecting comments that carry conversation forward. It is also important to teach that there can be many different offshoots of any person's topic so the participants have choices as to the direction they want the conversation to go.

When teaching "add-a-thought" comments, recognize those students who are already good at this. These tend to be your more "hyper-verbal" students. However, a lot of your students don't know how their own experiences can be blended into what someone else has already expressed.

 Tools & Materials

- Thought bubble "Add-a-thought" form - Appendix 7-6

- Initiating questions form - Appendix 7-3

- Chart paper or white board

How to use this lesson in the classroom:

1. Explain the "add-a-thought" concept to your students.

2. See Appendix 7-6. Copy the page and cut out each of the boxes. In each box is a "thought bubble" and the instruction, "add a thought."

3. Give each student four boxes.

4. Have one student start by telling the group a few things he did recently that he enjoyed (this weekend, last summer, what he did for the holidays, etc.). This student is not "adding a thought." He is merely providing a thought for the group to work with. You can use the "initiating questions" topics worksheet (Appendix 7-3) from an earlier lesson to help students generate other ideas.

5. With each topic statement put forth, explore the different spin-off topics this original statement can generate. For example, if the student says, "I like to go to grandpa's house to celebrate Christmas but he never gets a tree," the students can discuss possible spin-off topics. These could include "Christmas experiences," "visits to relatives," "traditions around the holidays," "Christmas trees," etc.

6. The students are to "add a thought" to the student's initiated comment. They do this by adding a comment that connects their own experiences or thoughts of the world in some way to each speaker's previous comment.

7. Each time a student connects to another person's response by "adding a thought" they put their "add a thought" slip of paper on the table. The next person to add a thought then puts their slip of paper on top of the other one. Over time a pile forms, visually representing the layers of thoughts that make up conversational language.

8. Beware: If a student asks a question of another student, rather than providing an "add-a-thought" comment, gently remind the student that right now we are focusing on the concept of "add-a-thought." It is important to keep your students focused on the specific strategy and how to use it for social communication, rather than letting them do whatever they want. At this point in the therapy they are learning to sharpen specific conversational tools. To encourage your students' open, spontaneous socializing, build time into the start and/or end of the session for them to just relate and interact. Provide this opportunity for more spontaneous interaction only if they are gaining enough skills to relate a bit to each other. Some of your groups may not yet use this time well!

 Another option is to introduce this lesson by starting with "Conversation 1 and Conversation 2," presented earlier in this lesson. Have your students figure out how each comment is related to a previous statement.

Lesson 47: Bridging Questions (Baiting Questions): Asking Questions to Make People Talk About Your Area of Interest

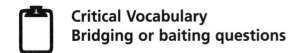

Critical Vocabulary
Bridging or baiting questions

Sometimes questions can serve as a way to lure people into a discussion about one's own area of interest or thoughts. An example of this type of question would be if I asked, "Have you ever been to China?" fully knowing that I am going to go to China very soon and I want to be able to talk about the upcoming trip.

These "bridging" or "baiting" questions are fairly commonplace in most day-to-day conversations. When used occasionally, they allow the speaker to introduce a preferred topic while seeming interested in other people's thoughts. These questions allow the speaker to more indirectly focus on his own interests.

Problems arise when this type of questioning is the only one used by a speaker. We need to clearly distinguish between asking a person a follow-up question with the intention of talking about that person, versus using a bridging question to talk to other people about yourself or your interests.

I don't usually teach students this type of bridging question. Instead, I teach students about the intentionality that different types of questions suggest. Ultimately, as each of us communicates, our partners are trying to figure out the intention behind the message. This is an interesting area to explore with older kids (middle school and above). Figuring out people's plans can be accomplished not only by observing them, but by figuring out their communicative intent.

Lesson 48: Conversation Stoppers:
Saying "Nothing" Gives Others Nothing to Think About!

Critical Idea

Don't respond by saying "nothing."
That means you give someone "nothing" to think about.

Work with students so they can offer informative responses to people's questions rather than responding with "I don't know," or "nothing." Typically, teens will answer with "nothing" when asked what they have done lately or what they think about something. We want our students to learn they need to provide informative responses by sharing their thoughts or experiences with the communicative partner so that the interaction continues.

Tools & Materials

- Rubber chicken

- Stop sign or other visual tool indicating a conversation stopper

How to use this lesson in the classroom:

1. When a student responds to a question such as, "What did you do this weekend?" by saying "Nothing" you can respond by throwing the rubber chicken in the air and saying, "You just stopped/killed the conversation. By saying 'nothing' you give us nothing to think about." This is obviously done with humor and exaggeration.

2. Remind students that language is supposed to trigger our partner's imagination or sense of wonder through each of our responses. If a student responds by saying "nothing," he effectively cuts off the fuel to ignite other people's connection to him.

3. Encourage the student to provide at least one descriptive response to any question asked. For example, if asked "What did you do last night", rather than say "nothing" the student can say "I had to clean the garage with my brother and then I just played some computer games."

Lesson 49: How Long is Too Long to Talk?
Start Short and Add On

Critical Idea

Shorter talking times are appropriate at the start of a conversation

As students respond with related comments, they need to learn they cannot talk as long as they desire. Communicative remarks, especially when they are for purely social connection, should start out rather short and brief (10 - 15 seconds). If someone is interested in what is being said, they will likely ask a question to encourage the speaker to expand on the topic. It is important our students learn they are not supposed to tell someone everything they know about a topic when simply asked, "What do you like to do?"

As we help students get a better sense of providing shorter, more succinct responses, we also need to let them know there will be times people go past the "10-15 second" speaking time in their initial remarks. Most people don't literally time the length of their responses, but they often do consider how long they have been talking. We have to use a flexible brain to figure out if the length of our response matches the interest level of the communicative partners.

Tools & Materials

• A timer, watch or clock with a second hand

How to use this lesson in the classroom:

1. Have students provide brief responses to questions about their day or favorite topics. Limit their responses to 30 seconds when you start to work with them on this concept. Use a timer that will ring/go off after 30 seconds.

2. Set the timer and encourage them to think about the most important part or main idea they want to relate. You will find that many of your students will not think they can share ideas of any significance in only 30 seconds. When they practice with a given time limit, they will start to get better at focusing in on their main ideas.

3. Once they have started to succeed within the 30 second time period, decrease talking time to 15 seconds. Encourage them to focus on the main idea or only one or two key points.

4. Once the students have responded in 15 seconds or less, practice having them modulate their further responses based on the listener's interest level. For example, if the listener responds to the student by shifting the topic to something else, then the student needs to learn to also move his response in this new direction. However, if the listener responds to the student by asking a question that relates back to the original topic, the student can then provide a bit more information (another 15-30 seconds worth). Then, if the listener asks yet another question about the topic (implying real interest in the topic), the student can expand the response even further.

6. Encourage students to recognize the enjoyment they feel when someone seems interested in them or their topic. For this reason they should provide reciprocal enjoyment for others by also asking them questions about their areas of interest! Communication is a dance that needs both partners!

Lesson 50: Whopping Topic Change (WTC)
(WTCs mess with people's minds)

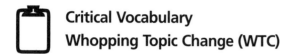

Critical Vocabulary
Whopping Topic Change (WTC)

Communicative partners are always trying to figure out how each person's shared thoughts build on what has already been stated. When each person's questions or comments are understood in the context of what has been stated, we call this "maintaining the topic".

In contrast, "Whopping Topic Changes" (WTCs) happen when a person's comment or question cannot be understood within the current context of the discussion or environment. WTCs (questions or comments) appear to be made "out of the blue" or "off the wall". We say the comments are "out of the blue" since we cannot figure out how the speaker's most recent comment(s) relate to prior comments(s) made. An example of a WTC would be if I said "I had a good weekend!", but my communicative partner responded by saying, "I like bananas." Since I was trying to figure out the intention behind my partner's message, I got confused because I could not figure out how my comment about my "good weekend" connected to his thinking about how much he "likes bananas".

Students usually find the concept of WTCs humorous. WTCs earn a light tap on the shoulder from the rubber chicken (only if the student enjoys this type of playful humor).

Lesson 51: Rude Interruptions versus Acceptable Interruptions

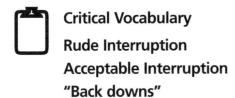

Critical Vocabulary

Rude Interruption

Acceptable Interruption

"Back downs"

From the time they are very young, we actively teach children not to interrupt others. We may also teach them not to let their words "bump" into those of others. However, the reality is that people engaged in an active conversation often interrupt each other as a sign of conversational motivation and momentum. As we listen to other people wind down their thoughts and predict how someone is going to complete their sentence, the motivated conversational partner may interrupt by adding his next thought before the current speaker has literally finished his sentence. We call this an "acceptable interruption" since it is a welcome and fair part of the normal, fast-paced flow of conversation. However, some of our rigid thinking students, even in high school and adulthood, can get very upset with someone they they perceive is interrupting them for any reason. At some point in their life they had probably been taught a rule that interruptions are always bad.

I define interruptions in two ways:

1. **"A Fair/Acceptable Interruption"** is when someone interrupts the speaker's thoughts because they are motivated to connect with the speaker on the topic. They don't wait until the speaker has finished every word before they add their own. The person who uses the "fair interruption" is actively engaged in the quick pace of the communicative exchange. When someone is eagerly adding to what has been said, the speaker realizes his thoughts were winding down and may cease saying the last few words to allow the communicative partner's idea to take center stage.

2. A **"Rude Interruption"** is an interruption that occurs near the start of one's message, or does not allow the speaker to express the majority of what he had to say. It may involve a WTC comment or question as well.

A. A repair strategy for an accidental "rude interruption" is called a "back down." This is when two people start talking at almost the exact same time, neither meaning to interrupt the other. By coincidence, they just started talking at the same time. In this case, one person has to "back down" to let the other share his thought. The person who is willing to back down often says, "oh, sorry" and then stops talking.

B. The speaker who was able to finish his/her thoughts can then recall this other person had "backed down" and overtly invite the comments to be restated by saying to this other person, "what was it you wanted to say?"

Tools & Materials

• Chart paper or white board

How to use this lesson in the classroom:

1. Review the following with your students:

   A. When you are with other people and having a lively discussion, people DO interrupt other people. Interruptions can actually be considered a very HEALTHY part of the interaction, if done at the right time in the discussion.

2. Explore "acceptable interruptions":

   A. Acceptable interruptions occur toward the end of someone's comments when the listener can predict the end of the speaker's point and wants to jump in to add a thought.

   B. Acceptable interruptions usually relate in some way to the topic being discussed.

   C. Acceptable interruptions show the listener is motivated to contribute to the overall discussion.

   D. Acceptable interruptions are not to be challenged or even taken notice of by the person who was 'interrupted.' The interrupted conversational partner is to "go with the flow."

E. What other rules can you or your teams discuss to better understand interruptions?

F. Challenge your students to consider what strategies they can use to help them monitor and adjust to other people's acceptable interruptions when talking as part of a group.

3. Explore "rude interruptions":

A. Rude interruptions occur when a person starts talking prior to the speaker having a chance to finish stating his main idea.

B. Rude interruptions can also happen when a person accidentally start talking at the same time and does not notice someone needs to "back down."

C. Rude interruptions occur when a person hears most of what the speaker has to say, but he completely dismisses the speaker's idea by failing to acknowledge it and just goes on to state his own idea. (Discounting the speaker's message.)

D. Rude interruptions occur when a person listens to some of what is said then creates a WTC to move the conversation onto what they want to talk about.

If your students demonstrate significant anxiety with any and all types of interruptions, continue to work with them on understanding people have to be aware of each other, but communication goes too fast for people to avoid all types of interruptions on a regular basis. Help them understand that "acceptable interruptions" should be interpreted as a person being highly motivated to talk to you. Whereas "rude interruptions," even if they are accidental, require subtle conversation repair skills to get a person back on track within the conversation.

If the person with anxiety or rigid rules about interruptions ends up yelling at the person who interrupted him, discuss that he actually appears to be ruder than the person who initiated the interruption in the first place. Our students must always keep in mind how complicated serial communication can be due to its rapid pace.

4. Teach the idiom, "cut people some slack," to help students understand that we all have to be forgiving of social errors, even in social conversations.

5. Challenge your students to consider what strategy they can use to help them monitor and adjust to other people's rude interruptions without becoming too rude themselves.

6. Regarding interruptions when people are talking in a larger social group: Once a group has four or more people in it, the group often breaks up into smaller conversational groups. If a student (Jeff) begins a topic and another person (Sue) shows interest by looking at Jeff, but the other two students are off on their own topic, then Jeff should continue to look at and speak directly to Sue. Jeff should not expect that the other kids must listen to him as well. Groups that get larger in size have a hard time maintaining one topic. What Jeff should NOT do is tell the other students they are rude because they did not listen to him. In groups of four or more, it is really common that the discussion splits into multiple topics. This is the reality of "hanging out".

This rule does not usually carry over to more formal settings such as meetings; however it may happen when working as part of a larger group in the classroom.

Lesson 52: Practicing Language Concepts: Conversation Tree and Conversation Street

Critical Vocabulary
Conversation Tree
Conversation Street

The Conversation Tree and Conversation Street are two visual strategies that help students explore ways in which communicative partners contribute to a conversation. Each of these techniques suggests ways participants can contribute to a social conversation. These strategies can also help "hyper-verbal" participants visually recognize how much they tend to dominate the discussion, and help the "hypo-verbal" participants recognize how little they contribute. The educator can then modify the demands placed on each participant to more strongly encourage participation by the hypo-verbal student, while encouraging stronger nonverbal and less verbal participation from the hyper-verbal student.

These techniques have already been described in great detail in Chapter 7 of my book *Thinking About YOU Thinking About ME, 2nd Ed* (2007). To avoid duplication of information, please review these techniques there.

Tools & Materials

- Language comment, question and body language forms, Appendix 7-4, 7-5, 7-7 and 7-8

- Colored copy paper

How to use this lesson in the classroom:

1. Teach students to increase their awareness of the techniques they are using:

An additional technique, not described in *Thinking About YOU Thinking About ME*, is one in which the teacher provides information to students about the type of language forms used in their conversational efforts. After students have learned to explore and become more proficient in their use of questions about other people, supporting comments/responses and "add-a-thought" strategies, the educator should provide direct confirmation about the students' use of these skills through the following steps:

A. Copy Appendices 7-4, 7-5, 7-7 and 7-8, each page on a different color of paper to visually distinguish one from the other.

B. Cut out the boxes on each page.

C. Put the slips of paper into color-coded piles.

D. At the start of each session, encourage the students to just talk or "hang out." Listen to their language. Each time a student asks a question about another person, place one of these slips of paper in front of the student. When another student gives a supporting comment, place one of these slips of paper in front of this student. When a student "adds a thought" put the matching slip of paper representing this language concept in front of that student. While monitoring the students to keep their bodies and eyes in the group while relating to others, occasionally provide one of these slips of paper to the students who are doing well with that.

E. Students will earn a small pile of slips of paper in front of them, showing them what types of language they are using spontaneously with other students. If a student is not receiving any papers, this student needs some further encouragement and help with learning and using specific skills.

F. Once the students have a pile of papers, review each student's pile. Is one student only "adding a thought" but never asking questions? Is another student always asking questions but never responding? Through this monitoring technique you allow students to become more aware of what they are doing well and what language forms they may have to keep pushing themselves to use.

G. If a student has received a blend of all the slips, congratulate him and encourage him to think about how he can use these same skills outside the therapy room.

2. Use the color-coded language concept slips to up the ante.

A. Use the same color-coded slips of paper as described in the previous task, but this time, allocate a certain number to each student at the start of the task.

B. You should give all students the same total number of slips, but you can give each student a different assortment depending on the skill you want to work on with that particular student. For example, the following group of students were each given 10 slips, but each student had a different array of slip types:

- Joe does not like to initiate but he responds really well. Joe gets five "ask others questions" slips, two "add-a-thought" slips and five "response slips." Joe really needs to continue to work on how he uses language to show others he is thinking about them.

- Rob has now become quite good at asking questions of other people, so he only gets two "question" slips. He is not as skilled at adding his own thoughts so he gets eight "add-a-thought" slips. He has no problem with responses, so he receives none of those.

- Will does a great job adding his own thoughts, but does not consistently respond to others nor does he ask others many questions. He is given six "ask a question" slips and four "supporting comment/response" slips.

3. You may observe your students trying to trade slips with their peers to get more of the ones they feel are easier for them to accomplish. Laugh with them, in recognition of what concepts are more difficult for them, but insist they keep their own slips.

4. Encourage the students to just talk or "hang out" but make clear they are not able to pull themselves out of the discussion until all their slips are used up. If students have difficulty initiating topics for this discussion, go back to using the initiation index card topics or provide a specific topic for them to talk about.

5. This activity allows students to practice very specific areas of language, which in turn helps them build self-awareness and self-accomplishment in the process.

Lesson 53: Talking About Topics no one Thinks People Actually Talk About, but They Do!

Critical Idea

Conversations are made up of a range of topics, including those that may be perceived as mundane!

Some of our students truly don't feel they are capable of talking about anything other than their topic of interest. In this lesson we help students learn they are capable of talking about a range of topics based on their experiences in the world.

It is always important to remind our students practicing social conversational skills, their underlying ability to relate to another person is far more powerful than the actual words spoken in the conversation.

Tools & Materials

• Paper or white board

How to use this lesson in the classroom:

1. On strips of paper, write out a number of "weird" or unfamiliar topics that we usually don't think to discuss. Suggested examples:

   a. Paper grocery bags   f. Doorbells

   b. Mold on trees   g. Cell phone rings

   c. Their sibling's area of interest   h. Full moons

   d. Bloody noses   i. Sleep

   e. Cafeteria food

2. Put the paper strips into an envelope.

◎ ′ ′

3. Remind your students when we talk to people we can talk about whatever comes up based on what we have experienced and learned about the world.

◎ ′ ′

4. Tell the students they are going to practice talking about topics that are a bit unusual.

◎ ′ ′

5. Ask a student to pull a strip of paper out of the envelope, read the topic and then have the student generate a comment about the topic. Encourage other students to add their own comments or to ask questions about the topic.

◎ ′ ′

6. Humor is usually born from this task. Encourage students to have fun with it. They are using their flexible brains to think of things to say. It is fine if students wander off the topic, through their own add-a-thought comments and onto another topic, as long as it is obvious how one thought is connected to another.

◎ ′ ′

7. Remind the students that hanging out and talking to other kids is often not about sharing really "smart" ideas or even things that someone knows a lot about. Conversing with other people mostly has to do with connecting to other people's thoughts and emotions and showing them you are interested in what they say. This shows you are relating to a person. This is how we use language to develop a friendship or relationship (e.g. "small talk"). It is a very different type of language than just telling people all you know about your area of interest. Most people do not like other people to act like they know everything. A person who is only willing to talk about topics that he or she is "smart" about, can be perceived as annoying by his peers.

8. After doing this prescribed topic list once, encourage the students to generate their own list of topics people often talk about but whose content is not considered "important" or "smart."

Lesson 54: Initiating Topics: Exploring Ways to Start a Conversation.

📋 **Critical Idea**

Remembering shared events
Seasonal topics
News events of interest
Specific enjoyable experiences you can share

How to use this lesson in the classroom:

1. Explore with your students that there are a number of different ways we "kick off" or get a conversation going. To follow are some ideas we discuss at the clinic – perhaps you can think of more?

   A. Remembering shared events: Once you have been with people and have shared experiences with them, you can talk about the experiences you both remember. By being part of the social thinking group, our students end up sharing a number of experiences and funny moments. However, these students rarely reference their prior shared experience when talking to each other. Neurotypical friends, though, often talk about things they have done together, or even events experienced separately but about which they both have knowledge (for example, both have been to Hawaii, but not at the same time).

   Below are some sample initiating comments about a shared experience:

   • "I remember that time when Michelle tripped over the rubber chicken!"

   • "Remember that time we all went bowling? That was fun!"

   • "I have been to Disneyland too. Did you ride on the new "Tower of Terror"?

B. Seasonal topics: These are topics that are generated by specific dates or commonly shared events on the calendar. For example, we talk to people about what they are going to do for summer, Fourth of July, Christmas, Hanukkah or Kwanzaa. We can also ask broader questions about common events linked to the calendar such as, "Are you going skiing during break?", "Is your family going on a vacation this summer?", or "Where are you applying to colleges?" While this sounds obvious, your students need practice in recognizing how frequently seasonal topics serve as conversation openers in small talk.

C. News events of interest: We share an emotional reaction to news events in our own local community – the weather or a garbage strike – or world news, such as September 11th, the tsunami, terrorism, etc.

D. Specific enjoyable personal experiences: This broad category that covers not only topics you like to study or are interested in about the world, but may also include a good book you have read, a movie you enjoyed or something interesting you observed or were just thinking about. For example, noticing how many people attended the local holiday festival, how quiet the freeways are in summer or discussing an interesting website are worthy subjects for kicking off discussions.

E. Things we forget about other people: We can inquire about things we have forgotten about others by saying something like, "What did you tell me you really like to do after school?" This type of question indicates you have spoken to this person before about topics like this but that you don't specifically remember the details. This is a better alternative than acting like you have never spoken to the person before or that you have no desire to talk to the person.

2. Make copies for your group of Appendix 7-9, the worksheet on "Topic Initiators When Hanging Out With Folks."

   A. Review these topic categories with the students.

   B. Have them brainstorm different topics they could initiate with the group and write them in the column on the right. You will have to remind them the first item, "remembering shared events," refers to things they remember they have done with the group or an event everyone shared separately but have all enjoyed together, like going to the newest Star Wars movie.

   C. Practice initiating different topics with the students.

   D. Have your students stand in a circle and give them one of the topic categories. Have the students quickly call out sub-topics connected to the general topic. One of the elements of practice is helping students quickly and efficiently think how their life and memories relate to others. In this lesson the students are just generating topic ideas; they are not working on sustaining a conversation about one of the ideas.

   E. Next, have the students initiate their own topics, allowing the group to practice sustaining the general topic by connecting it to their own ideas.

   F. Discuss how they can initiate unique topics with other groups outside of the therapy room (family members, other friends, Boy Scout meetings, etc.).

Lesson 55: Exploring Thoughts and Feelings of Others: Shared Experiences

Critical Vocabulary

Exploring other's emotions or personal experiences around a shared event

Many of our students do not talk about a commonly shared activity with others because they think they already know what the other person experienced. However, we want our students to learn even though we may have shared a common experience with another person, we never really know the other person's thoughts or feelings until we ask them. The critical lesson is we NEVER know how people really feel or think unless we talk to them about it. We should not presume to know this information.

For example: *Tammy went to Hawaii for the summer with her mom, therefore she did not think there was any point talking about the trip to Hawaii since they did it together. While in Hawaii they were caring for a friend's dog but the dog ran away. Tammy remembered it was really funny watching her mom chase the dog. Tammy did not think her mom had any other reaction to or memory of this event. Furthermore, since she had experienced this with her mom, there was NO need to talk about it.*

Only after Tammy was prompted to ask her mom about that experience did she find out this was actually a pretty stressful event for her mom. Her mom explained she was worried about whether the dog would return and what the friend would say if she had lost the dog.

Asking how people think or feel allows each person to further understand different people's points of view or perspectives. Work on this lesson often; there will be numerous "teachable moments." You can elaborate upon this lesson by having students practice asking each other questions about their thoughts or feelings in any situation shared with other students in the group.

Lesson 56: Exploring Thoughts and Feelings of Others: Unshared Experiences

Critical Vocabulary

Seeking other's emotions or personal feelings around an event NOT shared by the communicative partners

This lesson encourages our students to be curious about what people may think and feel when they do NOT know what the other person did.

Many of our students often think they know what another person might have done, thought or felt, rather than ask the person a question. Since they presume they know, they don't think they should have to find out for sure. Asking questions shows interest in the other person and also helps the student learn what the other person thinks and feel. This skill is essential in forming friendships with others.

For example, many of our students never ask what someone has done on a particular day, how they felt about what they did, or if they had an opinion about their experiences (e.g., how did you like going to China?). They get mad if their parents ask them what they did or how they felt about the day. Help your students understand why people are interested in each other. What sets this lesson apart from just asking questions of a person about that person is the underlying motivation for doing so: to more deeply learn about people's feelings and opinions about their activities.

Work on this lesson often during "teachable moments."

Lesson 57: Admitting You Don't Know: Being Willing to Talk About a Topic You Don't Know About

Critical Idea

It is OK to let people know you don't know about a topic!

Many of our students believe they should know everything. If they don't know much about a topic another person is talking about, they may get defensive and even refuse to engage in the discussion. Work with your students so they more fully understand:

1. No one can ever know everything. At times we have to work with students on the concept, "It is ok to not know!" or "You are not expected to know!"

2. People feel good when we ask them about things they know. We can teach students that asking these questions makes someone feel more important. Since most of us like to feel important, at times this is a worthy strategy in forging new friendships and maintaining existing ones.

If a student refuses to talk about a topic because he does not know enough about it, use humor and make this a "rubber chicken moment."

Lesson 58: Body Language as Part of Communication: Stand up and Move!

Critical Idea

Our bodies are central in the communicative process!

It is important for our students to realize that people communicate most frequently while standing, moving, or engaged in some activity. Most social communication does NOT occur when people are sitting around a table.

Make an effort to work with students away from the therapy table. Push the table to the corner of the room, if necessary, to encourage students to become aware of their physical stance, posture, use of body language, and thinking with their eyes while engaged in verbal interaction.

Students may resist standing, saying they are tired. Don't give in! Getting students to develop an awareness of their physical presence is critical when creating successful communication skills.

It is also important to note that on school campuses students often sit on the ground to talk to friends. Have the group practice communicating this way. Some students may sit, or stand, or do both during a conversation. Make it real life!

Most of the previous activities in this section can be practiced while standing or sitting on the floor.

How to use this lesson in the classroom:

1. As students become more efficient at asking questions, making supportive and add-a-thought comments without needing the index card topics as prompts, have them practice these same skills while standing up or sitting on the ground. Changing this one feature increases the complexity of the task, so be patient!

2. Practice joining and leaving conversations.

   A. As two students stand together talking, have a third student enter into the group. Teach students to enter the group quietly while "thinking with their eyes" to learn what other people are talking about and how they are feeling. Teach students, "Enter as a nobody to become a somebody" to convey the idea that they enter a group quietly and as an observer, so when they do start to talk they are connected to the topic and are aware of those around them.

3. Practice leaving the group without making a huge interruption.

   A. Exit a group by first making some nonverbal indication that you need to leave. This may be a subtle movement such as looking at your watch, asking someone else about the time, or looking out of the group.

   B. Between people's comments, make an exit comment such as "I have to go but I'll catch you later."

   C. Turn and walk out of the group.

   D. Avoid having students just turn and walk out of the group without acknowledging to others they are leaving. Sometimes they can just acknowledge nonverbally that they are leaving by pointing to their watch and giving a quick wave of "bye" (making it clear it is time to go).

4. Practice walking and talking. Walk around your building and encourage students to work on asking questions, making supportive comments and/or add-a-thought comments, while staying within the group.

5. Have students practice different body movements while standing in a group. Discuss that the way our bodies look sends nonverbal messages to our communication partners.

   A. Explore how people's bodies naturally move slightly and at times wander while standing. If someone adjusts their body and moves into another student's physical space, then that student is also expected to adjust his body to keep an appropriate distance between them.

   B. If someone stands in front of the student, the student should adjust and move to the side of this other participant without getting angry.

   C If any of your students have a very stiff physical stance, demonstrate how we shift our weight from hip to hip rather than stand completely rigid and straight-legged.

   D. If a student does not turn his head, but only moves his eyes to follow other people, use movement activities to help him practice relaxing his head and shoulders. If the person has a good sense of humor, let him know he does not want to look like a "talking head," but rather he should talk with his whole body. Practice stretching and moving all body parts prior to starting your group just to get students engaged in physical movement and a little looser and more relaxed.

   E. If a student usually lets his arms and hands hang at his sides while he talks, work with him on using gestures to indicate his interest in the conversation topic.

6. In groups of four or more, people often subtly break into smaller conversation units. Some students do not know how to adjust their body when in a large group to show they are part of one of these smaller units. Have students practice shifting their body to physically show where they are directing their attention. This is done through subtle movements of the hips, shoulders and head, and directed eye gaze. Let students practice shifting their body between two different conversations going on within a larger group that is hanging out together.

 To teacher and parent: each of these tasks seems basic to communication, but your students will often need years of practice to learn these techniques. Do not assume your student, who has difficulty connecting socially, does not need to be taught them because he is "too smart" or "too gifted with language."

Lesson 59: Clarifying Needs and Asking for Help.

Critical Idea

Asking for help and clarification

Questions to people are not just for social wonder; they also help us gain information we need to keep working calmly and efficiently with each other.

How to use this lesson in the classroom:

1. Explore with students why they need to ask for help.

   A. No person can know everything there is to know.

   B. Teachers and assistants help in school because they realize even really smart students cannot know how to do every task in every class.

   C. All people feel good when they can help another person. If you let someone help you then, in turn, you help that person have good thoughts about you.

   D. Sometimes we ask for help not because we don't know anything, but because we need to make sure we are thinking about it in the right way. For older students we can call this, "asking for clarification."

   E. Asking for help is something we do across our day and throughout life. It is not just something students do at school. Explore how students can ask for help at home as well.

   F. We ask for help not just to learn factual information but also to try and figure out what people are thinking. For example, we can ask "what did you mean by what you just said?"

Video Moments Self-Monitoring Checklist - Section 7

Our Language Makes Others Have Different Thoughts and Feelings

Student's Name _____ Date _____

We are learning to watch people's social behavior and figure out how these behaviors are making other people feel.

Every once in a while you are going to be a "behavior checker," meaning you will be checking on someone's behavior in the group.

Sometimes the person you are going to check on is you, other times it is someone else in the group.

The person you are going to check on today is _____

Behavior to check	Put a check here if the student is making others feel like he is doing a good job.	Put a check here if the student is having a hard time keeping track of how others are feeling about him or her during this behavior.
Asking a person questions about their experiences, feelings and thoughts.		
Answering questions with supporting comments and add-a-thoughts, without talking too much.		
Using follow up questions.		
Initiating thoughtful topics.		
Keeping their bodies and their eyes in the group.		
Asking for help or clarification.		

Based on what you checked, do you think this person would be a good person to work with on a project?

Circle: YES or NO

If not, what is one behavior the student could try and think about more to help people want to work with him?

Review for Teachers & Parents
🔊 Section 7

Our Language Makes Others Have Different Thoughts and Feelings

Teaching social communication skills and behaviors is quite complicated. We can introduce these lessons in the therapy room, resource room, special needs classroom, and even the regular classroom, but to have the student really learn to grasp how these skills impact him all day, every day, we need educational professionals and paraprofessionals, along with family members, to become acquainted with how to break down the information, teach and reinforce these skills on a regular basis as the need comes up in the environment.

We have developed a set of lessons for the student to become more efficient at social thinking and understanding the related social skills. We need all persons who work or live with the student to also become familiar with the social thinking concepts and to use them during "teachable moments."

Please review the vocabulary terms and concepts on the other side of this sheet and use them with the student as they apply.

If you have any questions on how to use these terms please contact your child's teacher, _____ at (phone number) _____.

Thanks for helping _____ learn to use these skills throughout his/her day, at home and school!

Remember the concepts we have introduced in previous sections:

Section 1: Doing what is "expected" in the group; doing what is "unexpected" in a group; "You can change my feelings"; observing others through imitation; big problem - little problem; three parts of play: set up, play and clean up.

Section 2: Whole body listening; think and thinking with our brains; thinking with your eyes; thinking about what other people think.

Section 3: Your body is in the group; your body is out of the group! Your brain is in the group; your brain is out of the group!; Just ME/ Thinking about You; good thoughts/weird thoughts; "I've got a secret"; video moment to watch what other people are doing.

Section 4: Figuring out other people's plans; smart guess/wacky guess; identifying one's own feelings; Social Behavior Mapping.

Section 5: Body language and spoken language (verbal and nonverbal); literal and figurative language; indirect language; figuring out meaning using four clues; figuring out people's intentions; flexible brain.

Section 6: Thinking about what others are thinking; synchronizing our movements; imagination; wonder, world wonder, social wonders; social curiosity; asking wonder questions; sharing in someone's wonder bubble.

VOCABULARY & CONCEPTS

Our Language Makes Others Have Different Thoughts and Feelings

Critical Vocabulary		Definitions
Whopping topic changes (WTC)		Comments made that people cannot follow and that interrupt the conversational flow. WTCs often confuse people or make people feel like you aren't interested in them.
Initial and follow-up questions		When we are asking people questions, it is best to listen to a person's response and then ask a follow-up question related to the same topic. This is how we move from small talk (rapid questions about different topics) to a deeper discussion about a topic area.
Supporting comments/ responses		These can be very simple responses such as "cool," "nice," or "bummer," or they can be nonverbal, such as showing body language and eye contact.
Bridging or baiting questions		These are questions aimed at getting others to talk about what the speaker wants to talk about. An example of a bridging question is, "Have any of you been to the mall lately?" if the speaker wants to talk about the mall. This is not a bad strategy as long as it is used sparingly.
Our bodies are part of communication		Teach students that keeping their bodies and brains in the group during active communication is crucial for good participation.
Clarifying needs and asking for help		Questions are not just for social wonder; they are also to help us gain information we need to keep us working calmly.
Initiating topics		Four general categories can be referenced to initiate topics with others by thinking about: 1) Shared experiences or memories, 2) Seasonal topics, 3) News events 4) General interests or thoughts.
Rude interruptions/ Acceptable interruptions		Not all interruptions are rude. Rude interruptions usually happen when someone cuts off your thoughts before you have really been able to state them, or they disregard your stated thoughts. Acceptable interruptions are those made before you finish stating all your ideas but your communicative partner has listened to your message and is highly motivated to add his or her thoughts on top of yours. Students have to determine the intention of the interruption before responding with anger or a reprimand to their communicative partner.

VOCABULARY & CONCEPTS *continued*
Our Language Makes Others Have Different Thoughts and Feelings

Critical Vocabulary	Definitions
How long is too long to talk?	Communicative partners need to keep a balance in the time they each talk. We teach that as a general rule, the first comment or response should be relatively short (10-15 seconds). If a person is interested in what you have to say, then the second response is welcome but also fairly short. If the person asks for even more information, the speaker is now welcome to provide a more elaborate, specific response as long as he or she continues to monitor the level of interest of the communicative partners.
Saying "nothing" gives people nothing to think about	Language allows us to share our thoughts, experiences and feelings with others. People pose questions to promote a communicative exchange. The person who responds to a question about his thoughts and feelings by saying "nothing" is effectively killing the conversation by giving the communicative partners nothing to think or talk about!

Goal Suggestions - Section 7
Our Language Makes Others Have Different Thoughts and Feelings

 __Based on curriculum activities in Section 7 and California Content Standards__

Goal #	Goal Suggestions
7-1	The student will talk about how he feels about himself and how he feels about his communicative partners when they pay attention to him by asking him questions or making comments (being good social thinkers), versus when they don't pay attention to him (being weak social thinkers), ____% of the time in the intervention setting.

7-1a   After a structured social interaction, _____ will describe how he/she feels about him/herself and the communicative partners when others pay attention to the student with their language (asking questions or offering comments – being good social thinkers) ____% of the time.

7-1b   After a structured social interaction, _____ will describe how he/she feels about him/herself and the communicative partners when others don't pay attention to the student with their language (**not** asking questions or offering comments – being weak social thinkers) ____% of the time.

7-2   The student will define and give examples of when others think the student is "friendly" versus "unfriendly," ____% in the intervention setting.

7-2a   When asked to contrast the concept of "friendly" versus "unfriendly", _____ will define these concepts and give ____(#) examples of why he applies those labels at times to his own and/or to other's behavior with ____% accuracy in the intervention setting.

7-3   The student will describe what it means to keep "people files" and will then recall information in his people files about other people and ask these people questions based on what he remembers about them, ____% of intervention session, and then using these concepts beyond the therapy room ____% of the time.

7-3a   The student will describe what it means to keep "people files" and will then recall information in his friend file about ____(# of) students with ____% accuracy in the intervention setting.

Goal #	Goal Suggestions
7-3b	The student will ask other people questions based on what he remembers about these people with ____% accuracy in the intervention session. *Take this skill beyond the intervention setting: There the student will recall information about people he meets across the home/school day and then ask questions of these people based on what he remembers ____(#) times per day.*
7-4	**The student will define the difference in conversational outcomes when a) using language to ask other people questions about themselves versus b) when asking people questions that encourage talk about the student's area of interest. The student will then monitor his use of the types of questions being asked of his conversational partners, ____% of intervention session and then use these concepts beyond the therapy room ____% of the time.**
7-4a	The student will define the difference between using language to ask other people questions about themselves versus asking them questions that encourage persons to only talk about the student's area of interest with ____% accuracy in the intervention setting.
7-4b	The student will then monitor his use of the different types of questions he is asking other people, ____% of intervention session. *Take this skill beyond the intervention setting: There the student will monitor the types of questions asked to conversational partners across the home and school day, decreasing his self-serving question asking to a small percentage of the total questions asked with ____% accuracy (student will provide self-report).*
7-5	**The student will define and describe the related emotional responses of communicative partners and use examples to describe how conversational partners react when the student uses these different concepts: questions to find out about others, add-a-thought comments, and whopping topic changes, with ____% accuracy during the intervention session, and then use these concepts beyond the therapy room ____% of the time.**
7-5a	The student will define and describe the related emotional responses of communicative partners when the student uses add-a-thoughts comments, with ____% accuracy during the intervention session.
7-5b	The student will define and describe the related emotional responses of communicative partners when the student uses whopping topic changes, with ____% accuracy during the intervention session. *Take this skill beyond the intervention setting: There the student will monitor when he uses questions to find out about others, add-a-thought comments and whopping topic changes to encourage others to have positive thoughts about the student during communicative exchanges, with ____% accuracy (student will provide self-report).*

Goal #	Goal Suggestions
7-6	The student will define two language-based behaviors he is willing to monitor and then will modify each in the presence of others to help the student be perceived as "more friendly" or a better social thinker, ____% of the intervention session and then using these concepts beyond the therapy room ____% of the time. *Take this skill beyond the intervention setting: There the student will define two language based behaviors he is willing to monitor and then will modify in the presence of others to help the student be perceived as "more friendly" or as a better social thinker, ____% of the time during the home/school day. (Student will provide self-report).*
7-7	The student will chart his own production of targeted language-based behaviors (list here _____ _____) ____% during the intervention session. *Take this skill beyond the intervention setting: The student will chart his or her own production of these language-based behaviors beyond the therapy room, ____# of times per day.*
7-8	Based on what others are saying, the student will use his imagination and ask social wonder questions of his communicative partner, ____% of intervention session and then use these concepts beyond the therapy room ____% of the time.

7-8a   The student will define the difference between social wonder questions and world wonder questions, and give examples to support their knowledge, with ___% accuracy.

7-8b   The student will ask who, what, when, where or why questions related to what they are imagining of another person's experience, ___# of times in the intervention setting.

7-8c   The student will use his/her imagination based on what others are saying and then ask further social wonder questions to the communicative partner; ___% of intervention session.

Take this skill beyond the intervention setting: There the student will ask social wonder questions based on what he imagines the experience of his communicative partners to be, ____# times per day during the home/school day. (Student will provide self-report).

Goal #	Goal Suggestions

7-9 After asking an initial question to people about other people, the student will ask follow-up questions pertaining to the topic, ____% of intervention session and then use these concepts beyond the therapy room ____% of the time.

📂

7-9a After asking an initial question to people about other people, the student will ask follow-up questions to maintain the topic, ____ (#) times during the intervention session.

Take this skill beyond the intervention setting: There the student will ask follow-up questions to maintain the topic shared by the communicative partners, ____ (#) times during the home/school day. (Student will provide self-report) .

7-10 The student will connect other people's experiences to his own by making add-a-thought comments, ____% of intervention session and then use these concepts beyond the therapy room ____% of the time.

📂

7-10a The student will connect other people's experiences to his own by making add-a-thought comments, ____% of intervention session.

Take this skill beyond the intervention setting: There the student will make add-a-thought comments to connect the student's experiences with those of the communicative partners, ____ (#) times during the home/school day. (Student will provide self-report).

7-11 The student will make supporting comments and/or use body language to demonstrate interest and understanding of other people's comments, ___% of intervention session and then using these concepts beyond the therapy room ____% of the time.

📂

7-11a The student will make supporting comments and/or use body language to demonstrate interest and understanding of other people's comments, ____% of intervention session.

Take this skill beyond the intervention setting: There the student will make supporting comments and/or use body language to demonstrate interest and understanding of other people's comments, ____% of the time across the home/school day. (Student will provide self-report).

Goal #	Goal Suggestions

7-12 The student will monitor the length of his talking time to offer shorter responses (up to _____ seconds) that provide more direct information about the topic rather than secondary details, _____% of the time during structured settings, and _____% in less structured setting.

7-12a The student will monitor the length of his talking time to provide shorter responses (up to _____ seconds) that provide more direct information about the topic rather than secondary details, _____% of the intervention session.

Take this skill beyond the intervention setting: There the student will monitor the length of his talking time to provide shorter responses (up to _____ seconds) that provide more direct information about the topic rather than secondary details, _____ (#) times per day across the home and school day. (Student will provide self-report).

7-13 The student will define and provide examples of whopping topic changes and then will monitor and then modify his own whopping topic changes during a communicative exchange, _____% of the time during the intervention session.

7-13a The student will define and provide examples of whopping topic changes and will monitor and then modify his own whopping topic changes during communicative exchanges, _____% of the time during the intervention session.

Take this skill beyond the intervention setting: There the student will monitor and then modify his own whopping topic changes during communicative exchanges, _____% of the time across the home/school day. (Student will provide self-report).

7-14 The student will define and provide examples of fair interruptions versus rude interruptions. The student will stay calm when others use fair interruptions and will monitor and modify his own use of interruptions, _____% of the time during structured settings, _____% in less structured setting.

7-14a The student will define and provide examples of fair interruptions versus rude interruptions, _____% of time during the intervention sessions.

7-14b The student will stay calm when others use fair interruptions, _____% of time during the intervention sessions.

Take this skill beyond the intervention setting: There the student will monitor and then modify his own reaction to other's fair interruptions _____% of the time across the home/school day. (Student will provide self-report).

Goal #	Goal Suggestions

7-15   The student, when faced with being one of two students starting to talk at the same time, will either immediately back down to let the other person talk, or will invite the other student to talk after he has finished his short message, ____% of the time during the intervention session.

      7-15a   The student, when faced with being one of two students starting to talk at the same time will notice the other person is talking and silence himself, ____% of the time during the intervention session.

      7-15b   The student, when faced with being one of two students starting to talk at the same time will either immediately back down, to let the other person talk, or will invite the other student to talk after he has completed his short message, ____% of the time during the intervention session.

              Take this skill beyond the intervention setting: There the student when faced with being one of two students starting to talk at the same time will either immediately back down to let the other person talk, or will invite the other student to talk after he has completed his short message, ____ (#) times across a home/school day. (Student will provide self-report).

7-16   The student will identify at least four different categories of topics often used to initiate conversational language, and then initiate a topic in each of these four categories, ____% of the time during structured settings, and ____% of the time in less structured setting.

      7-16a   The student will identify at least four different categories of topics often used to initiate conversational language during the intervention session, with ____% accuracy.

      7-16b   The student will initiate a topic in each of these four categories ____(#) times during an intervention session.

              Take this skill beyond the intervention setting: There the student will initiate a range of topics with conversational partners, ____(#) times across a home/school day. (Student will provide self-report).

7-17   The student will ask questions to find out what others think or feel about a discussed experience and then will share what he thinks or feels, ____% of the time during structured settings, and ____% of the time in less structured settings.

      7-17a   The student will ask questions to find out what others think or feel about a discussed experience, ____# of times during an intervention session.

Goal #	Goal Suggestions
7-17b	The student will share what he thinks or feels, ____(#) times during structured settings.
	Take this skill beyond the intervention setting: There the student will ask questions to find out what others think or feel about a discussed experience and then will share what he thinks or feels, ____(#) times across a home/school day. (Student will provide self-report).
7-18	The student will monitor and adjust his physical presence while engaging in a communicative exchange, ____% of intervention session, and then use these concepts beyond the therapy room ____% of the time.
7-18a	The student will monitor and adjust his physical presence while engaging in a communicative exchange, ____% of intervention session.
	Take this skill beyond the intervention setting: There the student will monitor and adjust his physical presence while engaging in a communicative exchange ____% of the time across a home/school day. (Student will provide self-report).
7-19	The student will define why people ask for help and provide examples. The student will then ask for help and/or clarification, ____% of intervention session and then use these concepts beyond the therapy room ____% of the time.
7-19a	The student will define why people ask for help and provide examples of times this is necessary with ____% accuracy in the intervention session.
7-19b	The student will then ask for help and/or clarification ____(#) times during intervention session.
	Take this skill beyond the intervention setting: There the student will ask for help and/or clarification ____(#) times across a home/school day. (Teacher report).
7-20	When reviewing videotaped footage of the social thinking group in which the student participates, the student will be able to identify the targeted conversational/communicative behaviors first in other students with ____% accuracy; and then in himself (focusing on identifying when "expected behaviors" happened), with ____% accuracy, during the intervention session.

California Content Standards - Section 7
Our Language Makes Others Have Different Thoughts and Feelings

Grade	Area of the curriculum	Essential Intervention California State Standard
K	Reading	Ask & answer questions about essential elements of text (fact questions)
1	Organization: Pragmatics	Stay on topic
1	Organization: Pragmatics	Use descriptive words
1	Reading	Respond to who, what, when, where, how questions
2	Organization: Pragmatics	Organize to maintain a clear focus
2	Reading	Ask clarifying questions about essential text elements of expositions (why, what if, how)
3	Listening and Speaking: Pragmatics	Respond with appropriate elaboration
4	Listening and Speaking: Pragmatics	Ask thoughtful questions with appropriate elaborations
4	Listening and Speaking: Pragmatics	Give precise directions/instructions
4	Writing	Write information reports, frame central question, include facts/details; multiple sources
5	Listening and Speaking: Pragmatics	Ask questions that seek information not previously discussed
6	Writing	Choose form of writing to best meet intended purpose
6	Writing	Create multi paragraph expository composition: engage reader with clear purpose, paint a visual image in the reader's mind, conclude with detailed summary linked to intro/purpose
6	Listening and Speaking: Pragmatics	Deliver narrative presentations: context, plot, sensory details; use narrative devices: dialogue, tension, suspense, humor. Also: 8
6	Listening and Speaking: Pragmatics	Deliver informative presentations/pose relevant questions, develop topic
6	Listening and Speaking: Pragmatics	Deliver oral presentations about literature (interpret, organize, develop). Also: 8
6	Listening and Speaking: Pragmatics	Deliver persuasive presentations. Also: 7, 8

Grade	Area of the curriculum	Essential Intervention California State Standard
6	Listening and Speaking: Pragmatics	Deliver presentations on problems/solutions
6	Writing	Write expository composition (describe, explain, compare, contrast...), state thesis, explain situation, follow organizational pattern, offer persuasive evidence and conclude as needed
6	Writing	Write persuasive compositions: clear purpose, support/organized, anticipate reader concerns or arguments. Also: 7, 8
7	Writing	Support all statements and claims with anecdotes, descriptions, facts
7	Writing	Strategies of note-taking, outlining and summarizing to impose structure on composition drafts
7	Listening and Speaking: Pragmatics	Narrative presentations: context, plot line, describe characters, setting. Also 9, 10
7	Listening and Speaking: Pragmatics	Oral summaries of articles/books
7	Listening and Speaking: Pragmatics	Research presentations: pose relevant and concise questions Also: 8
8	Writing	Create compositions that establish a controlling impression, have coherent thesis and make clear, well-stated conclusions
8	Writing	Support conclusions with analogies, paragraphs, quotes, opinions of authorities, etc.
8	Writing	Write responses to literature: careful interpretations/insight, connect student's own responses to writer's techniques, draw supported inferences, and support judgments.
9	Writing	Develop main ideas within body of composition through supporting evidence (scenarios, commonly held beliefs)
9	Writing	Write responses to literature in a comprehensive group of ideas, support ideas with detailed references, demonstrate stylistic devices used, identify impact of perceived ambiguities, nuances, etc.

People Files Interview Form

An interview demonstrates your interest in another person. When people see that you are interested in them they are more motivated to play or talk with you!

Interview another person in the group. Use the following questions to help you practice your interviewing skills. If you can think of extra questions to ask, that is a bonus!

Write their answers on the lines next to the questions:

1. What do you like to do? _____

2. What do you like to eat? _____

3. Where is one of your favorite places to go? _____

4. Who is in your family? _____

5. What is your favorite restaurant? _____

6. What books do you like to read? _____
Or TV shows to watch? _____

Once you complete the interview, pick out three answers that were the most interesting to you. This information DOES NOT have to fascinate you, but instead is just more interesting compared to the other things you learned about the person. These are the three things you are going to try and remember about the person.

You will put this information in your People File in your brain. The next time you see the person you try and remember this information so you can use it as a topic for conversation. For example, if you remember they like horses, the next time you see them you can ask if they have been able to ride a horse lately.

Appendix 7-2
Using WH- Words to Help Form Questions

Who?

What?

Where?

When?

Why?

How?

Do you.....?

For example:

What is your favorite..........?

Where do you like to ......?

Why do you like....?

Topics for Initiating Questions and Discussions

1.   Favorite teacher.

2.   Worst food you have had to eat.

3.   Best place to vacation.

4.   Things you like about Thanksgiving.

5.   Gifts you like to receive for Christmas.

6.   Worst teacher.

7.   People in your family.

8.   Things you like to shop for.

9.   What you like to do at a beach.

10. Dumb things your parents make you do.

11. Cool things your parents let you do.

12. Movies you like.

13. Things you like to build.

14. Sports you like.

15. Sports you don't like.

Feel free to add more topics to the list. You will use these cards often in the first year of working on these skills.

Appendix 7-4

Cut out each box and place one slip in front of the student each time he or she uses this skill correctly.

Asking questions to a person about that person.	Asking questions to a person about that person.
Asking questions to a person about that person.	Asking questions to a person about that person.
Asking questions to a person about that person.	Asking questions to a person about that person.
Asking questions to a person about that person.	Asking questions to a person about that person.
Asking questions to a person about that person.	Asking questions to a person about that person.
Asking questions to a person about that person.	Asking questions to a person about that person.
Asking questions to a person about that person.	Asking questions to a person about that person.
Asking questions to a person about that person.	Asking questions to a person about that person.
Asking questions to a person about that person.	Asking questions to a person about that person.
Asking questions to a person about that person.	Asking questions to a person about that person.

Appendix 7-5

Cut out each box and place one slip in front of the student each time he or she uses this skill correctly.

Supporting comment/response	**Supporting comment/response**
Supporting comment/response	**Supporting comment/response**
Supporting comment/response	**Supporting comment/response**
Supporting comment/response	**Supporting comment/response**
Supporting comment/response	**Supporting comment/response**
Supporting comment/response	**Supporting comment/response**
Supporting comment/response	**Supporting comment/response**
Supporting comment/response	**Supporting comment/response**
Supporting comment/response	**Supporting comment/response**
Supporting comment/response	**Supporting comment/response**

Cut out each box and give one to a student each time he or she uses this skill correctly.

Add A Thought

Add A Thought

Add A Thought

Add A Thought

Add A Thought

Add A Thought

Add A Thought

Add A Thought

Appendix 7-7

Cut out each box and give one to a student each time he or she uses this skill correctly.

Body and Eyes in the Group.	Body and Eyes in the Group.
Body and Eyes in the Group.	Body and Eyes in the Group.
Body and Eyes in the Group.	Body and Eyes in the Group.
Body and Eyes in the Group.	Body and Eyes in the Group.
Body and Eyes in the Group.	Body and Eyes in the Group.
Body and Eyes in the Group.	Body and Eyes in the Group.
Body and Eyes in the Group.	Body and Eyes in the Group.
Body and Eyes in the Group.	Body and Eyes in the Group.
Body and Eyes in the Group.	Body and Eyes in the Group.
Body and Eyes in the Group.	Body and Eyes in the Group.

Appendix 7-8

Cut out each box and give one to the student each time he or she uses this skill correctly.

Add-A-Thought	**Add-A-Thought**
Add-A-Thought	**Add-A-Thought**
Add-A-Thought	**Add-A-Thought**
Add-A-Thought	**Add-A-Thought**
Add-A-Thought	**Add-A-Thought**
Add-A-Thought	**Add-A-Thought**
Add-A-Thought	**Add-A-Thought**
Add-A-Thought	**Add-A-Thought**
Add-A-Thought	**Add-A-Thought**
Add-A-Thought	**Add-A-Thought**

Topic Initiators When Hanging Out With Folks

Memory shared with a specific person: • Can be about a person you worked with together. • An event at work. • Talking about someone you both know. • A place you have both been, even if you were not there together. • A story, TV show or movie you have both watched.**	**What memories can you share with others in the group?**
General seasonal topics: • Talking about plans for upcoming holidays. • Talking about plans for upcoming seasons (summer vacations, snow trips, etc.). • Elections.	**What topics can you think of related to something coming up on the calendar?**
News events of interest: • For example: 9/11; earthquakes; global warming, etc.	**What news events can you think of that were of interest to you?**
**Specific enjoyable experiences you can share: • Books you have read. • Places you have gone. • Things you saw in your day (a traffic accident, a funny photograph). • Something you heard someone say that struck you as intelligent, stupid, etc., or sharing a story of interest you heard. • Many other things.... ** *Part of the reason to go to movies, watch TV shows, etc. is to keep on top of what other people may also experience. This gives you more opportunities to relate to them.*	**What are things you have done, observed or like to think about that you can share with others?**
Other topics?	**What information can you provide?**

Bibliography and References - Section 7

Our Language Makes Others Have Different Thoughts and Feelings

Winner, M. (2007). *Thinking About YOU Thinking About ME, 2nd Ed.* Think Social Publishing, Inc.: San Jose, CA. www.socialthinking.com

Videos:

"Napoleon Dynamite" (2004). 20th Century Fox.

"My Dinner with Andre" (1981). Fox Lorber Home Video: A WinStar Company.

Section 8

There is Still So Much More to Teach!

Touching on the complexity of communication...

This curriculum guide provides a series of introductory lessons for students who are weak in developing intuitive social knowledge and skills. It is impossible to cover all good therapy ideas and resources within this curriculum; ultimately, even with this tool the teacher/parent is left to continue to define this most important path for their student. The art of successful and effective interpersonal communication cannot simply be laid out in a step-by-step curriculum. There are so many individual factors and variables which contribute to the development of a "good communicator."

Competent communicators attend to complex and ever-changing variables that constantly surround them. Section 8 highlights some other areas explored in our social thinking groups. However, in this section, the concepts are introduced briefly. I leave it up to you, educators and parents, to create your own pathways to teach these concepts. Materials are available that help to guide your study of these concepts – they are noted on the following pages.

The concepts reviewed below are often taught during "teachable moments." Such lessons should be tailored to the unique needs of each individual and the context/environment. Hopefully, Sections 1-7 model ways to break down concepts into concrete, teachable lessons, allowing you to continue to create new ideas for the therapy and classroom setting.

Enjoy your discovery of more social thinking pathways.

Critical Vocabulary & Concepts

- Hidden Rules (Hidden Curriculum)
- Rules change across our lives
- Opinions and belief systems
- Personal problem solving and the size of a problem
- Exploring student's thoughts and emotions about being a person with a social learning disability

- Anxiety, stress and mental health team members
- Improving organizational skills
- Recognizing the needs of our parents
- The four steps of communication
- The end is the beginning

Tools & Materials

Plan a time to walk around the campus to observe different settings—visit the library, media center, administrative office, etc.

Seek out other published materials on problem solving, anxiety management, time management, etc. See the bibliography for some further resources.

Further ideas to be explored over time and at relevant moments

Worksheets! for Teaching Social Thinking and Related Skills (2005, Winner, Think Social Publishing, Inc.), provides many more lessons that extend far beyond this published curriculum to assist the educator with developing further intervention strategies.

Lesson 60: Hidden Rules (also called the "Hidden Curriculum")

Critical Vocabulary

Hidden Rules (Hidden Curriculum)

We cannot simply send a child to school each day and expect that he will "be good today." Being good throughout the day is contingent on a variety of factors, many out of immediate control of the individual. Each environment has a set of "hidden rules" and children are expected to follow this hidden curriculum in order to navigate successfully across the day. Richard Lavoi first explored this concept in his lectures and videos related to persons with learning disabilities. (1994).

Examples of variables which may impact expectations of students:

• The plans of people who surround the student

• Time of day

• Who the student spends time with

• The expectations of the setting:
  Work time? Play time? Listening time?

• The behavioral expectations for the student in that particular context

The fact that a vast array of social rules exists, changing often, subtly and quickly within and across environments, is overwhelming for many of our students. This fact is also confusing for the adults who try to assist these students—they themselves may not realize the complexity of

the social information that has to be processed simultaneously throughout the day. To be perceived as "good," students need to process and comply with all of this information to "do what is expected."

Adults may not realize that social rules constantly change throughout the day. However, they notice when the student does not "transition well" or is not "appropriate" or "adaptable." These descriptions usually mean the student is having difficulty reading and understanding the ever-changing social rules. In addition, these students may not anticipate or be flexible enough in their social thinking to adapt while maintaining a calm demeanor or social engagement.

Think about the basic behavioral expectations of sitting at a desk in a classroom. Some of the "hidden" rules (the rules or expected behaviors not usually taught directly to children) that apply in the classroom are described below:

1. Students are expected to sit at their desks, listen attentively and raise their hands if they have questions throughout the school day and during formal class lectures.

2. Students can "hang out" with peers, while sitting in their desks, before the teacher officially starts to teach the class.

3. Students are expected to sit at their desks but they can call out their thoughts, questions, or responses during less formal instruction time throughout the day. However, most teachers do not clearly announce the less formal time in the class. Most students simply figure it out.

Across the school campus, in the community and at home there are many similar hidden rules that are prone to change based on the context or environment.

In her book *The Hidden Curriculum* (2004), Brenda Smith Myles, Ph.D. provides more details about the nature of this changing landscape.

She outlines some of the small, yet significant, hidden rules that we need to be aware of when preparing our students for the real world of complex information processing. Like any author who explores the myriad of details regarding social thinking, her purpose is to help develop the awareness of teachers and parents so they can readily identify and then explicitly teach the hidden curriculum in each child's environment.

A lesson on the hidden rules related to visiting the library follows. This lesson is also explored in a worksheet found in my book, *Worksheets! for Teaching Social Thinking and Related Skills* (2005).

How to use this lesson in the classroom:

1. Prepare for a visit to the school library or a large public bookstore. Before the visit, explore the concept of "hidden rules" with your students. Explain that most people are not told about these social expectations and subtle social rules.

2. Go to the school library and spend time as "detectives" figuring out some of the rules in this environment. Observe and identify how many different hidden rules can be found. Some examples of hidden rules in the library relate to:

   • Waiting in line for the librarian

   • Using the computer

   • Looking for books on the shelf

   • Socializing at the tables

   • Working at the table

   • Are there more?

3. Discuss with students that most behaviors considered "inappropriate" are those that do not adapt to the hidden rules. Lack of awareness of these rules can result in a student unknowingly violating these social codes of conduct. Social Behavior Mapping, discussed in an earlier section in this curriculum, provides more information about this.

4. Practice moving about the library and adjusting to the different sets of rules. As the hidden rules are uncovered, students then need to learn to adjust their behavior to accommodate this information (e.g. using a loud voice in the library when we first arrive but figuring out to use a quiet voice when we realize the hidden rule is to be quiet in libraries).

5. Begin to explore other environments and situations on campus, at home or in the community and identify how many different hidden rules each student must adjust to within these different contexts.

  Social Stories™, created by Carol Gray, *is a very important strategy to help students learn more about the "hidden curriculums" and "hidden expectations" in specific settings. These stories provide a relatively simple description of the salient variables in a context through three elements:*

1. The description of the setting

2. The perspective of others in the setting

3.The directive to help the student understand social expectations within that setting.

Every parent and educator should make it their homework to learn how to write social stories for students of all ages. Ms. Gray has written many books and articles about social stories. Research also proves their effectiveness. For up-to-date information on Ms. Gray's work in our field, visit her website: www.thegraycenter.org (The Gray Center for Social Learning and Understanding).

Lesson 61: Social Rules Change Across our Lifetime

Critical Idea

Rules change across our lives

Social rules are not static in nature. Social rules change as we mature and deal with a variety of people and a range of experiences. For example, we think it is cute (or acceptable) when a three-year-old points at strangers in an airport, but this same behavior would be considered very rude if exhibited by a 10-year old.

Because social rules and expectations are constantly evolving, teachers and parents have to be aware that ideas or rules we teach children at one age may dissolve or become inappropriate at an older age. Our more concrete-minded students may find it confusing and difficult to "unlearn" previous lessons that were once relevant.

Example 1: In kindergarten through approximately second grade, we teach students to apologize when they make a mistake or hurt someone by accident or even on purpose. ("Tell him you're sorry for pushing him.") However, this rule gradually changes – by middle school a whole different set of social expectations is in place for making an apology successfully. At this point, if you make a social mistake or hurt someone, your words of apology may mean very little. Now, the social rule dictates that you show you are truly sorry by adjusting your behavior around that person, being sincerely nice or at least polite to them. Conflict resolution in mid-

dle school is about working through a process after making mistakes. We have to teach our students that, as they get older, they cannot just say "I'm sorry" anymore. I explain the shift in social rules as people age by stating, "As you get older, some of the rules change."

Example 2: A fourth grade student fell on the floor laughing when someone said something funny. I said to him, "Do you know that the rules have changed and that fourth graders are not supposed to fall on the floor when things are funny?" I then asked him, in what grade might it be okay for kids to fall on the floor laughing when something is funny? He responded appropriately: "Probably in kindergarten, maybe first grade." I agreed and explained that people have "weird thoughts" when fourth graders use behavior that is only expected of much younger kids. Fourth graders are expected to remain standing (or seated), looking at the person who is funny, and laughing. Many times this is not even a really big laugh, but just a laugh to show you understand the humor. He was comfortable with this information. We then practiced establishing awareness and using social thinking skills more representative of fourth grade behavior.

Students require social thinking lessons that span their childhood and possibly, adulthood. In high school, we help students understand this dynamic process by letting them know they are now working on the "nuance and sophistication" of understanding social information.

Think about the thousands of social behavioral rules that change across students' school years. Discuss this concept often, that social rules change, with your students.

Some areas where rules change include:

• Organizational skills

• The way children play, interact and then "hang out" with their peers

• Their humor: what may be funny in kindergarten may no longer be as funny to the fifth grader

• How to get attention

• How to interact with the other gender or same gender

• How to participate in the classroom

• How to be helpful at home

• Working independently

Lesson 62: Opinions and Belief Systems

Critical Idea

Opinions, Beliefs

We often have to work with our students in the areas of acceptance and tolerance. Some students are not aware of the fact that many people have different opinions and belief systems. We need to explore the idea that people have values, likes and dislikes, priorities and thoughts that may be very different from their own. People have different preferences and opinions on virtually any and all subjects or issues (music, dress, food, studies, hobbies, weather, etc.).

Belief systems reflect core personal truths people hold, even if these beliefs are radically different from those of their neighbors or friends. Belief systems are fundamental to our being and may include our cultural, geographic, religious, sexual, political, and monetary beliefs. Differences in belief systems can be much more offensive to others than merely having differences in opinions. As people, we often develop strong prejudices about different aspects of people's belief systems. Not to be taken lightly, differences in belief systems can cause discomfort in relating to people who have very different beliefs. At the most intense end of the spectrum, different beliefs can be the cause for violence and war.

We need to address these issues with students, teaching them to not openly seek the beliefs of others, nor openly share their own beliefs with people they don't know very well. Just inquiring about someone's belief system, prior to developing a solid relationship, is generally thought to be inappropriate and a cause for embarrassment unless there is a valid reason for asking. It may be viewed as being rude or impolite. For example, a student might ask me, "What religion are you?" as soon as I meet them, leading me to question the motives or prejudice of my client. Ultimately this type of question makes others feel uneasy.

While most of us find that people's different opinions or beliefs can make the world more interesting, for many of our students this makes the world more stressful. It is one more factor to consider in the social world around us.

Teach students ways to discover and appropriately interact with others when they find out, or do not know, the different beliefs or opinions others might have. For example, it would be an "unexpected behavior" to ask people who are wearing unusual or "weird" clothes why they dress the way they do. However, it would be "expected" to notice someone's clothing and have a "weird thought" about it quietly in your head, not saying it out loud.

To be fair, this is a difficult lesson for all kids and adults to learn. Our sophistication in dealing with these types of social rules (also thought of as one way we demonstrate politeness) slowly emerges in elementary school and continues to evolve well into adulthood. We cannot expect any student, as he moves through elementary towards secondary school, to do this well. This is true for all students, even those without diagnostic labels!

However, students with social thinking challenges often stand out as being exceptional in their inability to deal with people's different ideas or opinions. Even in elementary school we may need to teach lessons on how to cope with and respond to people's differences.

Share with students that navigating around different people's opinions and beliefs can also be difficult for some adults. Yet to be successful we have to pay attention to who we are with and what we know about them, before we decide to share a joke or make a statement which may diminish their race, sexuality or beliefs. One complicated variable is that students often think that

jokes are funny, not offensive. The complexity of humor is a whole different topic! However, TV shows such as "South Park" and "The Simpsons" are based on challenging people's belief systems through humor.

It is also important to note that even lessons contained within a social thinking curriculum may challenge people's belief systems. One teenage student I worked with came from a family with very different and concrete belief systems than my own. After having taught a lesson on the reality that we all tell small "white lies" to protect the feelings of those around us (e.g. "oh, that dress looks nice on you," when you really don't think it does), the student's family decided this lesson was too far removed from their own beliefs (never lie), and they removed their student from the social thinking program.

Lesson 63: Personal Problem Solving and the size of the problem

Critical Vocabulary

Personal problem solving

The complexity of personal problem solving is discussed in my first book, *Inside Out: What Makes a Person with Social Cognitive Deficits Tick.*

Teaching our students strategies for becoming better personal problem solvers requires teaching them strategies for breaking down this complex task into segments, and then exploring numerous solutions. For example, in order to problem solve one has to:

- Identify the problem

- Explore why it became a problem

- Consider the problem from other people's perspectives

- Evaluate the good and bad choices that may solve the problem

- Decide which choice(s) to use based on desired consequences

- Initiate action plans to move towards problem solving, which may include talking to other people

It is also important for students to learn that problems and their related emotional-behavioral responses come in different sizes. If on a scale from 1-10 an earthquake or hurricane is a "10" and getting accidentally bumped by another person is a "1," then we can understand a student getting really upset and nervous due to an impending hurricane. However, if he gets equally upset by an accidental bump, then others become confused as to why he is so upset. Helping students learn that there are different levels of problems and related reactions is important. This lesson has proven invaluable not only to the kids on my caseload but to my adult clients as well!

Another key to problem solving is to become more aware and alert social thinkers, which is a primary focus of this curriculum.

New books related to problem solving continue to become available on the market. In my bibliography I note a number of books I use at my clinic to help teach this concept.

Lesson 64: Exploring Student's Emotions and Thoughts About Being a Person with a Social Thinking Learning Disability

As our students age, they develop greater awareness of their social differences. While one may appreciate that they are not as good at math as other students, this is only a problem in the math class. However, weaknesses in social thinking can be problematic in every environment in which a student shares space with other people. Increased anxiety, paranoia, stress and depression are common by-products.

Older students (middle school and older) benefit from learning more about their social thinking difficulties and often feel comfortable sharing their observations, emotions and experiences with other students with similar issues. However, I encourage our students to explore strategies they can learn to help themselves, rather than allow the students to just complain about the diagnostic label. One of our themes at our clinic is to help students realize they have too many other strengths to allow their "label" to be their excuse. In fact, we do relatively few discussions about the labels themselves (many of our social thinking groups are formed with kids having a number of different but overlapping diagnostic labels).

We have found the work of Dr. Mel Levine to be very helpful in teaching students about their own strengths and weaknesses. The bibliography provides some extra resources to help students explore these issues.

Lesson 65: Anxiety, Stress and Mental Health Team Members

Students who do not have easy access to the safety of a strong social group often develop anxiety, stress and/or depression. When this occurs, mental health providers (psychologists, psychiatrists, counselors) need to work with the student's parents, teachers, speech language pathologists, and occupational therapists as part of the intervention process. (No one profession can meet all the needs of our students; an interdisciplinary approach is best. With this treatment model we all share a similar intervention methodology, and then each professional adds his or her own expertise to the total intervention program.)

Stress and anxiety require concrete cognitive behavioral strategies to help students learn to navigate through them. Dr. Tony Attwood has recently published some workbooks to help students learn more about these challenges.

While stress and anxiety are very frustrating for the student to learn to cope with, these factors cannot be separated from the original social thinking/skill problems. If we treat the stress (or anxiety or depression) without providing intervention for the social issues that lead to these mental health issues, we treat the symptoms but never get to the core reasons for the stress.

Lesson 66: Executive Function Deficits:
Weak to Dysfunctional Organizational Skills

The majority of students with social cognitive deficits have significant problems with multi-tasking or creating functional organizational systems to manage their academic and personal lives. While ALL students hit stages of difficulty when developing organizational skills, students with social cognitive deficits have much more profound problems in this area and maturity alone does not provide remedy.

I now give full-day workshops on this topic (www.socialthinking.com). These provide further understanding of the 10 steps that help our students develop improved organizational skills so they can function more independently at school and at home. While the process of teaching students improved organizational skills is too broad a topic for this curriculum, it is important to acknowledge that helping a student develop these skills must be woven into the school and home day, just like teaching social thinking and related skills.

A DVD is now on the market that reviews these 10 steps. Titled "Strategies for Organization: Preparing for Homework in The Real World," it was produced by and is available from The Gray Center (www.thegraycenter.org), and is accompanied by a book of the same name.

Lesson 67: Helping Parents Cope With Their Children's Social Challenge: Running a Parent Education and Support Group

This curriculum has been designed to share with parents. Lesson 67 is a reminder that a social cognitive disability affects students 24 hours a day. Social functioning is needed whenever we share space with others.

Parents can easily become overwhelmed by their child's social learning needs. Social thinking and related skills have to be learned in virtually every environment and during daily activities, family holidays, and vacations. While educators choose to work with children on these skills (and receive training to do so), parents did not choose this role, nor did they receive any education on how to handle this deficit. Because parents are obviously more psychologically invested in their own children, they experience stress and anxiety as they watch their child encounter a wide range of social and educational problems resulting from this disability.

(Furthermore, some parents express that they are so genetically like their children that they cannot easily discern the crucial lessons to teach since they are not masters of these skills themselves.)

School programs rarely provide funding to educate and support parents. Instead, school personnel often expect parents to help educate and support the schools! Fortunately, professionals who volunteer to run "parent education and support groups" bridge this gap in ways that are beneficial to all. Their efforts toward "team-building" help all parents and professionals develop better support systems for each other, ultimately providing a better education for the child. You will find a worksheet on the basics of running a parent education and support group in my book, ***Worksheets! for Teaching Social Thinking and Related Skills***.

I would be remiss if I failed to note that our students' 24 hour-a-day social deficits can also negatively impact the most dedicated educator's stress level as well. No individual or IEP team is expected to have all the answers. As parents and professionals we have to support each other through the process of educating the child and other members of the intervention team.

Lesson 68: The Four Steps of Communication: The Complex Act of Communication

Learning the "art" of communication is an endlessly complicated skill. Teachers, parents and students need to continually keep in mind that communication does not begin and end solely through spoken language. Instead, social communication is grounded in a keen awareness of others: who we are talking to, how we physically approach them, the manner in which we maintain our connection, and how we choose our words to communicate carefully and succinctly. As we age, this process becomes even more complicated. Communication becomes more subtle, abstract and sophisticated.

I end this curriculum where I began in the Introduction, reviewing the Four Steps of Communication:

1. Thinking about the people in your communicative space.

2. Establishing a physical presence (body in the group, shoulders turned to the group, etc.).

3. Using our eyes to think about others.

4. Using language to establish and maintain our communication with others.

We should directly teach students, at least by middle school, the Four Steps of Communication. To be successful they must understand the importance of their bodies, eyes, and thoughts as part of the overall communicative process. These lessons are essential in helping students recognize and appreciate that communication encompasses far more than just talking.

Lesson 69: The End is Only the Beginning

Many students with social thinking challenges will continue to need instruction and guidance over many years, and throughout their lives for them to synchronize their thoughts and movement to maintain connections to others.

Remember to encourage students to observe others and provide opportunities for them to watch TV or videotapes to analyze the communication process. Can they identify what was successful or expected/appropriate? Which parts broke down and were unsuccessful or unexpected/inappropriate? Understanding and applying the Four Steps of Communication helps students organize the process of interpersonal communication. Having these skills may encourage them to develop their own social motivation, and to explore and improve upon their own social thinking and related skills.

The movie "Napoleon Dynamite" (2004) is excellent for use with teens to explore the subtleties of communication and the problems associated with making subtle, but persistent, errors. In process at our clinic is a new curriculum exploring the Four Steps of Communication via the nuances of the social triumphs and errors demonstrated in the film.

For our work with adults, we have used the movie, "My Dinner with Andre," which consists of a long dinner conversation between two adult men. Any movie with adult characters can be used to explore social thinking with adult clients.

To be a skilled and effective teacher of social thinking and related skills is to truly appreciate the complexity of communication. Failing to recognize the deep and multifaceted nature of social thinking may cause the intervention team to be unrealistic in goal setting, which may lead the team to work on skills a student is not yet ready to pursue. This can leave a team feeling frustrated by the student's limited learning, or increase the student's behavioral issues.

From a professional and educational standpoint, we are in our infancy in teaching complex communication skills. Hopefully, each of us will continue to explore and discover new ways to better equip our students with ideas and strategies that increase their social knowledge and behaviors during their lifetime. At our clinic, we have never "cured" a person of their social thinking challenges. Yet it is exciting to realize we have provided significant and important lessons for our students and their families to incorporate into their lives, helping them better understand, respond to, and empathize with the people around them. The social connections our students experience are real and tangible, and better their world.

Review for Teachers & Parents
🔊 Section 8

There is Still So Much More to Teach!

Teaching social communication skills and behaviors is quite complicated. We can introduce these lessons in the therapy room, resource room, special needs classroom, and even the regular classroom, but to have the student really learn to grasp how these skills impact him all day, every day, we need educational professionals and paraprofessionals, along with family members, to become acquainted with how to break down the information, teach and reinforce these skills on a regular basis as the need comes up in the environment.

We have developed a set of lessons for the student to become more efficient at social thinking and understanding the related social skills. We need all persons who work or live with the student to also become familiar with the social thinking concepts and to use them during "teachable moments."

Please review the vocabulary terms and concepts on the other side of this sheet and use them with the student as they apply.

If you have any questions on how to use these terms please contact your child's teacher, _____at (phone number) _____.

Thanks for helping _____ learn to use these skills throughout his/her day, at home and school!

Remember the concepts we have introduced in previous sections:

Section 1: Doing what is "expected" in the group; doing what is "unexpected" in a group; "You can change my feelings"; observing others through imitation; big problem - little problem; three parts of play: set up, play and clean up.

Section 2: Whole body listening; think and thinking with our brains; thinking with your eyes; thinking about what other people think.

Section 3: Your body is in the group; your body is out of the group! Your brain is in the group; your brain is out of the group!; Just ME/ Thinking about You; good thoughts/weird thoughts; "I've got a secret"; video moment to watch what other people are doing.

Section 4: Figuring out other people's plans; smart guess/wacky guess; identifying one's own feelings; Social Behavior Mapping.

Section 5: Body language and spoken language (verbal and nonverbal); literal and figurative language; indirect language; figuring out meaning using four clues; figuring out people's intentions; flexible brain.

Section 6: Thinking about what others are thinking; synchronizing our movements; imagination; wonder, world wonder, social wonders; social curiosity; asking wonder questions; sharing in someone's wonder bubble.

Section 7: Social thinking; friend files; world wonders and social wonders; add-a-thought; WTCs; bridging/baiting questions; conversation tree and conversation street; rude versus acceptable interruption; conversation stoppers; being willing to talk about what you don't know.

VOCABULARY & CONCEPTS

There is Still So Much More to Teach!

Critical Vocabulary		Definitions
The hidden curriculum or hidden rules		These are the untaught rules that exist within any environment and change within different environments (e.g. from structured teaching to group work). We need to be aware of these changes across contexts or environments and then explicitly teach these rules to the students.
Social rules change across our lives		Once a social rule has been taught to a child, it will most surely change as the child matures. The social rules we teach to a five-year-old are not the same rules that apply for 15-year-olds. By 15, children have to deal with much more nuance driven and sophisticated concepts. Teach students to be aware that the social rules change as they age.
Opinions and belief systems		Each of us has personal opinions and even stronger belief systems (e.g. religious, cultural, monetary, political, etc.). We need to teach our students to be aware of people's different values and belief systems. They must be taught to be careful with the questions they ask and not overtly announce their opinions and beliefs when establishing communication with others.
Problem solving		The student needs to learn a set of specific strategies for recognizing and addressing social problem solving. Seek more information about this from the student's social thinking teacher.
The Four Steps of Communication		The Four Steps of Communication speak to the multiple variables that create communication, and represent a hierarchy of actions of successful communication: 1. Thinking about the people in your communicative space. 2. Establishing a physical presence (body in the group, shoulders turned to the group, etc.). 3. Using your eyes to think about others. 4. Using language to relate to what other people are thinking.

Goal Suggestions - Section 8
There is Still So Much More to Teach!

Based on curriculum activities in Section 8 and the California Content Standards

<u>Goal #</u>	<u>Goal Suggestions</u>

8-1 The student will define what is meant by the hidden curriculum or hidden rules, and then define and follow the hidden rules for a specific context, ____% of intervention session and then use these concepts beyond the therapy room ____% of the time.

8-1a When asked, _____ will define "hidden curriculum" or "hidden rules," providing ____# examples with ____% accuracy within the intervention setting.

8-1b When given the hidden rule (e.g _____)
_____ will follow the rule with ___% accuracy within the intervention session.

Take this skill beyond the intervention setting: There the student is expected to follow the hidden rules (or seek clarification(s) needed to follow the rule) ____% of the time.

8-2 The student will be able to define how specific social rules change with age and provide related examples. The student will then produce the more sophisticated social behavior as defined for his present age, ____% of intervention session and then use these concepts beyond the therapy room ____% of the time.

8-2a When given a social scenario that involves various age-related options of "social rules," _____ will define the appropriate variation of the social rule for the student's age with ____% accuracy within the intervention setting.

8-2b After defining how a social rule is to be followed given the student's age, the student will produce the more sophisticated social behavior, ____% of intervention session.

Take this skill beyond the intervention setting: There the student is to use the more mature social behavior discussed in the above goal to correlate with the age appropriate version of the social rules, ____% of the time across the home and school day. (Parent, teacher and student report).

Goal #	Goal Suggestions

8-3   The student will describe the steps of problem solving. He will use the steps to solve his own personal problems, ____% of intervention session and then then use the steps beyond the therapy room ____% of the time.

    8-3a   When asked, _____ will describe the ___ steps of problem solving with ____% accuracy, in the intervention setting.

    8-3b   When in a social situation that requires a decision, _____ will use the steps to solve his own personal problems, with ____% accuracy within the intervention session.

Take this skill beyond the intervention setting: There the student is to use the strategies or steps of problem solving in the school and home environment with initial cues ____% of the time across the home and school day. (Parent, teacher and student report).

8-4   The student will define and apply a specific strategy to reduce stress/anxiety during the school/home day, ____% of intervention session and then use the strategy beyond the therapy room ____% of the time.

    8-4a   When faced with a stressful/frustrating situation in the social thinking group environment, _____ will reduce his stress/anxiety by utilizing (able to define and apply) a specific strategy with ____% accuracy within the intervention session.

Take this skill beyond the intervention setting: There the student is expected to utilize available stress reduction strategies within a situation with peers, teachers or at home with initial cues from educators, ____% of the time. (Parent, teacher & student report).

8-5   IT WILL BE IMPORTANT for educators to define and describe steps that help students develop better organizational and study skills. Write these goals out explicitly.

These issues are not covered in this curriculum, however the 10 Steps of Organizational Skills are reviewed in a videotape by Michelle Garcia Winner called "Strategies for Organization: Preparing for Homework and the Real World" (2005).

This 3.5 hour video workshop explores the process of getting organized for school and life. A set of handouts that further explain the concepts accompanies the video. (www.socialthinking.com)

Goal #	Goal Suggestions

8-6

The student will be able to describe the Four Steps of Communication and monitor his own use of these four steps after watching himself on the videotape.

8-6a After watching himself on the videotape, _____ will describe the Four Steps of Communication he observed in his interactions, with ____% accuracy within the intervention setting.

8-6b During a structured social interaction, _____ will monitor his use of the Four Steps of Communication, using a data collection system (e.g. chart) with ____ % accuracy, within the intervention session.

Take this skill beyond the intervention setting: There the student will monitor and modify his use of the Four Steps of Communication ____# times per day at home and school. (Parent, teacher and student report).

8-7

The student will be able to identify and describe which aspects of the Four Steps of Communication that he needs to consider and practice further. The student will monitor his use of these skills by reviewing videotape and then by monitoring himself during communication, ____% of intervention session and then use these concepts beyond the therapy room ____% of the time.

8-7a After a self assessment, _____ will identify with ____% accuracy which aspects of the Four Steps of Communication he needs to consider and practice further within the intervention setting.

8-7b After reviewing videotaped segments, _____ will monitor his use of selected focus skills (Four Steps of Communication) by rating what he observed on a data system (e.g. graph or chart), within the intervention session with ____ % accuracy.

8-7c While in a social interaction with familiar people, _____ will monitor his use of the Four Steps of Communication during communication, ____% of the time during the intervention session.

Take this skill beyond the intervention setting: There the student is expected to monitor and utilize the Four Steps of Communication while interacting with peers, teachers or family ____% of the time. (Parent, teacher and student report).

Goal #	Goal Suggestions

8-8

The student will be able to define the difference between fact and opinion and then allow others to state their opinion with the student supporting the right of the communicative partner to have an opinion different from his own, ____% of intervention session, and then do the same beyond the intervention room ____% of the time.

    📁

8-8a   When asked to utilize concepts within the social thinking context, _____ will define the difference between fact and opinion, citing at least ____(#) key points with ____% accuracy within the intervention setting.

8-8b   While in a social interaction with familiar people, _____ will allow others to state their opinion which may be different from his, ____% of intervention session.

Take this skill beyond the intervention setting: There the student is expected to accept the differing opinions of others (or at least allow others to state their opinions without argument) while listening or engaging in a discussion with peers, teachers or family ____% of the time.

8-9

A very tricky area, to say the least!

The student will be able to define the types of opinions that are considered part of our "belief systems" along with the hidden rules we follow to discourage overt discussions about less familiar communicative partners beliefs, ____% of intervention session, and then do the same beyond the therapy room ____% of the time.

    📁

8-9a   When given varied scenarios that illustrate the use of opinions, _____ will define the types of opinions that are considered part of our "belief systems" (as discussed within the context of the social thinking group) with ____% accuracy in the intervention setting.

8-9b   Being aware of the hidden rule(s) followed to discourage overt discussions about less familiar communicative partners' beliefs, _____ will refrain from stating comments that are possibly offensive to less familiar people or to people who the student knows share different belief systems, ____% of time within the intervention session.

Take this skill beyond the intervention setting: There the student will refrain from stating comments that are possibly offensive to less familiar people or to people who the student knows share different belief systems, ____% of time in a less structured setting. (Parent, teacher, student report).

California Content Standards - Section 8
There is Still So Much More to Teach!

Grade	Area of the curriculum	Essential Intervention California State Standard
2	Writing	Create graphic organizer or outline to practice prewriting skills
3	Writing	Create a single paragraph, develop topic sentence and simple supporting facts/details
4	Writing	Create multi-paragraph compositions: intro paragraph with topic sentence and supporting sentences, supporting paragraphs and conclusion paragraph
4	Listening and Speaking: Pragmatics	Ask thoughtful questions with appropriate elaborations
4	Listening and Speaking: Pragmatics	Give precise directions/instructions
4	Reading	Distinguish between cause and effect and between fact and opinion
5	Listening and Speaking: Pragmatics	Ask questions that seek information not previously discussed
6	Speaking Applications: Pragmatics	Determine the adequacy and appropriateness of the evidence.
7	Listening and Speaking: Pragmatics	Respond to persuasive messages with questions/challenges/affirmations
8	Oral Media Communication: Pragmatics	Evaluate the credibility of the speaker (Hidden agenda, are they biased?)

Bibliography and References - Section 8
There is Still So Much More to Teach!

Attwood, T. (2004). *Exploring Feelings: Cognitive Behaviour Therapy to Manage ANGER.* Future Horizons Inc.: Arlington, TX. www.fututurehorizons-autism.com

Attwood, T. (2004). *Exploring Feelings: Cognitive Behaviour Therapy to Manage ANXIETY.* Future Horizons Inc.: Arlington, TX. www.futurehorizons-autism.com

Bunnell, Steve (1988 and 1998). *Handling Relationships: 60 Problem Solving Activities.* J Weston Walch Publisher: Portland, ME.

Johnson, P. (1998). *Crash Course for Problem Solving: Strategizing, Prioritizing, Managing Emotions, Diagramming.* Linguisystems: East Moline, IL. www.linguisystems.com

Lavoie, Richard, (1994) *Last One Picked, First One Picked On* (video); PBS video; Alexandria, VA. www.ricklavoie.com

LoGiudice, C. and McConnell, N. (2004). *Room 28 Complete Kit* (formerly The Conflict Resolution Program: Activity Book). therapybookshop.com

LoGiudice, C., McConnell, N. and Warner, M. (2003). *NWhitso-Glamour® Social Language/Behavior Cards for Problem Solving.* Linguisystems: East Moline, IL. www.linguisystems.com

Mayo, P. and Gajewski, N. (1987) *Transfer Activities: Thinking Skill Vocabulary Development.* Thinking Publications: Eau Claire, WI. www.thinkingpublications.com

McGann, W. & Werven, G. (1999). *Social Communication Skills for Children: A workbook for principle centered communication.* Pro-ed, Inc. Austin, TX. www.proedinc.com

McGraw, Jay (2000). *Life Strategies for Teens.* Simon and Schuster: New York, NY.

Myles, B; Trautman, M.; & Schelvan, R. (2004). *The Hidden Curriculum: Practical Solutions for Understanding Unstated Rules in Social Situations.* Autism Asperger Publishing Co., Shawnee Mission, KS. www.asperger.net

Semrud-Clikeman, M. (2007). *Social Competence in Children.* Springer, Springer Science+Business Media; www.springer.com.

Winner, M. (2005). *Worksheets! for Teaching Social Thinking and Related Skills.* Think Social Publishing, Inc.: San Jose, CA. www.socialthinking.com.

Winner, M. (2005). *Strategies for Organization: Preparing for Homework in The Real World.* Companion DVD available. The Gray Center Publishers; Grand Rapids, MI. www.thegraycenter.org

Videos/DVDs:

Lavoie, Richard. (1994). "Last One Picked, First One Picked On" (video); PBS video; Alexandria, VA. www.ricklavoie.com

Winner, M. (2005). "Strategies for Organization: Preparing for Homework in The Real World." The Gray Center: Grand Rapids, MI. www.thegraycenter.org

Goal Suggestions

A Comprehensive List of Goal Suggestions from All Sections

Contents - Goal Suggestions

Goal Suggestions - Section 1
Being Part of a Group and Recognizing Expectations

 Based on curriculum activities in Section 1 and California Content Standards

Goal #	Goal Suggestions

1-1   Student will be able to use the terms "expected and unexpected" related to behaviors observed in his or her presence, and then describe his own behaviors as expected or unexpected, ____% of intervention session, and then using these concepts beyond the intervention room ____% of the time.

    1-1a   When in a small intervention group situation and provided a range of behaviors to critique, _____ will label observed behaviors of others as "expected or unexpected" ____% of intervention session.

        Take this skill beyond the intervention setting: There the student is expected to label observed "expected or unexpected" behavior in others, when asked by teachers or parents ____% of the time.

    1-1b   When in a small intervention group situation and provided a range of situations, _____ will describe his own behaviors as "expected or unexpected," ____% of intervention session.

        Take this skill beyond the intervention setting: There the student is expected to label his own behavior as "expected or unexpected," when asked by teachers or parents ____% of the time.

1-2   Student will be able to explain how expected and unexpected behaviors can impact how someone else feels, when observing others and then when describing how people are reacting to this student, ____% of intervention session, and then using these concepts beyond the intervention room ____% of the time.

    1-2a   When in a social situation and observing others, _____ will be able to explain how "expected and unexpected" behavior can impact how someone else feels, ____% of the intervention session.

        Take this skill beyond the intervention setting: There the student is expected to explain how "expected and unexpected" behaviors can change how someone else feels, when asked by teachers or parents ____% of the time.

    1-2b   When in a small group session and asked, _____ will describe how other group members are reacting to him during ____% of intervention session.

        Take this skill beyond the intervention setting: There the student is expected to describe how others are reacting to him, when asked by teachers or parents ____% of the time.

Goal #	Goal Suggestions

1-3   The student will predict how people will feel based on the possible presence of certain behaviors and then the child will modify his own behavior to help create specific positive/desired feelings in other people, ____% of intervention session, and then using these concepts beyond the intervention room ____% of the time.

📁

1-3a   When in a structured intervention group session, _____ will predict how people will feel based on the presence of certain behaviors, ____% of the intervention setting.

Take this skill beyond the intervention setting: There the student is expected to predict how others will feel based on the presence of certain behaviors, ____ % of the time.

1-3b   When in an intervention group situation, _____ will modify his own behavior to help create specific positive/desired feelings in other people, ____% of intervention session.

Take this skill beyond the intervention setting: There the student is expected to modify his/her behavior to create positive and desired feelings in others, ____ % of the time.

1-4   The student will observe other students and imitate discrete group play skills (group drumming, etc), with verbal or physical cues to maintain attention and synchronize movements and timing with the other members of the group, ____% of intervention session, and then using these concepts beyond the intervention room ____% of the time.

📁

1-4a   After observing other students' actions and being given verbal or physical cues to maintain attention, or to synchronize movements and timing with the other members, _____ will imitate specific group play skills (ie. group drumming, etc), ____% of intervention session.

Take this skill beyond the intervention setting: There the student is expected to appropriately imitate the specific actions of others when participating in a social game, ____% of the time.

Goal #	Goal Suggestions

1-5   When getting frustrated, the student will determine the size of the problem (big problem, little problem), describe their own and others emotional reactions to problems based on the size and then minimize their own emotional response to problems they acknowledge to be relatively small, ____% of intervention session, and then using these concepts beyond the intervention room ____% of the time.

1-5a   Given a situation that involves a "glitch" or problem that is frustrating to the student, _____ will accurately determine the size of the problem (big problem, little problem), ____% within the intervention setting.

Take this skill beyond the intervention setting: There the student is expected to determine the "appropriate" size of a frustrating situation ((big problem/little problem) when asked to evaluate the situation by his teachers or parents, ____ % of the time.

1-5b   When in a frustrating situation, _____ will describe <u>**his/her own**</u> <u>**emotional reactions**</u> to their own problems based on the perceived size of the problem, ____% of the time within the intervention setting.

1-5c   When in a frustrating situation, _____ will describe <u>**other people's**</u> <u>**emotional reactions**</u> to their own problems based on the perceived size of the problem, ____% of the time within the intervention setting.

Take this skill beyond the intervention setting: There the student is expected to describe the emotional reactions of himself or others based upon the size of the problem encountered, when asked by teachers or parents, ____ % of the time.

1-5d   When faced with a "small" problem or glitch, _____ will display a minimized emotional response to problems they acknowledge to be relatively small, ____% within an intervention session.

Take this skill beyond the intervention setting: There the student is expected to display a minimized emotional response to a "small" problem, ____ % of the time.

Goal #	Goal Suggestions
1-6	The student will be able to describe the three parts of play and then will regulate his or her own behavioral reactions during the "set up of play" to allow more time for all students to enjoy play, ____% of intervention session, and then use these concepts beyond the intervention room ____% of the time.

   📂

1-6a   After a structured play session, _____ will label or describe the three parts of play, ____% of the time within the intervention setting.

1-6b   During a play session or group activity, _____ will regulate his own behavioral reactions during the "set up of play" to allow more time for all students to enjoy play, ____% of intervention session.

Take this skill beyond the intervention setting: There the student is expected to regulate his behavior during the three different steps of play during group activities, _____% of the time, to allow for the most play time.

Goal Suggestions - Section 2
Our Whole Body and Mind Help Us Be Part of the Group

 Based on curriculum activities in Section 2 and the California Content Standards

Goal # | **Goal Suggestions**

2.1 The student will be able to identify how effectively others are using whole body listening and then be able to monitor and modify his or her own behavior with verbal cues to use whole body listening, ____% of intervention session, and then using these concepts beyond the intervention room ____% of the time.

2-1a While participating in a small group setting, _____ will describe how effectively others are using "whole body listening" ____% of the time within the intervention setting.

Take this skill beyond the intervention setting: There the student is expected to observe and describe how others use whole body listening when asked by a teacher or parents ____% of the time.

2-1b Given verbal cues to use whole body listening, _____ will monitor and modify his own behavior ____% of intervention session.

Take this skill beyond the intervention setting: There the student is expected to monitor and modify his whole body listening, when cued by teachers or parents ____% of the time.

2-2 The student will be able to predict what other people are looking at and thinking about based on where the student observes them to be looking, ____% of intervention session, and then using these concepts beyond the intervention room ____% of the time.

2-2a While observing the eye gaze and eye directions of others, _____ will determine and state what that person is looking at and maybe thinking about ____% of intervention session.

Take this skill beyond the intervention setting: There the student is expected to observe and predict what others are looking at and thinking ____% of the time.

Goal #	Goal Suggestions

2.3   The student will modify his or her own behavior based on what he sees others looking at/possibly thinking about (e.g. will think with his/her eyes to determine whose turn it is in a game, etc.), _____% of intervention session, and then using these concepts beyond the intervention room _____% of the time.

2-3a   When in a structured situation (e.g. a game which involves turn taking), _____ will modify his behavior based on what he sees others looking at/possibly thinking about _____% of the opportunities within the intervention session.

Take this skill beyond the intervention setting: There the student is expected to modify his behavior by watching for the eye gaze of others in a turn-taking activity with peers, teachers or parents _____% of the time.

Goal Suggestions - Section 3
Self-awareness and Self-monitoring Our Behavior in a Group

 Based on curriculum activities in Section 3 and the California Content standards

Goal #	Goal Suggestions

3-1
The student will monitor other students as well as his/her own ability to stay central in a group of students by monitoring if their brains and body are in the group or out of the group, ____% of intervention session, and then using these concepts beyond the intervention room ____% of the time.

3-1a
When in a structured small group activity, _____ will monitor other students' as well as his/her own ability to stay central by determining if their brains/body are "in the group" or "out of the group" ____% of intervention session.

Take this skill beyond the intervention setting: There the student is expected to monitor if his mind/body is in the group discussion ____% of the time.

3-2
The student will be able to define and use the concepts of being a "Just ME" versus a "Thinking of You" kid, when considering if other people think the student is working as a member of the group or not appearing to be part of the group ____% of intervention session, and then using these concepts beyond the intervention room ____% of the time.

3-2a
While in a small group interaction and asked to assess his behaviors, _____ will use the concepts of being a "Just ME" versus a "Thinking of You" kid, to evaluate how other people think he is working as a group member (vs. not appearing to be part of the group) ____% of intervention session.

Take this skill beyond the intervention setting: There the student is expected to use the terms "Just ME" or "Thinking of You" to describe his behavior when interacting with others, when asked by teachers or parents, ____% of the time.

3-3
The student will monitor and modify his or her own behavior to keep his body and brain in the group, allowing him/her to be considered a "Thinking of You" kid by other people, ____% of intervention session, and then using these concepts beyond the intervention room ____% of the time.

3-3a
While in a small group interaction, _____ will monitor and modify his own behavior to 'keep his body and brain in the group', allowing him to be considered a "Thinking of You" kid by other people, ____% of intervention session.

Take this skill beyond the intervention setting: There the student is expected to monitor and modify his body and brain to be considered a "Thinking of You" kid while in a small group interaction with peers, teachers or family members ____% of the time.

Goal #	Goal Suggestions

3-4

The student will be able to use the concepts "good thoughts, weird thoughts" to describe his/her thoughts about other people's behavior and then to regulate how people are thinking about his/her behavior, ____% of intervention session, and then using these concepts beyond the intervention room ____% of the time.

📂

3-4a
While in a structured small group activity, _____ will use the concepts "good thoughts, weird thoughts" to describe his thoughts about other people's behavior, ____% of the intervention session.

Take this skill beyond the intervention setting: There the student is expected to observe the behavior of others and determine his reactions using the concept of "good thoughts, weird thoughts" and share those thoughts when asked by others who want constructive feedback ____% of the time.

3-4b
When given feedback regarding his behavior (which may be generating "weird thoughts" from others), _____ will attempt to regulate his own behavior based on how people are thinking about him ____% of the intervention session.

Take this skill beyond the intervention setting: There the student is expected to modify his behavior so others have a more positive thought about him ____% of the time.

3-5

When reviewing videotaped footage of the social thinking group in which the student participates, the student will be able to identify the targeted behaviors first on other students and then on himself/herself, focusing on identifying when "expected behaviors" happened; ____% of the intervention session.

📂

3-5a
When reviewing videotaped footage of the social thinking group in which _____ participates, _____ will be able to identify at least two - three targeted behaviors in other students, focusing on identifying when "expected" behaviors happened, ____% of the intervention session.

3-5b
When reviewing video taped footage of the social thinking group in which _____ participates, _____ will be able to identify at least two - three targeted behaviors in himself, focusing on identifying when "expected" behaviors happened, ____% of the intervention session.

Goal Suggestions - Section 4
Starting the Detective Agency: Learning More About Observing Others

 Based on curriculum activities in Section 4 and the California Content Standards

Goal #	Goal Suggestions
4-1	The student will be able to reliably "read someone's plan" or report how someone is feeling based on observing their body language in the environmental context, ____% of intervention session, and then using these concepts beyond the intervention room ____% of the time.
4-1a	While in a small group activity and asked to assess the situation, _____ will be able to reliably "read someone's plan" and then report how someone is feeling based his observation of that person's body language (and using the environmental context) ____% of the intervention session.
	Take this skill beyond the intervention setting: There the student is expected to assess others' intents & plans of actions by observing their body language ____% of the time.

4-2	The student will be able to modify his or her own actions based on what he/she determines someone else is doing or going to do, ____% of intervention session and then using these concepts beyond the intervention room ____% of the time.
4-2a	When in a brief social interaction that involves movement, _____ will modify his own actions based on what he determines someone else is doing or going to do ____% of the intervention session.
	Take this skill beyond the intervention setting: There the student is expected to modify his actions in anticipation of what he thinks another peer, teacher or family member is doing ____% of the time.

4-3	The student will be able to distinguish between a smart guess and a wacky guess, and then be able to attempt to make a smart guess, ____% of intervention session and then using these concepts beyond the therapy room ____% of the time.
4-3a	After gathering information in the intervention room, followed by a request to make a guess, _____ will distinguish between a "smart guess" and a "wacky guess" ____% of the intervention session.
	Take this skill beyond the intervention setting: There the student is expected to assess whether his guess was a "smart guess" based on the information he or she was considering ____% of the time.

Goal #	Goal Suggestions
4-4	The student will define what it means to be a flexible thinker; he/she will then be willing to make choices, once they are presented to the student by the teacher, ____% of intervention session and then using these concepts beyond the therapy room ____% of the time.
4-4a	When asked, _____ will define what it means to be a flexible thinker and identify times during the social thinking groups when we use this skill ____% of the intervention session.
4-4b	When asked to make a choice, _____ will indicate his preference once they are presented to the student by the teacher ____% of intervention session.
	Take this skill beyond the intervention setting: There the student is expected to show his ability to be a "flexible thinker" by making a choice or considering options presented to him by peers, teachers or parents____% of the time.
4-5	The student will define what it means to be a flexible thinker and will then be willing to make self-generated choices, ___% of intervention session and then using these concepts beyond the therapy room ____% of the time.
4-5a	Using the concepts of being a "flexible thinker" _____ will make 2 -3 **self-generated** choices in a small group interaction ____% of intervention session.
	Take this skill beyond the intervention setting: There the student is expected to make self-generated choices that indicate his ability to be a "flexible thinker"____% of the time.
4-6	The student will use what he knows about the person or character's emotions and actions in specific contexts to predict what the person/character will do next, or to predict if his motives are just or questionable, ____% of intervention session and then using these concepts beyond the therapy room ____% of the time.
4-6a	Using what is known about the person/character's emotions and actions in specific contexts, _____ will predict what that person/character will do next, ____% of the intervention session.
	Take this skill beyond the intervention setting: There the student is expected to read a short passage and predict (make a smart guess) about what the character will do next with ____% accuracy.
4-6b	Using what is known about the person/character's emotions and actions in specific contexts, _____ will predict if their motives are just or questionable ____% of intervention session.
	Take this skill beyond the intervention setting: There the student is expected to read a short passage and predict if the characters motives are just or questionable with _____% accuracy.

Goal #	Goal Suggestions
4-7	The student will be able to note people's facial expressions, body language, tone of voice within specific contexts to determine how that person is feeling, ____% of intervention session and then using these concepts beyond the therapy room ____% of the time.
4-7a	After watching a brief video involving a social interaction, _____ will identify a selected person's facial expressions, body language, and tone of voice, within specific contexts, to determine how that person is feeling, ____% of intervention session.
4-7b	While in a social interaction with at least three people, _____ will identify a selected person's facial expression, body language and tone of voice, within specific contexts, to determine how that person is feeling, ____% of the intervention session.
	Take this skill beyond the intervention setting: There the student is expected to utilize the nonverbal and verbal cues of others to determine how persons may be feeling____% of the time.
4-8	The student will define what it means to be a "social detective" and then observe people in his/her therapy room, school or home to identify how they feel and what they need from others, ____% of intervention session and then using these concepts beyond the therapy room ____% of the time.
4-8a	When asked by the instructor, _____ will define what it means to be a "social detective" and providing ____(# of) examples about this concept taught within the social thinking sessions with ____% accuracy.
4-8b	After an observation of ____ (# of) people in his therapy room, school or home, _____ will identify how each person may feel, using at least ____ (# of) vocabulary words taught in the social thinking sessions, with ____% accuracy.
4-8c	Based on what _____ has observed and stated as the feelings of others, _____ will make a "smart" guess as to what that person(s) may need from others with ____% accuracy.
	Take this skill beyond the intervention setting: There the student is expected to use "social detective" skills to observe others and determine how they may be feeling and what they may need from others during a brief social interaction ____% of the time.
4-9	The student will explain how the four columns of a Social Behavior Map are related to each other, and then complete his or her own Social Behavior Map for a specific environmental context with ____% accuracy.
4-9a	Given a visual model of the Social Behavior Map, _____ will explain how the four columns of a Social Behavior Map are related to each other using at least two (or other #) concepts for each column with ____% accuracy.
4-9b	Given a visual model with a blank Social Behavior Map, _____ will complete his own SBM for a specific environmental context with ____% accuracy.

Goal #	Goal Suggestions

4-10 The student will monitor his/her own production of expected behaviors identified on the student's Social Behavior Map, ____% of intervention session and then using these concepts beyond the therapy room ____% of the time.

4-10a Using his/her completed Social Behavior Map, _____ will monitor his own production of "expected" behaviors ____% of intervention session.

Take this skill beyond the intervention setting: There the student is expected to use his personal Social Behavior Map to monitor his "expected" behavior within a selected classroom or interaction at home ____% of the time.

4-11 The student will target two expected behaviors on the Social Behavior Map, keep his/her own data on the production of these behaviors and then chart the occurrence of these behaviors in the appropriate context, ____% of intervention session and then using these concepts beyond the therapy room ____% of the time.

4-11a Using his/her completed Social Behavior Map, _____ will target two expected behaviors to use within the intervention session.

4-11b Once target behaviors are selected, _____ will keep his/her own data on the production of these behaviors by charting their occurrence in the appropriate context, ____% of intervention session.

Take this skill beyond the intervention setting: There the student is expected to focus on the two selected expected behaviors in another classroom environment, using his established data tracking system ____% of the time.

4-12 When reviewing videotaped footage of the social thinking group in which the student participates, the student will be able to identify the targeted behaviors first in other students and then in himself/herself, focusing on identifying when "expected behaviors" happened; ____% during the intervention session.

4-12a When reviewing videotaped footage of the social thinking group in which he participates, _____ will identify the targeted behaviors of _____ in other student(s), with ____% accuracy.

4-12b When reviewing videotaped footage of the social thinking group in which he participates, _____ will identify the targeted behaviors in himself, focusing on identifying when "expected behaviors" happen, with ____% accuracy.

Goal Suggestions - Section 5
Figuring Out What People Mean by What They Say

 Based on curriculum activities in Section 5 and the California Content Standards

Goal #	Goal Suggestions

5.1   The student will define how spoken language and body language help to convey a larger meaning and then use this knowledge to interpret meaning of spoken phrases ____% of intervention session and then using these concepts beyond the therapy room ____% of the time.

5-1a   When asked to define how spoken language and body language help to convey a larger communicative meaning, _____ will give at least _____ (# of) examples explored in the social thinking sessions, with _____% accuracy.

5-1b   Utilizing the concepts of understanding verbal and nonverbal language, _____ will accurately interpret meaning of spoken phrases within a brief social exchange _____% of the intervention session.

Take this skill beyond the intervention setting: There the student is expected to utilize the concepts of understanding verbal and nonverbal language, _____ will accurately interpret the meaning of spoken phrases within a selected classroom, during a ____ minute interaction ___% of the time.

5-2   The student will define and give examples of the difference between literal language and figurative language, then make "smart guesses" to determine language meaning in context, _____% of intervention session and then using these concepts beyond the therapy room ____% of the time.

5-2a   When given (# ___) words/phrases, _____ will state the difference between literal language and figurative language in each with _____% accuracy.

5-2b   Using the selected list of words/phrases _____ will make "smart guesses" to determine language meaning in each context; with _____% accuracy within the intervention session.

Take this skill beyond the intervention setting: There the student is expected to demonstrate an understanding of figurative language contained in an academic context with ____% accuracy.

Goal #	Goal Suggestions
5.3	The student will define the Four Clues we use to interpret language meaning and then make smart guesses to determine language meaning in context, ____% of intervention session and then using these concepts beyond the therapy room ____% of the time.
5-3a	When asked, _____ will define the Four Clues used to interpret language meaning with ____% accuracy.
5-3b	While in the social thinking session, _____ will make smart guesses to determine language meaning in context with ____% accuracy.
	Take this skill beyond the intervention setting: There the student is expected to make "smart guesses" when interpreting language meaning in a selected reading context with ____% accuracy.
5-4	The student will define and give examples of indirect language and how they interpret indirect language by determining people's motives; they will then interpret indirect language meaning in context, ____% of intervention session and then using these concepts beyond the intervention room ____% of the time.
5-4a	When asked, _____ will define and give at least ____# examples of indirect language and how they interpret indirect language by determining people's motives with ____% accuracy.
5-4b	When provided with a short passage to read, _____ will interpret the indirect language meaning in context with ____% accuracy within the intervention session.
	Take this skill beyond the intervention setting: There the student is expected to demonstrate his understanding of indirect language meaning within the context of a selected academic assignment with ____% accuracy.
5-5	The student will try to predict what people will say next based on their behavior (emotions, body language, previous spoken language) in a specific context, ____% of the time in the intervention session.
	Take this skill beyond the intervention setting: There the student will try to predict what people will say next, based upon their behavior (emotions, body language, previous spoken language) in a specific context with ____ % accuracy.
5-6	When reviewing videotaped footage of the social group thinking group in which the student participates, the student will be able to identify the targeted behaviors first in other students and then in himself/herself, focusing on identifying when people need to interpret language meaning, ____% of the time during the intervention session.

Goal Suggestions - Section 6
Adjusting Our Participation and Language Based on What Other People are Thinking, Imagining or Wondering

 Based on curriculum activities in Section 6 and the California Content Standards

Goal #	Goal Suggestions

6.1   The student will be able to monitor and adjust his/her physical presence, modifying their own behavior based on the activity of the entire group, ____% of intervention session and then using these concepts beyond the therapy room ____% of the time.

6-1a   While in a social thinking group activity, _____ will monitor/adjust his physical presence (e.g. move closer, move more slowly or faster) which will facilitate social exchanges, based on the activity of the group members ____% of intervention session.

Take this skill beyond the intervention setting: There the student is expected to adjust his physical presence in order to be a member of a social interaction with peers, teacher or family members ____% of the time.

6-2   The student will be able to read the meaning of another's index finger points as well as use an index finger point to alert others to look in specific directions, ____% of intervention session and then using these concepts beyond the therapy room ____% of the time.

6-2a   While observing others in a structured activity, _____ will follow the direction of another group member's pointing index finger to understand its meaning ____% of the time.

6-2b   When in a small group situation, _____ will use an index finger point to alert others to look in specific/desired directions as needed with ____% accuracy within the intervention session.

Take this skill beyond the intervention setting: There the student is expected to use and understand the meaning of an index finger point when interacting with peers, teachers or family members ____% of the time.

6.3   While in a sequenced imaginary play activity (e.g. making a pretend sandwich together), _____ will share an "imagination" as demonstrated by taking turns ____% of the time during the intervention session.

Goal #	Goal Suggestions
6.4	During a structured activity that involves synchronizing movements based on the shared imagination of the group, _____ will perform those actions to demonstrate his ability to share an imagination with other students ____% of the time during the intervention session.
6.5	During a structured imaginative play activity _____ will make _____ (#) of related comments or ask questions to demonstrate his sharing an imagination when playing with others, ____% of the time during the intervention session.
6.6	The student will demonstrate the ability to follow the lead of another child in a shared imagination activity by synchronizing movements, making related comments and playing cooperatively, ____% during the intervention session.

6.6a	In a shared imagination activity that involves synchronizing movements, _____ will demonstrate the ability to follow the lead of another child by imitating at least _____(#) of the observed movements with ____% accuracy.
6.6b	In a shared imagination activity that involves synchronizing movements, _____ will make ____ (#) of related comments to indicate his active participation in the structured activity with ____% accuracy.
6.6c	In a shared imagination activity that involves synchronizing movements, _____ will play cooperatively as indicated by such actions as _____ _____ (list observable behaviors) ____% of the time during the intervention session.

6-7	During an imaginative play activity, _____ will allow other students to take the lead during play (use a flexible brain), ____% during the intervention session.
6.8	The student will define the difference between world wonder and social wonder questions, asking his/her peers social wonder questions, ____% of intervention session and then using these concepts beyond the therapy room ____% of the time.

6-8a	When asked, _____ will define and give at least ____(#) examples of indirect language and how he interprets indirect language by determining people's motives with ____% accuracy.
6-8b	When provided with a short passage to read, _____ will interpret the indirect language meaning in context with ____% accuracy in the session.
	Take this skill beyond the intervention setting: There the student is expected to demonstrate his understanding of indirect language meaning within the context of a selected academic assignment with ____% of accuracy.

Goal #	Goal Suggestions
6.9	When given an imaginary "job" _____ will act out _____(#) specific tasks/roles using his imagination (based on a "smart guess" about the world) with ____% accuracy during the intervention session.

6.10	When reading or relating to peers, the student will be able to imagine a person's/character's feelings, motives, actions in a specific context based on his own smart guesses about the world, even when he has not shared this same experience, ____% of intervention session and then using these concepts beyond the therapy room ____% of the time.

6.10a After reading a short passage, _____ will describe a person's/character's feelings (motives or actions) in the specific context based on "smart guesses" about the world, even when he has not shared this same experience, with ____% accuracy.

6.10b When relating to his peers within the familiar group, _____ will describe a person's feelings (motives or actions) in a specific context based on "smart guesses" about the world, even if he has not shared this same experience, with ____% accuracy.

Take this skill beyond the intervention setting: There the student is expected to describe others' feelings (motive or actions) using a smart guess even if he has not has the similar experience ____% of the time.

6.11	When relating to peers, the student will share in another's wonder bubble and ask questions and make comments related directly to what they are imagining other's experiences to be; ____% of intervention session and then using these concepts beyond the therapy room ____% of the time.

6-11a When relating to peers, _____ will share in another's "wonder bubble" by asking ____(#) questions related directly to what he is imagining others' experiences to be with ____% accuracy within the intervention session.

Take this skill beyond the intervention setting: There the student is expected to ask questions using his perceptions of an unfamiliar experience of a peer, teacher or parent ____% of the time.

6.11b When relating to peers, _____ will share in another's "wonder bubble" by making ____(#) comments related directly to what he is imagining others' experiences to be with ____% accuracy within the intervention session.

Take this skill beyond the intervention setting: There the student is expected to make comments using his perceptions of an unfamiliar experience of a peer, teacher or parent ____% of the time.

6.12	When reviewing videotaped footage of the social group thinking group in which the student participates, the student will be able to identify examples of the student and others in the group using an imagination to synchronize movements, ask questions and make related comments, with ____ % accuracy.

Based on curriculum activities in Section 7 and California Content Standards

Goal #	Goal Suggestions

7-1   The student will talk about how he feels about himself and how he feels about his communicative partners when they pay attention to him by asking him questions or making comments (being good social thinkers), versus when they don't pay attention to him (being weak social thinkers), ____% of the time in the intervention setting.

7-1a   After a structured social interaction, _____ will describe how he/she feels about him/herself and the communicative partners when others pay attention to the student with their language (asking questions or offering comments – being good social thinkers) ____% of the time.

7-1b   After a structured social interaction, _____ will describe how he/she feels about him/herself and the communicative partners when others don't pay attention to the student with their language (**not** asking questions or offering comments – being weak social thinkers) ____% of the time.

7-2   The student will define and give examples of when others think the student is "friendly" versus "unfriendly," ____% in the intervention setting.

7-2a   When asked to contrast the concept of "friendly" versus "unfriendly", _____ will define these concepts and give ____(#) examples of why he applies those labels at times to his own and/or to other's behavior with ____% accuracy in the intervention setting.

7-3   The student will describe what it means to keep "people files" and will then recall information in his people files about other people and ask these people questions based on what he remembers about them, ____% of intervention session, and then using these concepts beyond the therapy room ____% of the time.

7-3a   The student will describe what it means to keep "people files" and will then recall information in his friend file about ____(# of) students with ____% accuracy in the intervention setting.

Goal #	Goal Suggestions
7-3b	The student will ask other people questions based on what he remembers about these people with ____% accuracy in the intervention session. *Take this skill beyond the intervention setting: There the student will recall information about people he meets across the home/school day and then ask questions of these people based on what he remembers ____(#) times per day.*
7-4	The student will define the difference in conversational outcomes when a) using language to ask other people questions about themselves versus b) when asking people questions that encourage talk about the student's area of interest. The student will then monitor his use of the types of questions being asked of his conversational partners, ____% of intervention session and then use these concepts beyond the therapy room ____% of the time.
7-4a	The student will define the difference between using language to ask other people questions about themselves versus asking them questions that encourage persons to only talk about the student's area of interest with ____% accuracy in the intervention setting.
7-4b	The student will then monitor his use of the different types of questions he is asking other people, ____% of intervention session. *Take this skill beyond the intervention setting: There the student will monitor the types of questions asked to conversational partners across the home and school day, decreasing his self-serving question asking to a small percentage of the total questions asked with ____% accuracy (student will provide self-report).*
7-5	The student will define and describe the related emotional responses of communicative partners and use examples to describe how conversational partners react when the student uses these different concepts: questions to find out about others, add-a-thought comments, and whopping topic changes, with ____% accuracy during the intervention session, and then use these concepts beyond the therapy room ____% of the time.
7-5a	The student will define and describe the related emotional responses of communicative partners when the student uses add-a-thoughts comments, with ____% accuracy during the intervention session.
7-5b	The student will define and describe the related emotional responses of communicative partners when the student uses whopping topic changes, with ____% accuracy during the intervention session. *Take this skill beyond the intervention setting: There the student will monitor when he uses questions to find out about others, add-a-thought comments and whopping topic changes to encourage others to have positive thoughts about the student during communicative exchanges, with ____% accuracy (student will provide self-report).*

Goal #	Goal Suggestions
7-6	The student will define two language-based behaviors he is willing to monitor and then will modify each in the presence of others to help the student be perceived as "more friendly" or a better social thinker, ____% of the intervention session and then using these concepts beyond the therapy room ____% of the time. *Take this skill beyond the intervention setting: There the student will define two language based behaviors he is willing to monitor and then will modify in the presence of others to help the student be perceived as "more friendly" or as a better social thinker, ____% of the time during the home/school day. (Student will provide self-report).*
7-7	The student will chart his own production of targeted language-based behaviors (list here _____ _____) ____% during the intervention session. *Take this skill beyond the intervention setting: The student will chart his or her own production of these language-based behaviors beyond the therapy room, ____# of times per day.*
7-8	Based on what others are saying, the student will use his imagination and ask social wonder questions of his communicative partner, ____% of intervention session and then use these concepts beyond the therapy room ____% of the time.

7-8a   The student will define the difference between social wonder questions and world wonder questions, and give examples to support their knowledge, with ___% accuracy.

7-8b   The student will ask who, what, when, where or why questions related to what they are imagining of another person's experience, ___# of times in the intervention setting.

7-8c   The student will use his/her imagination based on what others are saying and then ask further social wonder questions to the communicative partner; ___% of intervention session.

Take this skill beyond the intervention setting: There the student will ask social wonder questions based on what he imagines the experience of his communicative partners to be, ____# times per day during the home/school day. (Student will provide self-report).

Goal #	Goal Suggestions

7-9   After asking an initial question to people about other people, the student will ask follow-up questions pertaining to the topic, ____% of intervention session and then use these concepts beyond the therapy room ____% of the time.

📁

7-9a   After asking an initial question to people about other people, the student will ask follow-up questions to maintain the topic, ____ (#) times during the intervention session.

Take this skill beyond the intervention setting: There the student will ask follow-up questions to maintain the topic shared by the communicative partners, ____ (#) times during the home/school day. (Student will provide self-report) .

7-10   The student will connect other people's experiences to his own by making add-a-thought comments, ____% of intervention session and then use these concepts beyond the therapy room ____% of the time.

📁

7-10a   The student will connect other people's experiences to his own by making add-a-thought comments, ____% of intervention session.

Take this skill beyond the intervention setting: There the student will make add-a-thought comments to connect the student's experiences with those of the communicative partners, ____ (#) times during the home/school day. (Student will provide self-report).

7-11   The student will make supporting comments and/or use body language to demonstrate interest and understanding of other people's comments, ____% of intervention session and then using these concepts beyond the therapy room ____% of the time.

📁

7-11a   The student will make supporting comments and/or use body language to demonstrate interest and understanding of other people's comments, ____% of intervention session.

Take this skill beyond the intervention setting: There the student will make supporting comments and/or use body language to demonstrate interest and understanding of other people's comments, ____% of the time across the home/school day. (Student will provide self-report).

Goal #	Goal Suggestions

7-12   The student will monitor the length of his talking time to offer shorter responses (up to _____ seconds) that provide more direct information about the topic rather than secondary details, _____% of the time during structured settings, and _____% in less structured setting.

     7-12a   The student will monitor the length of his talking time to provide shorter responses (up to _____ seconds) that provide more direct information about the topic rather than secondary details, _____% of the intervention session.

           Take this skill beyond the intervention setting: There the student will monitor the length of his talking time to provide shorter responses (up to _____ seconds) that provide more direct information about the topic rather than secondary details, _____ (#) times per day across the home and school day. (Student will provide self-report).

7-13   The student will define and provide examples of whopping topic changes and then will monitor and then modify his own whopping topic changes during a communicative exchange, _____% of the time during the intervention session.

     7-13a   The student will define and provide examples of whopping topic changes and will monitor and then modify his own whopping topic changes during communicative exchanges, _____% of the time during the intervention session.

           Take this skill beyond the intervention setting: There the student will monitor and then modify his own whopping topic changes during communicative exchanges, _____% of the time across the home/school day. (Student will provide self-report).

7-14   The student will define and provide examples of fair interruptions versus rude interruptions. The student will stay calm when others use fair interruptions and will monitor and modify his own use of interruptions, _____% of the time during structured settings, _____% in less structured setting.

     7-14a   The student will define and provide examples of fair interruptions versus rude interruptions, _____% of time during the intervention sessions.

     7-14b   The student will stay calm when others use fair interruptions, _____% of time during the intervention sessions.

           Take this skill beyond the intervention setting: There the student will monitor and then modify his own reaction to other's fair interruptions _____% of the time across the home/school day. (Student will provide self-report).

Goal #	Goal Suggestions

7-15 The student, when faced with being one of two students starting to talk at the same time, will either immediately back down to let the other person talk, or will invite the other student to talk after he has finished his short message, ____% of the time during the intervention session.

📂

7-15a The student, when faced with being one of two students starting to talk at the same time will notice the other person is talking and silence himself, ____% of the time during the intervention session.

7-15b The student, when faced with being one of two students starting to talk at the same time will either immediately back down, to let the other person talk, or will invite the other student to talk after he has completed his short message, ____% of the time during the intervention session.

Take this skill beyond the intervention setting: There the student when faced with being one of two students starting to talk at the same time will either immediately back down to let the other person talk, or will invite the other student to talk after he has completed his short message, ____ (#) times across a home/school day. (Student will provide self-report).

7-16 The student will identify at least four different categories of topics often used to initiate conversational language, and then initiate a topic in each of these four categories, ____% of the time during structured settings, and ____% of the time in less structured setting.

📂

7-16a The student will identify at least four different categories of topics often used to initiate conversational language during the intervention session, with ____% accuracy.

7-16b The student will initiate a topic in each of these four categories ____(#) times during an intervention session.

Take this skill beyond the intervention setting: There the student will initiate a range of topics with conversational partners, ____(#) times across a home/school day. (Student will provide self-report).

7-17 The student will ask questions to find out what others think or feel about a discussed experience and then will share what he thinks or feels, ____% of the time during structured settings, and ____% of the time in less structured settings.

📂

7-17a The student will ask questions to find out what others think or feel about a discussed experience, ____# of times during an intervention session.

Goal #	Goal Suggestions

7-17b   The student will share what he thinks or feels, ____(#) times during structured settings.

Take this skill beyond the intervention setting: There the student will ask questions to find out what others think or feel about a discussed experience and then will share what he thinks or feels, ____(#) times across a home/school day.
(Student will provide self-report).

7-18   The student will monitor and adjust his physical presence while engaging in a communicative exchange, ____% of intervention session, and then use these concepts beyond the therapy room ____% of the time.

7-18a   The student will monitor and adjust his physical presence while engaging in a communicative exchange, ____% of intervention session.

Take this skill beyond the intervention setting: There the student will monitor and adjust his physical presence while engaging in a communicative exchange ____% of the time across a home/school day. (Student will provide self-report).

7-19   The student will define why people ask for help and provide examples. The student will then ask for help and/or clarification, ____% of intervention session and then use these concepts beyond the therapy room ____% of the time.

7-19a   The student will define why people ask for help and provide examples of times this is necessary with ____% accuracy in the intervention session.

7-19b   The student will then ask for help and/or clarification ____(#) times during intervention session.

Take this skill beyond the intervention setting: There the student will ask for help and/or clarification ____(#) times across a home/school day. (Teacher report).

7-20   When reviewing videotaped footage of the social thinking group in which the student participates, the student will be able to identify the targeted conversational/communicative behaviors first in other students with ____% accuracy; and then in himself (focusing on identifying when "expected behaviors" happened), with ____% accuracy, during the intervention session.

Goal Suggestions - Section 8
There is Still So Much More to Teach!

 Based on curriculum activities in Section 8 and the California Content Standards

Goal #	Goal Suggestions

8-1 The student will define what is meant by the hidden curriculum or hidden rules, and then define and follow the hidden rules for a specific context, _____% of intervention session and then use these concepts beyond the therapy room _____% of the time.

8-1a When asked, _____ will define "hidden curriculum" or "hidden rules," providing _____# examples with _____% accuracy within the intervention setting.

8-1b When given the hidden rule (e.g _____) _____ will follow the rule with _____% accuracy within the intervention session.

Take this skill beyond the intervention setting: There the student is expected to follow the hidden rules (or seek clarification(s) needed to follow the rule) _____% of the time.

8-2 The student will be able to define how specific social rules change with age and provide related examples. The student will then produce the more sophisticated social behavior as defined for his present age, _____% of intervention session and then use these concepts beyond the therapy room _____% of the time.

8-2a When given a social scenario that involves various age-related options of "social rules," _____ will define the appropriate variation of the social rule for the student's age with _____% accuracy within the intervention setting.

8-2b After defining how a social rule is to be followed given the student's age, the student will produce the more sophisticated social behavior, _____% of intervention session.

Take this skill beyond the intervention setting: There the student is to use the more mature social behavior discussed in the above goal to correlate with the age appropriate version of the social rules, _____% of the time across the home and school day. (Parent, teacher and student report).

   Goal Suggestions

Goal #	Goal Suggestions

8-3 The student will describe the steps of problem solving. He will use the steps to solve his own personal problems, ____% of intervention session and then then use the steps beyond the therapy room ____% of the time.

8-3a   When asked, _____ will describe the ___ steps of problem solving with ____% accuracy, in the intervention setting.

8-3b   When in a social situation that requires a decision, _____ will use the steps to solve his own personal problems, with ____% accuracy within the intervention session.

Take this skill beyond the intervention setting: There the student is to use the strategies or steps of problem solving in the school and home environment with initial cues ____% of the time across the home and school day. (Parent, teacher and student report).

8-4 The student will define and apply a specific strategy to reduce stress/anxiety during the school/home day, ____% of intervention session and then use the strategy beyond the therapy room ____% of the time.

8-4a   When faced with a stressful/frustrating situation in the social thinking group environment, _____ will reduce his stress/anxiety by utilizing (able to define and apply) a specific strategy with ____% accuracy within the intervention session.

Take this skill beyond the intervention setting: There the student is expected to utilize available stress reduction strategies within a situation with peers, teachers or at home with initial cues from educators, ____% of the time. (Parent, teacher & student report).

8-5 IT WILL BE IMPORTANT for educators to define and describe steps that help students develop better organizational and study skills. Write these goals out explicitly.

These issues are not covered in this curriculum, however the 10 Steps of Organizational Skills are reviewed in a videotape by Michelle Garcia Winner called "Strategies for Organization: Preparing for Homework and the Real World" (2005).

This 3.5 hour video workshop explores the process of getting organized for school and life. A set of handouts that further explain the concepts accompanies the video. (www.socialthinking.com)

Goal #	Goal Suggestions

8-6

The student will be able to describe the Four Steps of Communication and monitor his own use of these four steps after watching himself on the videotape.

8-6a   After watching himself on the videotape, _____ will describe the Four Steps of Communication he observed in his interactions, with ____% accuracy within the intervention setting.

8-6b   During a structured social interaction, _____ will monitor his use of the Four Steps of Communication, using a data collection system (e.g. chart) with ____ % accuracy, within the intervention session.

Take this skill beyond the intervention setting: There the student will monitor and modify his use of the Four Steps of Communication ____# times per day at home and school. (Parent, teacher and student report).

8-7

The student will be able to identify and describe which aspects of the Four Steps of Communication that he needs to consider and practice further. The student will monitor his use of these skills by reviewing videotape and then by monitoring himself during communication, ____% of intervention session and then use these concepts beyond the therapy room ____% of the time.

8-7a   After a self assessment, _____ will identify with ____% accuracy which aspects of the Four Steps of Communication he needs to consider and practice further within the intervention setting.

8-7b   After reviewing videotaped segments, _____ will monitor his use of selected focus skills (Four Steps of Communication) by rating what he observed on a data system (e.g. graph or chart), within the intervention session with ____ % accuracy.

8-7c   While in a social interaction with familiar people, _____ will monitor his use of the Four Steps of Communication during communication, ____% of the time during the intervention session.

Take this skill beyond the intervention setting: There the student is expected to monitor and utilize the Four Steps of Communication while interacting with peers, teachers or family ____% of the time. (Parent, teacher and student report).

Goal #	Goal Suggestions

8-8

The student will be able to define the difference between fact and opinion and then allow others to state their opinion with the student supporting the right of the communicative partner to have an opinion different from his own, ____% of intervention session, and then do the same beyond the intervention room ____% of the time.

8-8a   When asked to utilize concepts within the social thinking context, _____ will define the difference between fact and opinion, citing at least ____(#) key points with ____% accuracy within the intervention setting.

8-8b   While in a social interaction with familiar people, _____ will allow others to state their opinion which may be different from his, ____% of intervention session.

Take this skill beyond the intervention setting: There the student is expected to accept the differing opinions of others (or at least allow others to state their opinions without argument) while listening or engaging in a discussion with peers, teachers or family ____% of the time.

8-9

A very tricky area, to say the least!

The student will be able to define the types of opinions that are considered part of our "belief systems" along with the hidden rules we follow to discourage overt discussions about less familiar communicative partners beliefs, ____% of intervention session, and then do the same beyond the therapy room ____% of the time.

8-9a   When given varied scenarios that illustrate the use of opinions, _____ will define the types of opinions that are considered part of our "belief systems" (as discussed within the context of the social thinking group) with ____% accuracy in the intervention setting.

8-9b   Being aware of the hidden rule(s) followed to discourage overt discussions about less familiar communicative partners' beliefs, _____ will refrain from stating comments that are possibly offensive to less familiar people or to people who the student knows share different belief systems, ____% of time within the intervention session.

Take this skill beyond the intervention setting: There the student will refrain from stating comments that are possibly offensive to less familiar people or to people who the student knows share different belief systems, ____% of time in a less structured setting. (Parent, teacher, student report).

Bibliography and References

Agassi, M. (2000). *Hands Are Not For Hitting.* Free Spirit Publishing Inc.: Minneapolis, MN.

Allard, H. & Marshall, J. (1977). *Miss Nelson is Missing!* Houghton-Mifflin Company: New York, NY.

Attwood, Tony (1998). *Asperger Syndrome: A Guide for Parents and Professionals.* Jessica Kingsley Publishers: London and Philadelphia, PA.

Attwood, T. (2003). "Cognitive Behavior Therapy (CBT)." In L.H. Willey (Ed.) *Asperger Syndrome in Adolescence: Living with the Ups and Downs and Things in Between.* Jessica Kingsley Publishers: London and Philadelphia, PA.

Attwood, T. (2004). *Exploring Feelings: Cognitive Behaviour Therapy to Manage ANGER.* Future Horizons Inc.: Arlington, TX. www.fututurehorizons-autism.com

Attwood, T. (2004). *Exploring Feelings: Cognitive Behaviour Therapy to Manage ANXIETY.* Future Horizons Inc.: Arlington, TX. www.futurehorizons-autism.com

Attwood, T. (2006). *The Complete Guide to Asperger Syndrome.* Jessica Kingsley Publishers: London and Philadelphia, PA.

Berry, Joy Wilt (2000). Book Series: *Let's Talk About Feeling Frustrated; Let's Talk About Feeling Disappointed; Let's Talk About Feeling Embarrassed; Let's Talk About Feeling Inferior; Let's Talk About Feeling Cheated; Let's Talk About Feeling Jealous; Let's Talk About Feeling Rejected;* Gold Star Publishing: Scottsdale, AZ.

Baron-Cohen, S. (1995). *Mindblindness: An Essay on Autism and Theory of Mind.* The MIT Press: MA

Baron-Cohen, S.; Tager-Flusberg, H.; Cohen, D.; Eds. (2000). *Understanding Other Minds: Perspectives from Developmental Cognitive Neuroscience.* Oxford University Press, Great Britain.

Briggs, R. (1978). *The Snowman.* Random House, Inc.: New York, NY.

Brown, L. and Brown, M. (1998). *How To Be A Friend: A Guide to Making Friends and Keeping Them.* Little, Brown and Company: Boston, MA.

Bunnell, Steve (1988 and 1998). *Handling Relationships: 60 Problem Solving Activities.* J Weston Walch Publisher: Portland, ME.

Cardon, T. (2004). *Let's Talk: Emotions.* Autism Asperger Publishing Company: Shawnee Mission, KS. www.asperger.net

Crooke, P.J., Hendrix, R.E., Rachman, J.Y., (2007). "Brief Report: Measuring the Effectiveness of Teaching Social Thinking to Children with Asperger Syndrome (AS) and High Functioning Autism (HFA)." *Journal of Autism and Developmental Disorders,* Online Publication: DOI 10.1007/s10803-007-0466-1

Curtis, Jamie Lee (1998). *Today I Feel Silly & Other MOODS That Make My Day.* Scholastic: New York, NY.

Day, A. (1990s). Book series: *Carl Goes Shopping, Carl's Afternoon in the Park; Carl's Christmas.* Farrar Straus Giroux: New York, NY.

Dobson, K. & Dozois, D. (2001). "Historical and philosophical bases of the cognitive-behavioral therapies." In K. Dobson, *Handbook of Cognitive Behavioral Therapies.* The Guilford Press: New York, NY.

Duke, M.; Nowicki, S.; Martin, E. (1996). *Teaching Your Child the Language of Social Success.* Peachtree Publishers: Atlanta, GA.

Duke, M.; Nowicki, S.; Martin, E. (2002). *Will I Ever Fit In?* The Free Press: New York, NY.

Dunn Buron, K. & Curtis, M. (2004). *Incredible 5-Point Scale: Assisting Students with Autism Spectrum Disorders in Understanding Social Interactions and Controlling Their Emotional Responses.* Autism Asperger Publishing Company: Shawnee Mission, KS. www.asperger.net

Emberley, E. & Miranda, A. (1997). *Glad Monster, Sad Monster.* Little, Brown and Company: Boston, MA.

Everly, N. (2005). *Can You Tell How Someone Feels.* Linguisystems: East Moline, IL. www.linguisystems.com

Everly, N. (2005) *Can You Think With Your Eyes?* Linguisystems Inc.: East Moline, IL. www.linguisystems.com

Feldman, David (1989). *Who Put the Butter in Butterfly...and Other Fearless Investigations Into our Illogical Language.* Harper & Row Publishers: New York, NY.

Felix, M. (1983). *The Further Adventures of the Little Mouse Trapped in the Book.* Green Tiger Press: La Jolla, CA.

Gray, C. (1994). *Comic Strip Conversations.* Future Horizons: Arlington, TX. www.futurehorizons-autism.com

Idioms Fun Deck, Super Duper publications. Greenville, SC. www.superduperinc.com

Johnson, P. (1998). *Crash Course for Problem Solving: Strategizing, Prioritizing, Managing Emotions, Diagramming.* Linguisystems: East Moline, IL. www.linguisystems.com

Koenig, T. & Meyer, B. (1999). *Caring Kids: Social Skills & Character Education Lessons for Grades 1-3.* Thinking Publications: Eau Claire, WI. www.thinkingpublications.com

Lavoie, Richard, (1994) *Last One Picked, First One Picked On* (video); PBS video; Alexandria, VA. www.ricklavoie.com

Leaf, M. (1939). *Fair Play.* Frederick A. Stokes Company: New York.

Levine, M. & Clutch, J. (2001). *Jarvis Clutch: Social Spy,* Educators Publishing Service, Inc.: Cambridge, MA.

LoGiudice, C. and McConnell, N. (2004). *Room 28 Complete Kit* (formerly The Conflict Resolution Program: Activity Book). therapybookshop.com

LoGiudice, C., McConnell, N. and Warner, M. (2003). *NWhitso-Glamour® Social Language/Behavior Cards for Problem Solving.* Linguisystems: East Moline, IL. www.linguisystems.com

Madison, L. (2002). *The Feelings Book: The Care and Keeping of Your Emotions.* American Girl Library. Pleasant Company Publications: Middleton, WI. www.americangirl.com

Mayo, P. and Gajewski, N. (1987) *Transfer Activities: Thinking Skill Vocabulary Development.* Thinking Publications: Eau Claire, WI. www.thinkingpublications.com

McAfee, J. (2002). *Navigating the Social World.* Future Horizons, Inc.: Arlington, TX. www.futurehorizons-autism.com

McGann, W. & Werven, G. (1999). *Social Communication Skills for Children: A workbook for principle centered communication.* Pro-ed, Inc. Austin, TX. www.proedinc.com

McGraw, Jay (2000). *Life Strategies for Teens.* Simon and Schuster: New York, NY.

Myles, B; Trautman, M.; & Schelvan, R. (2004). *The Hidden Curriculum: Practical Solutions for Understanding Unstated Rules in Social Situations.* Autism Asperger Publishing Co., Shawnee Mission, KS. www.asperger.net

Parish, P. or Parish, H. (1990s). Book series: *Amelia Bedelia 4 Mayor; Amelia Bedelia and the Baby; Amelia Bedelia Goes Camping; Amelia Bedelia Helps Out; Amelia Bedelia's Family Album; Good Work, Amelia Bedelia; Merry Christmas, Amelia Bedelia; Teach Us, Amelia Bedelia; Bravo, Amelia Bedelia; Good Driving, Amelia Bedelia.* Harper Trophy: New York, NY.

Perry, A. & Condillac, R. (2003). *Evidence-Based Practices for Children and Adolescents with Autism Spectrum Disorders: Review of the Literature and Practice Guide.* Ontario: Children's Mental Health Ontario: Toronto, Ontario, Canada.

Pro-Ed (1990s). **Emotions and Expressions:** Photographs. Imaginart: AZ. www.proedinc.com (ask for these in the speech and language materials section of their product line).

Semrud-Clikeman, M. (2007). *Social Competence in Children.* Springer, Springer Science+Business Media; www.springer.com.

Sheindlin, Judge Judy. (2001). *You Can't Judge a Book By Its Cover: Cool Rules for School.* Cliff Street Books. www.harperchildrens.com

Sofronoff, K., Attwood, T., & Hinton, S. (2005). "A randomized controlled trial of a CBT intervention for anxiety in children with Asperger Syndrome." *Journal of Child Psychology and Psychiatry,* 46(11), 1152-1160.

Speech Mark (1990s). *Color cards - Different boxes: Daily Activities; Emotions; Daily Living Cards.* www.speechmark.net

Spector, Cecile. (1997). *Saying One Thing, Meaning Another: Activities for Clarifying Ambiguous Language.* Thinking Publications: Eau Claire, WI. www.thinkingpublications.com

Speech Mark (1990s). *Color Cards - Different boxes: Daily Activities; Emotions; Daily Living Cards.* www.speechmark.net

Stallard, P. (2002). *Think Good-Feel Good: A Cognitive Behavior Therapy Workbook for Children and Young People.* John Wiley and Sons, LTD.: West Sussex, England.

Toomey, Marilyn (2002). *The Language of Perspective Taking.* Circuit Publications: Marblehead, MA.

Tovani, C. (2000). *I Read It, But I Don't Get It: Comprehension Strategies for Adolescent Readers.* Stenhouse Publishers: Portland, ME.

Webster's New World Dictionary and Thesaurus. (2002).

Winner, M. (2002). *Inside Out: What Makes the Person with Social Cognitive Deficits Tick?* Think Social Publishing, Inc.: San Jose, CA. www.socialthinking.com

Winner, M. (2004). "Perspective Taking Across the School and Adult Years for Persons with Social Cognitive Deficits." *Social Spectrum: Social Understanding*, Vol 4-03/04, The Gap, Australia.

Winner, M. (2004). "A Proposal for a Perspective Taking Spectrum." *The Journal of the Association of Educational Therapists,* Winter 2004, Vol 24, number 1, Burbank, CA.

Winner, M. (2007). *Social Behavior Mapping.* Think Social Publishing, Inc.: San Jose, CA. www.socialthinking.com

Winner, M. (2005). *Social Thinking Posters: Social Behavior Map Dry Erase surface, Social Behavior Map for the Classroom, The Boring Moment, Being Part of A Group.* Think Social Publishing, Inc.: San Jose, CA. www.socialthinking.com

Winner, M. (2007). *Sticker Strategies: Practical Strategies to Encourage Social Thinking and Organization.* Think Social Publishing, Inc.: San Jose, CA. www.socialthinking.com

Winner, M. (2005). *Strategies for Organization: Preparing for Homework in The Real World.* Companion DVD available. The Gray Center Publishers; Grand Rapids, MI. www.thegraycenter.org

Winner, M. (2007). *Thinking About YOU Thinking About ME, 2nd Ed.* Think Social Publishing, Inc.: San Jose, CA. www.socialthinking.com

Winner, M. (2005). *Worksheets! for Teaching Social Thinking and Related Skills.* Think Social Publishing, Inc.: San Jose, CA. www.socialthinking.com

Videos and DVDs:

Lavoie, Richard. (1994). "Last One Picked, First One Picked On" (video); PBS video; Alexandria, VA. www.ricklavoie.com

"My Dinner with Andre" (1981). Fox Lorber Home Video: A WinStar Company.

"Napoleon Dynamite" (2004). 20th Century Fox.

Park, N. (1993). "The Wrong Trousers." Wallace & Gromit Video Series. CBS-Fox.

"Toy Story" (1995). Pixar Films.

"Toy Story 2" (1999). Pixar Films.

Winner, M. (2007). "Growing Up Social." The Gray Center: Grand Rapids, MI. www.thegraycenter.org

Winner, M. (2007). "Social Behavior Mapping." The Gray Center: Grand Rapids, MI. www.thegraycenter.org

Winner, M. (2005). "Strategies for Organization: Preparing for Homework in The Real World." The Gray Center: Grand Rapids, MI. www.thegraycenter.org

Games

Taboo: The game of unspeakable fun. Milton Bradley.

The Superflex Series!

You Are a Social Detective!
Michelle Garcia Winner and Pamela Crooke

For parents and professionals to use with students 4 years - 5th grade

Every one of us is a Social Detective. We are good Social Detectives when we use our eyes, ears, and brains to figure out what others mean by their words and deeds and are planning to do next. This entertaining comic book teaches children how to develop their own skills and become successful Social Detectives!

Superflex... A Superhero Social Thinking Curriculum*
Stephanie Madrigal and Michelle Garcia Winner

Superflex Takes on Rock Brain and the Team of Unthinkables*
Stephanie Madrigal

For professionals and parents to use with students in 2nd - 5th grade

The Superflex Curriculum offers educators, parents, and therapists fun and motivating ways to help students with social and communication difficulties develop an awareness of their own social thinking and behaviors, then learn self-regulation strategies across a range of these behaviors.

Through a comic book format, students are introduced to Superflex, a superhero who lives inside each child, and Rock Brain, one of the Team of Unthinkables, characters that try to detour students from using their social thinking skills. Rock Brain makes kids get stuck on their ideas. Creative strategies to defeat Rock Brain are included.

* packaged and sold as a set; Curriculum includes CD with handouts and funwork.

All titles available at the Social Thinking website: www.socialthinking.com

Superflex Takes on Glassman and the Team of Unthinkables
Stephanie Madrigal and Michelle Garcia Winner

For professionals and parents to use with students in K - 5th grade

In this teaching comic book, Superflex swoops down to help Aiden overcome the Unthinkable, Glassman, who causes children to have over-sized reactions to small things. The setting: the first day of school!

Superflex Takes on Brain Eater and the Team of Unthinkables
Stephanie Madrigal and Michelle Garcia Winner

For professionals and parents to use with students in K - 5th grade

In this teaching comic book, Superflex swoops down to help Aiden overcome the Unthinkable, Brain Eater, who distracts people and makes it hard for them to focus on what they are supposed to be doing.

Of Related Interest

Whole Body Listening Larry at Home
Whole Body Listening Larry at School
Both books by Kristen Wilson and Elizabeth Sautter

For parents and professionals to use with students 4-9 years old

These colorfully illustrated storybooks provide fun ways to teach younger children an abstract but essential idea - that their eyes, hands, brains – their whole bodies! – communicate, engage with and affect the people around them. Scenarios range from at home and at school to in the car, with friends or grandparents.

Core Books About the Social Thinking Model & Related Teaching Strategies

Inside Out: What Makes a Person with Social Cognitive Deficits Tick?
By Michelle Garcia Winner

For professionals and parents to use with all ages!

The starting place to learn about the ILAUGH Model upon which Social Thinking is based. Discusses the direct connection between social thinking and academic problems such as reading comprehension and written expression, and helps readers pinpoint specific challenges in a child or student. Valuable insight on information we expect students to know to become strong learners but that doesn't develop "naturally" in everyone.

Thinking About YOU Thinking About ME, 2nd Edition
By Michelle Garcia Winner

For professionals and parents to use with all ages!

Learn more about social interaction and social awareness! Explains Michelle Garcia Winner's core Social Thinking concepts and treatment methods, with extensive curriculum content on perspective taking as well as assessment using the Social Thinking Dynamic Assessment Protocol®. Age-targeted lesson and activity ideas, templates and handouts included. A precursor to using books like Superflex, You Are A Social Detective, and more!

Think Social!
A Social Thinking Curriculum for School-Aged Students, 2nd Edition
By Michelle Garcia Winner

For parents and professionals to use with all ages!

A complement to Thinking About YOU Thinking About ME, this is the fundamental Social Thinking curriculum book to help individuals K-12 and into adulthood. The book sequences through eight chapters and 69 lessons that help students explore the basics of working and thinking in a group. Each chapter addresses how to use and interpret language (verbal and nonverbal) to further understand the context of communications.

Social Thinking books, curriculum, worksheets, and related products developed by Michelle Garcia Winner and Social Thinking Publishing

Core Books about the Social Thinking Model & Curriculum
Inside Out: What Makes a Person with Social Cognitive Deficits Tick?
Thinking About YOU Thinking About ME, 2nd Edition
Think Social! A Social Thinking Curriculum for School Age Students
Worksheets! for Teaching Social Thinking and Related Skills
Social Behavior Mapping: Connecting Behavior,
Emotions and Consequences Across the Day *

For School-Age Children
You Are a Social Detective! (co-authored by Pamela Crooke) * *
Superflex: A Superhero Social Thinking Curriculum (co-authored by Stephanie Madrigal)
Superflex Takes on Rock Brain and the Team of Unthinkables By Stephanie Madrigal
Superflex Takes on Glassman (co-authored by Stephanie Madrigal)
Superflex Takes on Brain Eater (co-authored by Stephanie Madrigal)
Social Town Citizens Discover 82 New Unthinkables for Superflex to Outsmart!
(co-authored by Stephanie Madrigal and Pamela Crooke)
Sticker Strategies: Practical Strategies to Encourage
Social Thinking and Organization, 2nd Edition
Whole Body Listening Larry at Home! By Kristen Wilson & Elizabeth Sautter
Whole Body Listening Larry at School! By Elizabeth Sautter & Kristen Wilson
We Can Make it Better! A Strategy to Motivate and Engage Young Learners
in Social Problem-Solving Through Flexible Stories By Elizabeth M. Delsandro
I Get It! Building Social Thinking and Reading
Comprehension Through Book Chats By Audra Jensen, M.Ed., BCBA
The Zones of Regulation: A Curriculum Designed to Foster Self-Regulation
and Emotional Control By Leah M. Kuypers, MA Ed., OTR/L
What is a Thought? (A Thought is a Lot) By Jack Pransky and Amy Kahofer
Movie Time Social Learning: Using Movies to Teach Social Thinking and Social Understanding By Anna Vagin, PhD

* Available in English and Spanish   * * Available in English, French, and Spanish

Teens and Young Adults
Socially Curious and Curiously Social: A Social Thinking Guidebook
for Teens and Young Adults (co-authored by Pamela Crooke)
Social Fortune or Social Fate: Watch Their Destiny Unfold
Based on the Choices They Make (co-authored by Pamela Crooke)
Social Thinking Worksheets for Tweens and Teens:
Learning to Read in Between the Social Lines
Social Thinking Across the Home and School Day
Strategies for Organization: Preparing for Homework and the Real World
Social Thinking at Work: Why Should I Care? A Guidebook for Understanding
and Navigating the Social Complexities of the Workplace (co-authored by Pamela Crooke)
Should I or Shouldn't I? A Game to Encourage Social Thinking and Social Problem Solving
Middle & High School Edition By Dominque Baudry, MS., Ed.
Movie Time Social Learning: Using Movies to Teach Social Thinking and Social Understanding By Anna Vagin, PhD

Related Products
You Are a Social Detective Interactive CD
Social Thinking Posters for the home and classroom
The Zones of Regulation Poster
Superflex Poster
Whole Body Listening Larry Poster

**Visit our website for more information on our books and products,
free articles on Social Thinking topics, and a listing of Social Thinking Conferences
across the U.S.**

www.socialthinking.com